Disordered Attention

Disordered Attention

How We Look at Art and Performance Today

Claire Bishop

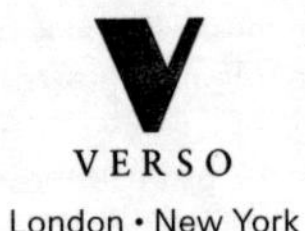

VERSO
London • New York

This paperback edition first published by Verso 2025
First published by Verso 2024

3 5 7 9 10 8 6 4 2

Verso
UK: 6 Meard Street, London W1F 0EG
US: 207 East 32nd Street, New York, NY 10016
versobooks.com

Verso is the imprint of New Left Books

ISBN-13: 978-1-80429-673-8
ISBN-13: 978-1-80429-289-1 (US EBK)
ISBN-13: 978-1-80429-290-7 (UK EBK)

British Library Cataloguing in Publication Data
A catalogue record for this book is available from the British Library

Library of Congress Cataloging-in-Publication Data

Names: Bishop, Claire, author.
Title: Disordered attention : how we see art and performance today / Claire Bishop.
Description: London ; New York : Verso, 2024. | Includes bibliographical references and index.
Identifiers: LCCN 2024000521 (print) | LCCN 2024000522 (ebook) | ISBN 9781804292884 (hardcover) | ISBN 9781804292907 (ebk)
Subjects: LCSH: Arts, Modern – 21st century – Philosophy. | Engagement (Philosophy) | Arts audiences. | Arts and society – History – 21st century.
Classification: LCC NX460 .B47 2024 (print) | LCC NX460 (ebook) | DDC 700.1/03 – dc23/eng/20240207
LC record available at https://lccn.loc.gov/2024000521
LC ebook record available at https://lccn.loc.gov/2024000522

Typeset in Sabon by Biblichor Ltd, Scotland
Printed and bound by CPI Group (UK) Ltd, Croydon, CR0 4YY

Contents

Introduction: OS XXI, Disordering Attention

Two recent performances seem emblematic of how we look at art and performance today. The first, *Sun and Sea (Marina)* (2019), is an opera about climate change. When it was staged at the Venice Biennale in 2019, viewers entered a former naval building onto a raised gallery overlooking a thick blanket of sand populated with sunbathers.[1] All ages, races, genders, and even a dog were hanging out on this makeshift 'beach'. For eight hours, they sang, chatted, napped, read books and magazines, looked at their phones, and occasionally wandered off. Only the children were conspicuously mobile – building sandcastles, running around, and playing various ball games. With all the continuous low-level peripheral noise and activity, combined with an elevated viewing position that flattened the beach-stage into a horizontal plane, it was often difficult to identify which performer was singing. The libretto largely took the form of complaints that oscillated between the personal and the environmental – the sea filling with algae, needing more sunscreen, the difficulty of relaxing, and species dying out. These sunbathing tourists on pastel-coloured towels seemed to occupy a suspended time at the edge of a climate abyss. They were also the audience's mirrors, reflecting our own inaction back to itself. As disconnected from the slow violence of climate change as the languid performers beneath us, we murmured to each other and took photographs.

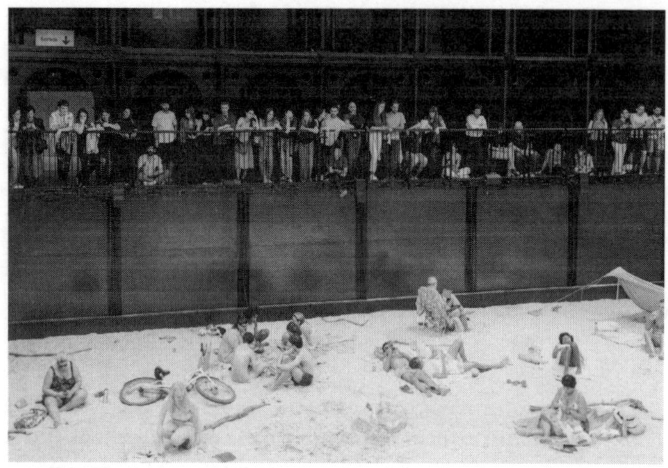

Rugilė Barzdziukaitė, Vaiva Grainytė, and Lina Lapelytė, *Sun and Sea (Marina)*, 2018. Performance view, Teatre Lliure, Barcelona, 2022.

Time passed. The beach occupants (under bright lights), like us (watching in the shadows), came and went as the hours ticked by – drifting in, staying a while, and wandering out again.

The second performance, Kevin Beasley's *The Sound of Morning* (2021), took place at a street intersection on the Lower East Side of Manhattan.[2] A group of Black dancers undertook activities that were casual to the point of being barely visible: dragging a piece of metal, fixing a bicycle wheel, bouncing a deflated basketball. Each set of actions created a sound that was amplified, mixed with others, and gradually came to the fore in an improvised composition. The city bled into the work not just sonically but visually: passers-by, cyclists, and delivery trucks constantly wove through and bypassed the performers. The four-way intersection offered multiple lines of sight. Backdrop and foreground melted into each other. Audience members followed the performers, watched, stepped out of the way, talked to neighbours, took photographs. We tuned in, we tuned out. The action was so understated that there wasn't that much to watch, so we coexisted with Beasley's abstracted material

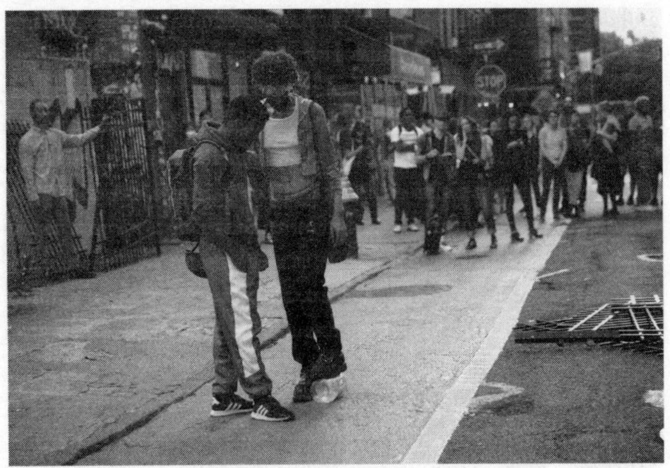

Kevin Beasley, *The Sound of Morning*, 2021. Performance view, New York, 14 October 2021. Performers: Raymond Pinto, Amadi Washington, Ley Gambucci.

sound – a sonic collage taken from and re-layered back onto that corner of the city.

In both performances – one indoors, one outdoors – the viewer's attention was radically dispersed, and not just because sonic and visual interference was embraced as a feature. Duration mattered, as did the free-flowing structure. At no point was it expected that the audience would watch each performance in reverent silence. Our conversations and observations took place in and alongside the work, as did our photography. This relaxed distribution of focus goes beyond previous strands of art, performance, and dance since the 1960s – work characterized by an all-over compositional dehierarchization, often using site-specificity (allowing the work to be permeated by its context) or duration (straining our capacity for sustained attention). The most important difference, though, lies in the photographic condition of contemporary spectatorship. Initially and hesitantly with digital cameras in the 2000s, and then rapidly with networked camera phones in the 2010s, we have come to document as we look. This reflex documentation has become collective, real-time, and distributed. We are physically present in the performance but also networked to multiple elsewheres. Looking is hybrid, occupying multiple spaces and times simultaneously: we are in the present with the work, interacting with those in our immediate vicinity, but also relaying this to others watching remotely, in real time or (more often) with a slight delay.

Today, documentation is in the hands of every viewer, not just the professional hired photographer. As a result, the hierarchies of distribution have been scrambled. This has changed the dynamic of looking at art and especially performance. The work is less self-important, less total; it grants us the space to be mobile and social, to react, chat, share, and archive as we watch. After both *Sun and Sea (Marina)* and *The Sound of Morning*, I was curious to check Instagram to see if other people had looked at the performance in ways that corresponded to my experience. Perhaps I would even be visible in their footage.

Much has been written about the impact of the internet, smartphones, and social media upon our attention spans – and most of it has been negative. But these debates do not adequately broach the new conditions of spectatorship that characterize contemporary culture. How has our attention been reorganized? How are artists processing, reacting to, or rejecting these developments – and how can we understand these shifts? This book is an attempt to answer these questions by engaging with two concerns. The first is the idea of 'contemporary art history', the field within which my research is situated. There is a tendency to treat this field, commonly understood as the period since 1989, as one historically unified unit: an era that began with the fall of the Berlin Wall and synchronized with economic globalization and widespread access to the internet. Yet there have been tectonic shifts in both the production and consumption of art in the decades between the pre-internet world of the early 1990s and the post-pandemic 2020s. Contemporary art and how we look at it exists not just in tandem with the uneven development of globalization but alongside unimaginable developments in technology. The rise of an attention economy and its flipside, attention deficit hyperactivity disorder (ADHD), form the contextual horizon for this book.

The second engagement is with naming and historicizing certain genres of making art since the early 1990s. Part of the work of historicization is mapping how these strategies have shifted in conjunction with the rise of digital technology. *Disordered Attention* charts four ways of making art that can be found more or less globally – although my examples reflect my context, which is Europe and North America. These strategies manifest a range of responses to new technologies of information and image circulation – responses that can be unconscious, oblique, internalized, or ambivalent. One of my arguments is that the effects of digital technology upon spectatorship are best seen in art that, at first glance, seems to reject digital technology most forcefully – for example, in performances that emphasize live presence, or installations that harness obsolete technology. I will return to these four strategies in due course.

How we define attention is inextricably connected to how we conceive of ourselves as human subjects. In this book, attention is understood not as a universal, deep-rooted faculty of the human mind, but as a capacity that is mutable – through technology, medication, and the presence of others. Further, how we define attention undergirds our idea of what constitutes an important cultural artifact and how it should be consumed. Modern Western culture has long cherished its esteemed cultural objects ('masterpieces') for the way they seem to elicit inexhaustible attention. Scholars in the humanities spend long hours writing about such objects. Over decades, and even centuries, these writings add layers of meaning and help to sediment a canon. I want to push back against this association between meaning and profundity, or what I call a depth model of culture. While some cultural objects have longevity and seem timeless, others are slight but have the virtue of being timely and provoking intense debate. This book tries to make space for a range of work, some of which has been neglected by art history – particularly those practices considered too ephemeral, recent, or unbounded to enter the canon.[3]

The depth model of culture has been rocked by the rise of digital technology. Memes and the viral have put a new model of engaged looking into circulation, predicated on quantity and speed rather than narrowness and depth. Modern spectatorship, premised on fully focused presence and deep attention, no longer seems appropriate or necessary.[4] This is not to say that we should abandon contemplation and automatically celebrate the fast feed. My point is that today's ways of seeing are not just so much dispersed and distributed as incessantly hybrid: both present and mediated, live and online, fleeting and profound, individual and collective – a condition that has only been compounded and intensified by the COVID-19 pandemic.

Throughout the 2010s, there were already flashpoints: tensions over the use of camera phones in theatres, grumbling about works of art that seemed designed to look better on screen than in real life, complaints about exhibitions too large to see in their entirety, and artists' frustrations over video clips of their works being circulated on social media. Even before the lockdowns of 2020 we were being edged into hybridized spectatorship, and traditionalists weren't happy. The rest of us, perhaps reluctantly, developed new habits – I felt that using my phone in a performance was somehow 'wrong', but couldn't resist taking a photo nonetheless. Faced with huge exhibitions, I learned to expedite and triage my time. Today I switch rapidly between different modes of attention. In a typical visit to an exhibition, I'll get lost in long periods of focus and presence. But I'll also scan the QR code to read the exhibition booklet later. I wonder if I can ask the curator for a link to stream the video at home. I take installation shots and a few close-ups. I respond to my partner's texts about childcare. I photograph the labels. I send an image to a friend and tell them they were right, this is (or is not) a good show. This perpetual oscillation between here and elsewhere, consuming and commenting, is central to how we look at art and performance today.

Normative Attention

Attention, in this book, is the unifying glue between four essays on contemporary art and performance. Yet it fits within, and pushes back against, a larger body of literature that could loosely be described as attention studies. The first publications date from the 1990s and comprise a euphoric business literature on the attention economy. Since then, in response to the rise of Web 2.0 and social media, and then to surveillance and right-wing disinformation, a more critical body of writing has emerged in the humanities. Distraction has been mobilized as a signifier of technological (and generational) unease: 'For teachers like myself,' writes cultural theorist Dominic Pettman, 'distraction is our nemesis, just as attention is our lifeblood.'[5] For others, navigating the attention economy has become a matter of 'wellness', to which techniques of coping, digital mindfulness, slow looking, and opting out are regularly offered as solutions. These books, which range from the scholarly to the popular, conjugate contemporary literacy, politics, education, social media, and mental health, but rarely mention visual art.[6]

The most cited history of attention, however, is by an art historian. Jonathan Crary has shown how attention first emerged as a preoccupation and problem in the late nineteenth century, in tandem with industrial capitalism, and was associated above all with the *individualization* of perception. The newly emergent disciplines of physiology and psychology sought to demonstrate that perception is constituted *internally* – as a capacity of the subject – rather than as an imposition from external phenomena.[7] The key protagonists of this emergent discourse were experimental psychologists in Germany (Hermann von Helmholtz and William Wundt) and in the United States (William James and W. B. Pillsbury). Wundt and James independently set up the first laboratories in 1875, devising experiments to test reaction times, divided attention, short-term memory, distractibility, and fatigue. One of their central questions concerned the locus of attention, which they came to frame as a capacity from within (as in Wundt's argument for voluntary attention) rather than a result of external stimulus from without. In *The Principles of Psychology* (1890), James offers a breezily confident definition of attention that remains much cited today: 'Everyone knows what attention is. It is taking possession by the mind, in clear and vivid form, of one out of what seem several simultaneously possible objects or trains of thought. Focalization, concentration, of consciousness are of its essence.'[8] Yet he goes on to prevaricate, unable to decide if attention is an effect of the perceived object's magnetism or a subjective imposition of individual will.

James lays the foundations for what I call 'normative attention': an attention directed at objects (rather than other subjects), that is intellectual and cognitive (rather than sensorial and affective), that is framed in terms of ownership ('taking *possession* of the mind'), and which is individual (rather than socially or collectively constituted).[9] Attention is a property, a force exuding *from* the subject, an expression of his interest (and it is always a *he*); it's autonomous and voluntary, even if most of us can't actually sustain exclusive focus for more than a few seconds at a time.[10] Attentive subjects have agency: they actively direct their gaze, holding it firm, seizing their object. Located in the subject, but directed towards an external entity, attention constructs both as poles: the subject selects his object and brings it into focus, allowing the rest of the visual/sonic field to recede into the background. Normative attention thus conforms to Enlightenment conceptions of the modern subject as conscious, rational, and disciplined. This model is, of course, paradigmatically white, patriarchal, bourgeois, colonial. It is synonymous with ownership, property, and optical mastery.[11]

It is not coincidental that attention came to be a research field as the phenomenal world was being transformed by the space and time of industrial capitalism. The modern city was fast, loud, crowded, and chaotic. The nineteenth-century reconfiguration of attention as a quality of the individual (rather than emerging from a common social context) enabled it to be quantified, optimized, and disciplined. A concern for workers' safety (for example, the need for vigilance when using factory machinery) dovetailed with the desire to regulate, monitor, and maximize productivity.[12] Workers were observed and controlled – and profits could soar. The time-and-motion calculations of Taylorist 'scientific management' in the 1900s offered a high point of scrutiny to attention in the workplace.[13] The contemporary algorithmic management and surveillance of workers in Amazon fulfilment centres continues this monitoring of bodies, now extended even to facial expressions. Yet the impulse to track workers' attention indicates the extent to which the norm is not in fact normative attention (focused, present, directional) but something more erratic and unfixed. Attention is so valued precisely because it is rare and unstable, continually unravelling from within.

During the 1870s, the same period that attention was emerging as a scientific research object, new types of urban architecture were redesigned to hone attention. Museums and theatres began to overhaul spectatorship in ways that emphasized a directionality of focus with conformity to collective behaviour.[14] The museum was conceived as a space of uplifting refinement: audiences were expected to be well behaved, to self-regulate their own bodies in relation to others, and to forgo the noisy social dynamics that formed part of public culture elsewhere (carnivals, pleasure gardens, sporting events).[15] By the 1870s, the conventional nineteenth-century 'salon hang' – works crowded in rows up to the ceiling – had been replaced in independent venues by one or two rows of paintings with more breathing space between them. These were displayed in settings that evoked a private apartment, in order to facilitate more intimate and focused attention.[16]

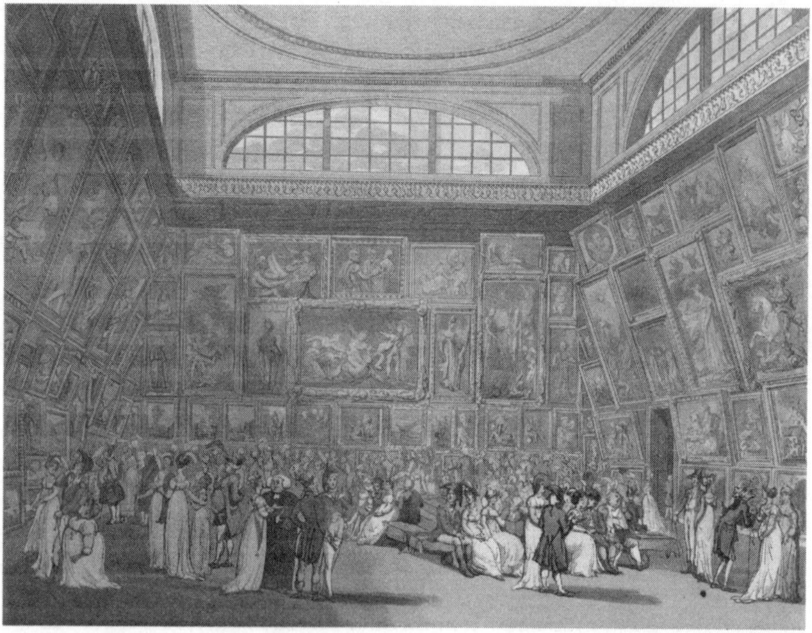

Thomas Rowlandson, Auguste Charles Pugin, and John Hill, *Exhibition Room, Somerset House*, 1808. Etching and aquatint.

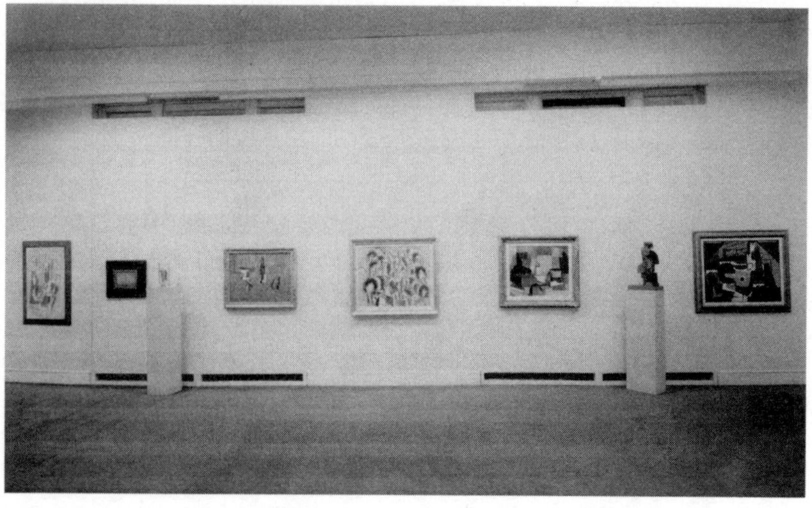

View of 'Cubism and Abstract Art', Museum of Modern Art, New York, 1936.

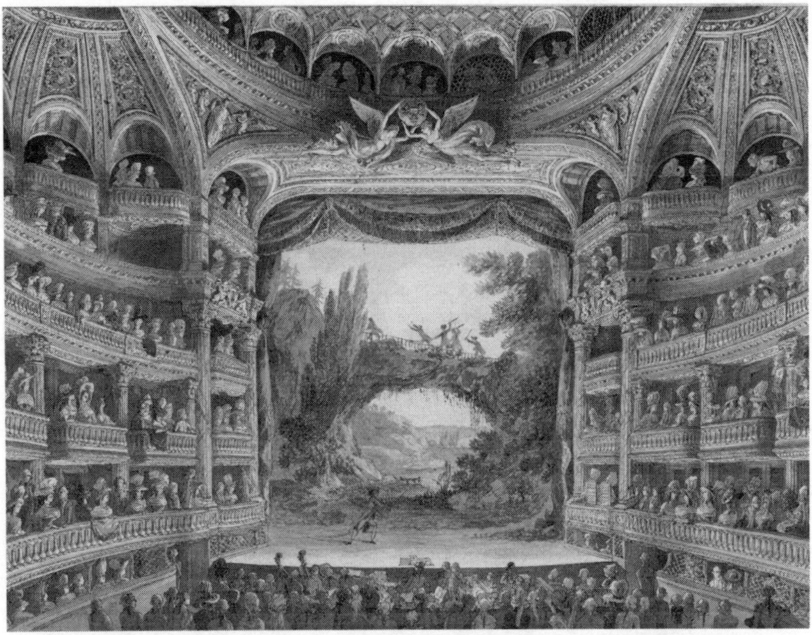

Antoine Meunier, *La Comédie-Française,* ca. 1790–1800. Pen, ink, and watercolour.

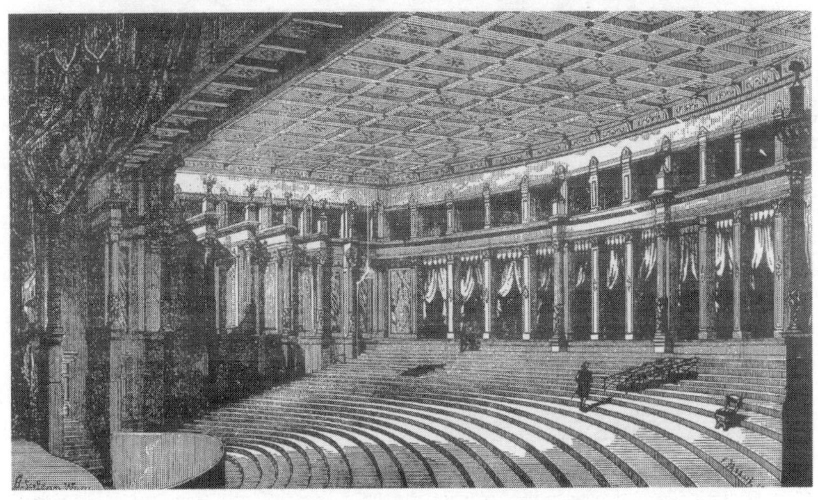

La vue intérieure du théâtre de Bayreuth (interior view of the theatre at Bayreuth). Illustration published alongside Édouard Dujardin's history of the Bayreuth Festspielhaus in *Revue Wagnérienne*, Paris, vol. V, 8 June, 1885.

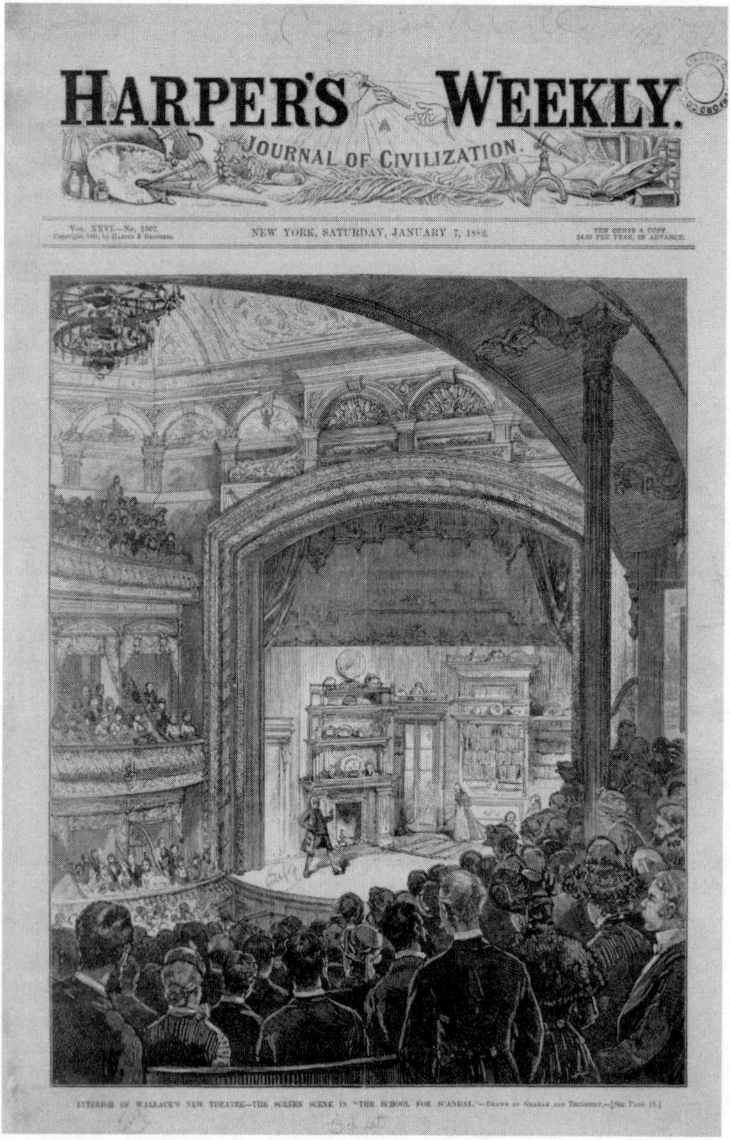

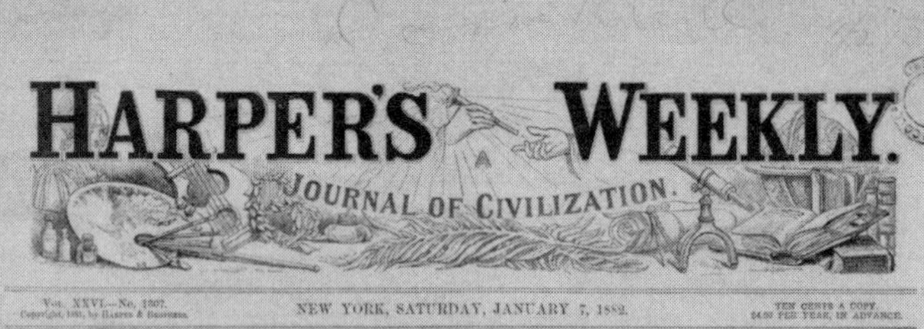

Charles Graham and Thure de Thulstrup, *Interior of Wallack's New Theatre (the screen scene in 'The School for Scandal')*, 1882. Wood engraving.

Around 1900, the modernist 'white cube' came into being, with a greater spatial separation between the paintings, which were treated as autonomous, mirroring the exhibition's ideal subject: an atomized, self-contained viewer.[17] Works hung in a single row, at eye level, on a white wall, facing the viewer one-to-one, continues to be the global norm.

In theatre, the best-known example of optical and behavioural reorganization is Richard Wagner's design for the Festspielhaus in Bayreuth, which opened in 1876. Prior to this moment, the arrangement of seating in theatres had been a horseshoe curve in which the majority of boxes faced each other rather than the stage; Wagner changed this to an unobstructed frontal alignment in which the entire audience looks forwards. To encourage greater optical surrender to the on-stage spectacle, boxes were eliminated, the auditorium was plunged into near darkness, and the orchestra concealed in a pit.[18] The goal was to produce ritual immersion in the *Gesamtkunstwerk* rather than boisterous participation in a social event. By the 1890s, in the major cities of Europe, darkness was a universal condition of the theatrical experience – with accompanying behavioural expectations of silence and respectful observation. Sociologist Richard Sennett notes,

> In the 1850s, a Parisian or London theatergoer had no compunction about talking to a neighbour in the midst of the play, if he or she had just remembered something to say. By 1870, the audience was policing itself. Talking now seemed bad taste and rude. The house lights were dimmed too, to reinforce the silence and focus attention on the stage.[19]

The affective hubbub of the sociable crowd was increasingly contained to popular culture, leaving the theatre and museum as discrete domains of polite self-abnegation. In these institutions, modern regimes of attention sought to create a space of individualized focus within a social sphere, one private bubble among others. To all intents and purposes, the theatre audience was alone except for the interval and the moment of applause. It's telling that when the historical avant-garde turned to performance in the 1910s and 1920s, they looked not to bourgeois theatre but to the more interactive, participatory, and working-class formats of cabaret and music hall for their model – spaces in which it was commonplace to smoke and sing along with, heckle, or even ignore the performers.

Recent scholars of audience have shown how class assumptions about silent viewing continue to inform the hegemonic model of theatre spectatorship as self-contained and reverential. Theatre historian Katy Sedgman argues that what is considered to be 'reasonable' audience behaviour in fact ends up enforcing an elite white able-bodied norm, while simultaneously policing other bodies (especially the neurodivergent and the non-white).[20] The recent fad for theatre etiquette manifestos has arisen as a direct consequence of modern modes of attention – privatized, immersive, transcendent – clashing with a contemporary culture of digital connectivity. The obsessive focus of these manifestos is the mobile phone: answering calls, responding to texts, and taking photographs are all considered social offences.[21] Museum etiquette guides are less draconian, but testify to the sense of class intimidation and anxiety that many people still feel on entering museums and galleries. Rather than forbidding mobile phones entirely, advice tends to focus on reducing volume (using your 'indoor voice') and camera protocols: don't use flash or selfie sticks, don't photograph everything, and 'keep up with the pace' in crowded exhibitions ('your Instagram post doesn't actually need to be instant').[22] These viewing etiquettes underscore how a discourse of normative attention is embedded within these architectures of looking and their protocols for 'reasonable' behaviour, and the extent to which digital technology has introduced new forms of spectatorship that strain (and even shatter) modern attentional plenitude.

A final word about normative attention. By presupposing a universal human subject of vision, attention discourse creates inadvertent exclusions. The first time I assembled a graduate seminar on attention and technology, my syllabus disturbed me: so few women seemed to write about attention, and even fewer writers of colour. Did they simply have nothing to say about attention? The answer was slow to dawn on me: normative attention assumes a normative subject – privileged, white, straight, able-bodied, volitional – who confers his attention onto an exteriority thereby constituted as an object. For minoritarian subjects, the discourse of attention has little relevance because it is structurally difficult to occupy the position of attentiveness; historically, we have always been the objects of others' attention. To fold these perspectives into any discussion of attention thus requires a shift in terminology to adjacent discourses of visuality – such as the 'male gaze' and 'care' (in feminism), 'surveillance' and 'fugitivity' (in Black studies), 'passing' and 'realness' (in queer and trans theory), or 'staring' (in disability studies).[23] In each instance, normative attention is discursively sidestepped and reconstituted to deal with the complexities of seeing and being seen from a non-hegemonic perspective. This is one reason, then, why attention needs to be disordered.

Against Distraction

Thus far I have avoided using the word *distraction*, but from the moment of its emergence in the late nineteenth century, attention has always been defined as its opposite. James declares that attention 'implies withdrawal from some things in order to deal effectively with others, and is a condition which has a real opposite in the confused, dazed, scatterbrained state which in French is called *distraction*, and *Zerstreutheit* in German'.[24] I want to push back on this binary – indeed, to dismantle it – because any judgement about distraction tends to be underpinned by ideological assumptions about a productive work ethic, a virtuous life, and the dangers of sensory pleasure. In other words, 'distraction' is more of a moral judgement than a coherent description of how we look and think.

This subtle moralizing can be seen in reactions to new technology throughout the twentieth century. It can be found in critical responses to early cinema – from reformers' concerns over women and children attending the Nickelodeon cinemas of the 1900s, to disdain for workers spending their evenings in the enormous new movie palaces of Berlin and New York during the 1920s.[25] It is always the working classes who are the object of analysis – never the middle and upper classes, who presumably prefer opera and theatre. Newly emancipated women were seen as particularly vulnerable to ideological sway in movie theatres. Siegfried Kracauer's preferred term for distraction, *Zerstreuung*, carries connotations of diversion and being scatterbrained, and was gendered as female. In 'Little Shopgirls Go to the Movies' (1927), the German critic reads a number of recent films through the lens of an imaginary, small-minded female spectator.[26] Distraction, for Kracauer, nevertheless serves a function: by subjecting viewers to such a rapid onslaught of images that no time is left to contemplate, movies indirectly reveal the truth of social disorder. At the same time, he argues, cinema architecture works against this: the exorbitant decoration of the glittering new movie palaces serves to 'rivet viewers' attention to the peripheral so that they will not sink into the abyss'.[27]

In the postwar period, television was heir to these anxieties – at its worst exemplifying a loss of humanity, freedom, and self-determination.[28] Well into the 1980s, three decades after television had become a fixture of domestic space, critics lamented its presentism, its atomization of information, its speed, and its capacity to distract.[29] Women and the working classes continue to be the primary focus of concern ('daytime television plays a part in habituating women to interruption, distraction, and spasmodic toil').[30] Yet again, passivity and distraction are gendered. Raymond Williams's account of television's central logic as 'planned flow' is a rare exception in the television literature, both for its incisive analysis of the apparatus in terms of flow (rather than fragmentation), and for withholding value judgements on its spectators.

He argues that televisual flow produces a new form of attention and comprehension that differs from the rest of our lived experience, which is built around discrete events.[31] Williams's 'flow' anticipates the borderless penetration of networked technology into our lives with the iPhone (and similar gadgets) that merge portability and the prosthetic.

In the new century, it is children that have become the central focus of anxiety. After the introduction of the iPhone in 2007 and the rise of social media, there has been no shortage of writing denouncing the impact of this technology upon the human psyche and social relations.[32] Studies frequently draw upon neuroscientific research into synaptogenesis, the development of the brain's axons, synapses, and dendrites after birth. Do children have too much screentime, too early? Do digital screens affect their sleep, and thus their performance at school? Have younger generations lost traditional reading skills? Is digital technology rewiring their synapses? Sociologist Sherry Turkle describes the new 'tethered self' of children wedded to their devices, unable to develop their own ideas and identities independently, and thus suffering developmental inhibition.[33] French philosopher Bernard Stiegler, one of the most assiduous champions of deep attention, argues that the brain is structured differently in children raised on contemporary media, resulting in a 'generational mutation' that produces an inability to attend deeply and thus mature into adulthood.[34]

Across this literature on cinema, television, and social media, we repeatedly find that depth of attention connotes agency and self-determination, while distraction not only describes its loss but becomes a way to denigrate those who succumb to its trivialities.[35] Distraction is not the opposite of attention, then, but an accusation of *misplaced* attention, made in relation to an other perceived as deficient or vulnerable. It implies a weakness of character that can be reined in through will power and inner strength. In short, distraction is one of the ways in which a (dominant) social group expresses disapproval about another (subordinate) social group. When we refer to people as 'distracted' (for example, by social media), it's a way of saying that we think their attention is in the wrong place.

Philosopher Paul North has observed that distraction is basically a degraded or divided attention; when pushed, the two terms produce a tautological structure whereby distraction always becomes a *version* of attention. In his reading, attention and distraction are not opposites but points on a circular spectrum; when pushed, they collapse into each other.[36] This book goes further, claiming that attention and distraction are a false binary. The two terms are not a matter of individual subjective capacities: will power versus coercion, agency versus weakness, intense focus versus dispersed gaze, and so on. Rather, attention and distraction are cultural constructs emerging from a set of tacitly agreed norms and values. Distraction is not *opposed* to attention but is a *type* of attention – it's not individual and intrinsic but social and relational. As memes, fashion, crowds, and trending all indicate, we instinctively pay attention to what others pay attention to.

Hyperattention

In 2007, N. Katherine Hayles, one of the few female scholars to weigh in on the topic of attention, coined the term *hyperattention*. This is characterized as 'switching focus rapidly among different tasks, preferring multiple information streams, seeking a high level of stimulation, and having a low tolerance for boredom'.[37] She posits hyperattention as antithetical to the 'deep attention' characteristic of research in the humanities: absorption in a single object, usually via a single information stream, for a long period of time. Hayles sees the divide as generational, but she advocates a non-judgemental middle ground: both modes of attention are useful, she argues, and educators need to recognize this. Her pragmatism is echoed in the work of English scholar Cathy Davidson, who argues in favour of multitasking, and attributes students' lack of attention to pedagogic conservatism: attempting to shoehorn old methods of teaching into brains shaped through exposure to digital technologies. Rather than seeing 'continuous partial attention' as a lack or problem, she argues for it as a digital survival skill and an opportunity for collaboration.[38]

Hayles's work, widely cited, today appears curiously outdated. During the COVID-19 lockdowns, all forms of research, hyper and deep, took place on digital interfaces. The association of hyperattention with digital media, and deep attention with print culture, finally disintegrated. But was humanities research ever only about deep absorption in a single cultural object? Research involves gaining a handle on adjacent discourses more broadly – work that requires skimming as much as lingering, regardless of the technological interface. Humanities research, for better or worse, is a constant shuttling between phases of furious searching for the gist (both print and online) and phases of slow thinking and writing (on paper and onscreen).[39] My experiences of total absorption have almost entirely taken place online, when I've slipped down a research rabbit hole and become oblivious to the physical world and the passing of time. The biggest difference between research today and research prior to digitalization in the 2000s is not depth but *speed*: I am never in the situation of waiting for a book to be delivered to my desk and wondering what to read in the meantime. The next pdf is always available, and I race through it with the help of command-F.

Old patterns of thinking are nevertheless hard to overcome. Deep attention continues to be seen not just as superior but as constitutive of our humanity. Stiegler, for example, dismisses hyperattention as 'a form of attention without consciousness, a characteristic of wild animals'.[40] He sees dehumanization as a perpetual threat. Unlike creatures who vigilantly scan their whereabouts for danger, humans have the capacity for deep attention: the ability to set aside immediate urges (eating, sleeping, reproduction – the priorities of the animal world) in order to focus in unhurried stretches of quiet thought and observation. Such arguments also feel out of sync with today: given the climate emergency, increased vigilance about our surrounding environment can only be an asset, rather than an impediment. Stiegler laments the erosion of deep attention by the 'programming industries' (film, television, videogames, the internet), and while not wholly against new technologies, he nevertheless finds it hard to articulate a positive role for them. The 'industrial capture of attention', he writes, systematically 'de-forms' the psyche away from the transmission of intergenerational knowledge and *savoir-vivre*. Education has the capacity to resist this because it cultivates the brain like a piece of land, enabling the collective production of transgenerational memory. While there is much to admire in Stiegler's passionate theorization of transindividuation, there is also a fatal pessimism: the sense that humanity is fighting a losing battle against attention's destruction by 'psychotechniques' – the unspecified forces of consumer-capitalist programming.[41] His outlook is dark, yet the cause of his gloom partly resides in his own capture by the European philosophical tradition and an unwillingness to think outside or beyond it.

Crary's recent work, on the other hand, makes an effort to factor in anticolonial, postcolonial, and decolonial perspectives but ends up equally disenchanted. His books *24/7* (2013) and *Scorched Earth* (2022) both form a marked contrast to his landmark surveys of nineteenth-century attention, which balance an account of the historical emergence of attention as a discourse with artistic efforts to metabolize the new convergence of industrial modernity and popular spectacle.[42] Although Crary attempts to stay focused on a critique of capitalism rather than a denunciation of technology per se, he sees no possible redemption for what he calls 'the internet complex'. This phrase denotes a cascading array of problems: technological hardware (including the extraction of minerals like coltan from the global south), software and apps (and their production of compulsory consumerism), and the impending climate apocalypse (the needless electricity required to power a global digital infrastructure). Any potential benefits of social communication or activism through networked technology are secondary, claims Crary, to the toxic powers of the internet complex as an 'implacable engine of addiction, loneliness, false hopes, cruelty, psychosis, indebtedness, squandered life, the corrosion of memory, and social disintegration'.[43]

Crary's diagnosis of capitalist ecocide has undeniable moral force. Yet it also prevents him from taking seriously the new modes of perception, attention, and communication that have emerged in the last twenty years. He can only see and reinforce the ways in which these have been stigmatized as insufficiently human and inhibiting self-determination. To his eyes, digital skills are not even legible as skills. As befits a professor, his concern is with students rather than children: young people on their phones and videogames, he laments, who are being 'dispossessed of their youth' as 'addictive stimulation and electroluminescent homogeneity' replace the flourishing of friendships, sexuality, and creativity.[44] His language is searing but too totalizing to be a rallying cry. It alienated my students, who struggle to recognize themselves in his description. Their position, like mine, is that this technology isn't going away; we need to engage with and work through it.

Attention Disorders

Any discussion of attention in art soon finds itself engaging with two related discourses since the 1990s: Attention Deficit Hyperactivity Disorder (ADHD) and the attention economy. Attention in the classroom has become a central issue since ADHD was officially categorized as a mental disorder by the American Psychiatric Association in 1980.[45] Today, diagnoses are rampant in the US, less so in Europe, and barely exist elsewhere in the world. It's estimated that 11 per cent of US schoolchildren have received a medical diagnosis of ADHD, and that two-thirds of these are on Ritalin or Adderall.[46] The majority of these children are white, middle-class boys.

ADHD medication seeks to treat biologically a set of behavioural and environmental conditions, turning to the individual brain rather than pointing to a larger sociocultural structure.[47] It's not hard to see why this has come about. A more systemic analysis would necessitate a critical evaluation of the link between attention and contemporary capitalism. In turn, this would inevitably lead to a critique of a neoliberal Western education system that overemphasizes metrics, benchmarks, testing, and 'normal' development, and thereby inculcates a pressure to succeed, produce, and be competitive in the labour market. In classic neoliberal style, ADHD diagnoses shift the responsibility for distraction onto the 'innocent' neurobiological individual, rather than addressing an underfunded public education system, privatized healthcare, Big Pharma, unaffordable childcare, and the normalization of competitive individualism. As one doctor was quoted as saying in the *New York Times*: 'We've decided as a society that it's too expensive to modify the kid's environment. So we have to modify the kid.'[48]

Given this context, the critiques by Stiegler and Crary are not incorrect, but by refusing to see any benefits to digital technology they remain attached to a traditional model of pedagogy (and quite possibly risk driving more students towards ADHD meds). At the same time, the meet-you-half-way pragmatism of N. Katherine Hayles and Cathy Davidson feels unsatisfyingly conciliatory; both authors tend to paper over the neoliberal context of contemporary education and a profit-driven pharmaceutical industry. For Hayles, the rise in diagnoses simply indicates a generational 'shift in the mean toward the ADHD end of the spectrum' as a result of exposure to media stimulation.[49] For Davidson, pedagogy needs to be rethought for a generation reared on multitasking, making use of videogaming, blogging, self-grading, and collaborative learning. Both advocate a redesign of US education that seems comfortably in tune with a digital economy.

It is salutary to contrast their work to that of media historian Kenneth Rogers, who demonstrates how, beginning in the 1980s, attention started to be thought of less as a capacity than as a *resource*, and thus contributed to a neoliberal reframing of the self.[50] ADHD and the attention economy, he argues, exert such pressure on the social field precisely because they form a two-pronged attack. When this bifurcated pressure coincided with portable, networked digital technology in the 2000s, it opened up attention to new forms of measurement and instrumentalization for profit – clicks, views, downloads, shares, likes, followers. ADHD medication became a neuro-technology for enabling the individual to self-regulate their *own* biological capital and thereby to meet the needs of political and economic liberalism. We are now at the point where ADHD medication is arguably the pharmaceutical wing of the attention economy: on platforms like TikTok (2017–), the algorithm comes full circle to suggest ADHD self-diagnoses and medication to users who exhibit certain interests and preferences.

Of course, when the term *attention economy* first appeared in the 1990s, it was in relation to advertising on television, not to social media.[51] Georg Franck, a German philosopher, economist, and urban planner, produced a series of articles that pointed out the asymmetry between celebrities in the media and the 'work' of people sitting in front of television screens and reading magazines, 'paying' attention that gets monetized for others' profit.[52] Contemporaneously, US net theorist Michael Goldhaber began describing an attention economy in relation to the internet – at this point still largely a free space without ads, banners, pop-ups, and other forms of clickbait.[53] In an attention economy, he writes, our capacity to focus is conceived as a limited resource because the brain can only take in so much information; we are thus compelled to make decisions about what to attend to and for how long. Business is like a performance in search of an audience, even fans – and there is no limit to how much attention you (or your business) can receive, unlike material goods (food, clothes, cars), where you tend to reach a saturation point. When you have people's attention, Goldhaber claims, you 'own' a bit of property in their mind.

Unsurprisingly, Goldhaber's perspective won out – not least because attention was already being described and expressed economically, in phrases like 'paying', 'lending', 'spending', and 'investing' your time. Attention was ideally poised to fill a gap in business theory at a moment when information, experiences, and services were becoming the foundations of a post-Fordist service economy. It didn't hurt that attention could also be medicated into existence. Some of the earliest business literature on the attention economy even makes this connection: the first line of Thomas H. Davenport and John C. Beck's landmark publication, for example, asks 'Does your company suffer from organizational ADD?'[54] The attention economy and attention deficit coexist as two sides of the same lucrative coin, both seeking to optimize and monetize our capacity to focus.

This is not to deny that many families have been helped by ADHD medication. It enables kids to function better at school, to fit in and make friends. Behavioural problems like hyperactivity, hyperkineticism, and delinquency became controllable and less stressful for parents. For many students and working adults, medication is a way to handle the pressures of the contemporary workplace: to be productive, competitive, and boost cognitive performance. And yet . . . how rapidly these become economic calculations. Focus and concentration matter because they lead to improved qualifications and a return on educational investment. Even when schools embrace neurodiversity and offer therapy, it is always towards the goal of conventionally measured academic achievement. The fact that one can medicate oneself into high performance normalizes the idea that it is natural and right to increase the quality, quantity, and speed of one's output. It shifts the locus of repair onto the individual, rather than pointing to decades of disinvestment in public education and welfare. And it obviates the idea that other forms of attention are equally valid, and potentially more resistant, vital, creative, and fulfilling. Imagine if children didn't need to be medicated for 'underachievement', and if there were multiple educational paths to allow children's diverse and disparate energies to flourish without imposing (and rewarding) conformity to an outdated, metrically evaluated norm. Art, dance, and music are some of the places where these energies might find alternative outlets for exploration.[55] The goal should not be greater economic efficacy but greater collective happiness in all its wild plurality.

Ecologies of Care

The pathologization of attention enforces a split between mind and body, individual and society. It lets you off the hook, because it's your brain that has the deficit, not you. And yet it's you, the individual, that gets medicated – not society. French scholar Yves Citton puts forward an alternative way of thinking that starts from the assumption that attention is a transindividual, relational, and collective phenomenon. He theorizes an 'ecology of attention', arguing that the direction of any single person's attention is always influenced by that of others. Attention is thus reframed away from individualist and economic paradigms and towards the collective and ecological: '*through "me", it is always "our" collective thinking and feeling who is paying attention*'.[56] An ecological approach to attention, he suggests, would entail not just a breakdown of its conventional dual horizon (subject and object) but a consideration of the environmental consequences of any image sphere. When looking at art, Citton speculates, this would mean redirecting attention away from the 'first material ground' (the ostensible subject matter of an image) and towards the 'second ground', its concrete material substrate, and asking, in turn, how this interacts with the environment. Using the example of an undated watercolour by Rajarshi Mitra titled *Storm in Calcutta*, Citton points to the paints, the printed page on which we see the reproduction, and the pixels (if we are reading on a screen):

> the water that the Bengalese painter used to mix his watercolour may have been polluted by uncontrolled industrialization; the

> production of my liquid-crystal screen emitted sulphur hexafluoride, which is the most powerful greenhouse gas . . . As we watch the rain fall on the Calcutta pedestrians in Rajarshi Mitra's watercolour, we must learn to see how the circulation of images and texts, along with the circulation of barrels of oil and rare metals, contribute to the climate imbalance that threatens to engulf this city.[57]

Such an expanded frame, Citton proposes, would allow us to unite an ecology of attention with attention to the ecology. For art historians, such an attention to art's materiality as a 'second ground' is nothing new, but positioning this in relation to the climate crisis is arguably a less familiar move. Still, it is telling that Citton saves this example for the final pages of his book. Pursuing this approach in any further detail would necessarily lead to a study whose primary focus is the bad Anthropocene. This book has a much smaller frame – the analysis of some operations in recent art and performance – and admits that it fiddles while Rome burns.

Citton conscripts attention into *care*, an important subtheme in twenty-first-century attention studies.[58] An attention ecology, for Citton, is rooted in the ethics and politics of care, understood as solidarity with and responsibility towards others. Care as a discourse emerged in the 1980s, when white feminist scholars proposed an ethics of individual care and consideration as opposed to an abstract concept of justice.[59] Attention was thus reframed as *attentiveness* to context, emphasizing interdependent relationships that develop over time. Since the mid-2000s, Black feminists have taken up this discourse in two further ways. First, by framing care as *self-care*, a radical and transgressive self-love that became prominent in the aftermath of Black Lives Matter activism and burnout; second, as care for the dying and those who continue to live with the consequences of slavery, as explored in Christina Sharpe's *In the Wake* (2016).[60]

Care is characterized by quiet nurturing, reminding us that the word *attention* derives from the Latin *attendere*: combining *at* (proximity) and *tendere* (to tend to, incline towards). The connotations are less of grasping and owning than tending towards, and reciprocity – attending to that which preoccupies others.[61] It's a prominent term throughout Tina Campt's *A Black Gaze* (2021), where it is constitutive of ethical attention – a 'being with' rather than 'looking at'.[62] Campt uses care to describe both the artists' relationship to their subjects and the viewers' interaction with the resulting work; for both, intimacy and duration are central. She describes the attentiveness bestowed by Black artists on their subjects of video and performance as a 'slow ethics of care'. Elsewhere, she recalls sitting on the floor of photographer Deana Lawson's studio, pen and notebook in hand, allowing herself to be captured by the gaze of the artist's portraits, thereby reversing visual mastery. Campt's book takes up a long tradition of thinking the gaze as haptic, moving beyond the possessive associations of the optical.[63] Her concept of care is powerfully reparative. At the same time, it leaves me uneasy. I don't find myself turning to art for care or to be cared for (there's enough of that already in my life). It shifts the discussion to ethics and away from politics. It also returns us to the depth model of a fully present beholder. In art history, this model is most often associated with the writing of Michael Fried.[64] While Campt's approach to absorption is quite different – she emphasizes reciprocity, Fried admires transcendence – both admire a type of work that is unitary and graspable, be this a large-scale photograph or an abstract sculpture. For both writers, presentness is grace.

The works discussed in the first three chapters of this book offer none of the formal unity endorsed by Fried and Campt, only partial and fragmentary views: installations that aggregate more material than can be digested; performances that last for weeks; interventions that exist more for media circulation than for first-hand viewing. Since full attention is compromised from the get-go, they abandon a modernist aesthetics of rapt enthrallment and plenitude. Instead, they suggest modes of collective attention that are hybrid, disordered, and almost certainly less satisfying.

And they imply a different model of the viewing subject: not a poised and centred spectator, but one whose perception is tugged in multiple directions by other people and technology. The dichotomies of depth versus shallowness, slow versus fast, are appealing and tenacious, but we need to find other ways to describe the disorderly operations of attention today.

Disordering Attention

While *Disordered Attention* is framed by the reality of an attention economy (the monetization of our limited capacity to absorb information), it is not a tirade against the experience economy. The latter term is frequently used to talk about flashy, photogenic installation art – from blockbuster exhibitions by Yayoi Kusama to commercial extravaganzas like *Van Gogh: The Immersive Experience*. My goal in this book is to provide some history and theory for four types of art and performance that are less obviously photogenic and more visually austere.

Here, ironically, my ambition is to impose some order where there seems to be little. Around 2010, the global expansion of art history and contemporary art seemed to provoke anxiety among scholars: the art world was becoming too baggy and sprawling to be meaningfully analysed, and there was simply too much to take into account.[65] By contrast, this book tries to make the case that it is necessary and possible to identify some of the artistic strategies that have emerged in the last thirty years, and to analyse these synchronically and diachronically. Although my examples are drawn primarily from Europe and North America, they represent approaches that can be found globally: archival installations, durational performance, and unauthorized interventions. (Chapter 4, for reasons explained therein, is less widespread.) Although regional variants exist, they are united by a shared relationship to digital technology that is itself historical. Each chapter is premised on the idea that our relationship to the digital has changed drastically in the last three decades – from the utopian early days of the internet, to the participatory euphoria of Web 2.0, to the antidemocratic manipulations of social media. Noticing these shifts allows us to identify transformations in artistic strategies and spectatorship within a period that is labelled as 'contemporary', while reflecting on how these technological developments have themselves become important research tools.

The four chapters cumulatively track various encroachments of digital culture into art, performance, and their audiences. The first chapter focuses on research-based art, a type of installation practice that emerged in the early 1990s, and which often deploys large amounts of *text* to convey information – in books, documents, ephemera, archives, faxes, slide shows, or databases. When we survey the trajectory of this work since the 1990s, we notice the changing valence of 'truth' – from a poststructuralist critique of universal truth to the right-wing assault on objectivity – reflected in artistic conceptions of what constitutes knowledge. Installations in the 1990s gave viewers a large role in sifting and synthesizing research materials. As literacy has evolved in tandem with the internet and social media, the audience's appetite for synthesizing large quantities of text has shifted – from a sense of empowered autonomy to feelings of information overload. It becomes difficult to take in everything so we triage our viewing. The mode of attention that results is *skimming* and *sampling* – reading quickly to get the gist, or sampling two or three parts of the installation rather than the whole.

The second chapter turns to exhibitions of performance and especially dance that began in the late 2000s, around the same time as the introduction of the iPhone. These performance exhibitions have been lacerated by art critics and dance critics alike, whose disparaging comments often draw comparisons to social media. Yet the relationship to digital technology is deeper: a matter of internal composition and structure. For performance exhibitions to exist in the gallery for the duration of opening hours, for example, choreographers organize time by *looping* and *refreshing*. The relocation of the performing arts into the gallery space is thus symptomatic: while performance exhibitions encourage photographic capture and circulation, they also prioritize an embodied physical presence and immediacy that is organized 'digitally'. I argue that performance exhibitions do not signal the end of fully focused attention but exemplify how we look at art today. They instantiate a new mode of *hybrid spectatorship* that returns us to aspects of pre-modern sociality, now triangulated between the live work, an in-person audience, and an online network.

The third chapter attempts to analyse artistic interventions, a way of working that has yet to be theorized and historicized. I define interventions as rapid-fire, ephemeral artistic gestures that are undertaken in public space and go viral. The disruptive ethos of this work goes back to the historical avant-garde, but 'intervention' as an artistic term was not used until the 1970s in Brazil, when US interference in Central and Latin America was beginning to be described as interventionist. Grounded in the brevity and immediacy of physical action in an urban milieu, interventions have always sought some form of media circulation – be this printed newspapers, television, or social media. Examples from the last decade have mobilized social media in ways that have changed our understanding of the artist-interventionist – from an anonymous outsider to a social media personality who feels emboldened to undertake actions with the support of their globally (dis)connected followers. The type of attention that interventions elicit is the peak-and-wane model of the *viral*: the spread, saturation, and fatigue that data scientists describe as the 'sigmoid curve'.[66]

The final chapter addresses a type of citational practice that has been prevalent since the early 1990s: the invocation of modernist architects and designers, which can be found across Eastern and Western Europe and North and South America. Invocation denotes a respectful, even reverential approach to a cultural precedent. The proper name of the modernist precedent plays a prominent role – most often, canonical male figures like Le

Corbusier, Mies van der Rohe, and Oscar Niemeyer, but increasingly 'minor' figures, especially women (e.g., Eileen Agar, Lina Bo Bardi, Charlotte Perriand). Although most of this work deploys traditional artistic media (i.e., painting, sculpture, photography, drawing, film, video), my image archive for this chapter was amassed online. Keeping track of the many examples has in turn required the creation of an online archive.[67] This ever-growing body of work raises the question of periodization (what does the artistic obsession with modernism tell us about the mindset of a period that calls itself contemporary?) but also speaks to the problem of researching contemporary art today (how to reckon with a glut of similar works at a moment when everything is online?). The repetitions found in this work are framed through the attentional mode of *scrolling*: a flatness of affect only occasionally punctured by curiosity.

While attention ebbs and flows as a focus in these four essays, temporal experience remains a recurrent theme: a time-pressure when faced with information overload, giving in to duration, the brevity of the viral, and numbing repetition. Four genres of work are each underpinned by a respective artistic strategy: aggregation, duration, disruption, and invocation. Each chapter describes a relationship between the subject, time, and technology, and articulates a variant of hybrid attention that has emerged since the 1990s: skimming and sampling, hybrid spectatorship, viral attention, and scrolling.

My methods are – in keeping with the book's theme – somewhat hybrid and disorderly. The four essays were originally conceived as independent texts; only belatedly did I realize the connecting theme was attention. They are not presented here in the sequence in which they were written, but have been reordered to begin with attention under a spotlight, which dims as the book proceeds. Each chapter leans on different intellectual traditions for its method. The first chapter is genealogical, drawing a trajectory for a type of work now thirty years old but never previously historicized. The second is more classically focused on three case studies and discourse analysis (the grey zone as the convergence of white cube and black box). The third mobilizes conjunctural analysis, a term taken from cultural theorist Stuart Hall to describe an expansive approach to periodization. The fourth is a critical revision of distant reading, accompanied by an online image database. The schema underpinning the book is outlined in the accompanying table.

Genre of practice	*Strategy*	*Mode of attention*	*Effect*	*Method*
Research-based art	Aggregation	Skimming and sampling	Information overload	Genealogy
Performance exhibition	Duration	Hybrid/social spectatorship	Grey zone	Case studies
Intervention	Disruption	Viral/S-curve	Interest and fatigue	Conjunctural analysis
Invocation	Citation/ appropriation	Scrolling	Déjà vu	Distant reading

The traditional unit of art historical analysis is the singular case study. I have eschewed this, preferring to stand back and survey a field, grasping conventional types and strategies rather than lingering on paradigmatic examples. This is for two reasons. The first is an unease with the monographic model. The aggrandizement of authorship by the market and museums constructs the (male) artist as an exceptional individual, and conceals the vast infrastructural network that supports him. In the city I call home, the art world is awash with ludicrous wealth for the winners (collectors and artists who make it big) and crippling debt and precarity for the losers (graduates, artists, and performers who struggle to get by). This discrepant economy spurs me to read art as a cultural symptom rather than as an expression of individual creative genius. Works of art do their best to think through our moment, but the world changes faster and more cruelly than even artists can grasp. McLuhan's observation that artists are the canaries in the mine is no longer true.[68] Some of the works discussed in this book are nostalgic and sentimental; others inadvertently exacerbate a situation. In the twenty-first century, works of art tend to be symptomatic of larger conditions, rather than anticipatory fortune tellers.[69]

The second reason is to retrieve a model of broad scope writing that used to be common practice in art criticism, but which has largely been replaced by affirmative monographic essays and book chapters. *Disordered Attention* thus attempts to tread a path between a disappearing model of synoptic art journalism and the method of 'distant reading' that emerged around 2000 in studies of world literature. As formulated by literary scholar Franco Moretti, distant reading at its most radical mobilizes the digitalization of literary works to draw conclusions from units that are smaller or larger than the text: 'devices, themes, tropes – or genres and systems'.[70] Not uncontroversially, this devalues the exceptional work in favour of the broader tendency. In following this approach, I present art as a collective phenomenon: a set of widely used strategies for making and doing, rather than the singular output of an extraordinary individual. In turn, attention itself becomes a collective phenomenon – hence my emphasis throughout on the 'we' of seeing and experiencing art and performance.

This is not to write off the value of close looking, which has been the most cherished mode of visual analysis for art historians since the discipline's inception. Even during the intellectual upheavals of the 1970s, when Marxism and feminism reframed what we value and how a canon is produced, and the 1980s, when deconstruction and postcolonial theory respectively challenged unity and universality, depth remained a constant value. In this, art history shares with related disciplines in the humanities a baseline equation of depth with meaning. More recently, literary scholars have advocated 'surface reading' as a rejection of unveiling and unmasking (as found in Marxist and psychoanalytic approaches) – but this still entails close looking.[71] I am not averse to this: one of the great pleasures of the humanities is spending sustained amounts of time with cultural artifacts, and being guided through another person's close looking and thinking. The attention in this book is close and long (as evidenced in the decade it has taken to write it); it is simply trained on *types* of practice more than individual works.

There are two more methodological assumptions underlying this book. The first is that technology (including digital technology) is not a discrete unit that 'impacts' the work of art, the artist, or the viewer. Technology as exteriority would presume a pure and essential concept of human nature. Instead, we are entwined with our technological objects as prostheses.[72] Bronze Age axe-heads, the printing press, pens, libraries, cars, books, iPhones – all are prosthetic technologies, both material and phenomenological. They are not fully interior or exterior to the subject, because technology is constitutive of human consciousness *and* an object of sensual engagement; it shapes the mind, but only because the mind is already embodied and social, biological and cultural, dependent upon and responsive to others.

For this reason, I have sought to avoid reductive statements about digital technology's 'effect' on human perception. In this I follow philosopher Brian Massumi, who describes television not as a perspectival 'window on the world' but as an 'operative event-space' that includes the content of the home, the screen, the mediated content – and, I would add, its viewers.[73] In Massumi's reading, technology isn't reducible to the television set that 'impacts' the viewers; it's an event-space assemblage of spectatorial behaviours, affects, gender conventions, and flows of power. The iPhone and social media are similarly intra-active, and even more dispersed and multidirectional than television. This technology forms part of a shifting entanglement of global financial investment (factory production, transnational distribution, stocks and shareholders), environmental pollution (mineral extraction, energy production), labour exploitation (Coltan miners in the DRC, Foxconn workers in China), aesthetics (design, branding, interfaces), social forms of participation and communication (news, texting, social media, digital literacy), and neurobiology (dopamine, serotonin).[74]

The second assumption of this book is that works of art construct particular ways of seeing. Attention is not a volitional state of focus that exists in opposition to distraction, but is a collective phenomenon. It is structured for us by a situation and a set of external conditions (the work of art, performance, exhibition, concert, webpage, social environment), which in turn encounter our internal predispositions and desires. We can therefore analyse how any given work of art *attempts* to steer and structure our attention – but this success is never guaranteed, and is contingent upon the audience (who may have competing impulses) and the context (poor acoustics, humidity, crowds). As a result, there is no 'ideal viewer', only a flow of possible approximations. We might feel obligated to be 'good' viewers and make a fair stab at looking at or watching everything in an exhibition, but equally feel overwhelmed and alienated by the amount of material it contains. We might want to be fully present for a performance and at the same time take a few photographs and a short video, and send them to our friends and respond to their comments. The artist's desires and intentions continually come into conflict with the contingencies of staging and circulation and the audience's own orientations and needs. When I refer to 'attention' in the rest of this book, it denotes this collision of artistic strategies, spectatorial conventions, individual inclinations, and unforeseen contextual eventualities.

Disordered Attention aims to move beyond the moralizing binary of attention/distraction, to dispense with attention's economic framing, to jettison plenitudinous modern attention as an impossible ideal, and to rethink contemporary spectatorship as neither good nor bad but perpetually hybrid and collective. Crary is right: the internet complex *is* environmentally ecocidal. Yet digital technology and the modes of contemporary attention it has engendered are not going away. New habits are forming, and new protocols are being established. Contemporary art and performance wrestle with these, and try to guide our attention in new ways – not always successfully – but they present challenges whose reactions and effects tell us about our ongoing adaptation to, and imbrication with, networked technology in the twenty-first century. Our task is to understand these emergent patterns of cultural production and consumption, rather than to fantasize their disappearance. Whether we like it or not, hybrid attention is 'OS XXI', the operating system of spectatorship in the twenty-first century.

1

Information Overload: Research-Based Art

Postcards, faxes, and email printouts lie wanly in a vitrine. A plywood shelving unit holds rows of informational leaflets. One gallery wall is plastered with graphs and charts. Another is covered in hundreds of seemingly identical photographs. On a bank of video monitors, talking heads are explaining something, but you'll need to sit down and put on headphones. In a darkened corner, a slide projector clunks slowly through a carousel of images. Nearby, a 16-mm film whirs alongside a soporific voice-over. An illuminated table is covered in papers and newspaper clippings marked up with Post-its. Every object on display is accompanied by a lengthy explanatory caption written by the artist, also available as a pamphlet.

If any of this sounds familiar, you've been in the presence of research-based art. Although the elements vary, the genre is characterized by a reliance on text – printed or spoken – to support an abundance of materials, distributed spatially. In place of the usual vertical arrangement on a wall (which announces itself as 'art'), items are reoriented horizontally in a vitrine or on a table (which reads as 'archive'). Although the individual elements may vary, the overall structure is always additive rather than distilled, obeying a logic of more is more. Whenever I encounter one of these installations, I start to experience a feeling of mild panic. How much time is it going to take to wade through this? Do I really need to read it *all*?

Rarely do I experience surprise. Today, research-based art is nothing novel; its presence is almost mandatory in any serious exhibition. Although the term *research-based art* has been in circulation for a good twenty years, and this type of work emerged at least a decade before that, the genre has never been clearly defined – or, for that matter, critiqued. It has much in common with other trends that have arisen since the 1990s, such as the artist-curated exhibition and the archival turn, but is not fully congruent with either.[1] While research-based art brings up similar issues of display and archival presentation, this essay seeks to examine a bigger issue: how changes in digital literacy since the 1990s have impacted our consumption of this type of contemporary art, and how artistic approaches to research and knowledge have similarly shifted over the same period. In what follows, I will offer a tentative genealogy for research-based art, before going on to chart four overlapping phases of this work from the 1990s to the 2010s. These periods, I argue, have evolved in tandem with changes in digital information delivery, which have consequences for display, spectatorship, and the relationship between knowledge and truth. While research-based art initially seized the utopian possibilities of the internet (making vast amounts of information available to a counter-public sphere), its more recent iterations seem to have fully internalized an internet logic (the epistemology of search, information overload). The archive and the library are no longer the first steps in a research process that led to a work of art, but have become the work of art itself.

Although research-based art is a global phenomenon, it is inseparable from the rise of doctoral programmes for artists in the West, especially in Europe, in the early 1990s. According to a 2012 survey conducted by art historian James Elkins, seventy-three institutions in Europe offered PhDs in studio art, forty-two of which were in the UK alone – striking statistics when compared to just five in Canada, seven in the US, and four in Brazil.[2] Unlike Master of Fine Arts degrees (the usual higher education qualification for artists), doctoral programmes generally expect that artistic practice be supplemented by written research – either as a separate but related dissertation, or made legible within the artwork itself. While some of the artists I discuss below were born outside Euro-North America, they have all passed through its art schools. Even if they don't have doctorates, the intellectual milieu of these programmes informs their work, along with the broader conscription of education to neoliberal systems of value.

This differs from previous models of education, in which knowledge – along with truth and reason – was one of the autonomous goals of a liberal model of education pursued for its own sake. Beginning in the 1990s, the neoliberalization of the university resignified knowledge as capital: externally funded, separated from teaching, directly linked to the functional imperatives of the economy, and evaluated using the language of finance and 'return on investment'. Such a shift from knowledge for the public good to 'knowledge production' for the information economy required a fundamental rethinking of education. In the UK especially, knowledge has been strategically reconceived as a form of capital that flows from academia to industry and government, a recognizable 'output' that leads to measurable 'impact': funded, created, acquired, transmitted, and protected through intellectual property laws.

Unsurprisingly, the literature on research-based art is overwhelmingly European. Practice-based PhD programmes in Northern Europe have resulted in a slew of anthologies presenting the results of doctoral studies in visual art, performance, and theatre.[3] These tend to fall into two categories: a collection of articles mired in the specifics of a given research project, often in an upbeat promotional register, or general surveys, often by faculty in administrative positions, with a more fraught tone of underlying ambivalence about the problematic contiguity between practice-based PhDs and the neoliberal knowledge economy. These surveys express anxiety about the marketization of higher education, even though many of them constitute 'research outputs' that are themselves symptomatic of the need to demonstrate accountability to a funding body.

There are many reasons to be sceptical of the PhD-in-Fine-Art boom. One is that it exacerbates hierarchies of economic privilege already endemic to art education. Paying for another two to four years of education on top of a BFA and MFA means that practice-based PhDs are largely the preserve of those who can afford them.[4] It also leads to the expectation, already prevalent in some countries, that artists should have a PhD to be able to teach. The result is an academicization of artistic practice, which becomes tamed, systematic, and professional. For artist Hito Steyerl, 'artistic research' has even become a new discipline: one that normalizes, regulates, and ensures the repetition of protocols.[5] Yet as Elkins points out, very few influential texts or manifestos by artists of the past would ever be granted a doctorate, because some of the best writing by artists has been dogmatic and impulsive rather than laboriously researched and peer reviewed.

My focus in this chapter is not the neoliberal university context, since this has been much discussed already.[6] Nor do I want to recap the longer history of postwar art education – the shift, identified by art historian Howard Singerman, from artisanal training in technical skills to discursive forms of practice that place a premium on the verbal articulation of the work of art.[7] Nor do I look at moving-image work in terms of research, even though it shares many of the same concerns as the practices discussed in this essay; this lineage has been well charted by Steyerl. Nor, finally, will I examine the curatorial endeavours that have supported and enabled the dissemination of research-based art.[8]

Instead, my task here is closer to recent writing that has made a fruitful attempt to analyse 'artistic research' – a broader historical category of which I take research-based art to be a recent subset – in terms of knowledge production and epistemology.[9] Yet none of these texts steps back to analyse the *forms* that artistic research adopts, the type of *knowledge* that artists produce, or how the viewer *attends* to the information that has been assembled.[10] My point is that research-based installation art – its techniques of display, its accumulation and spatialization of information, its models of research, its construction of a viewing subject, and its relationship to knowledge and truth – cannot be understood in isolation from contemporaneous developments in networked digital technology.

Three Genealogies

Not one but three art-historical genealogies converge in research-based art: photodocumentary (specifically, the tradition of lengthy captioning), the film essay, and Conceptual art. The first of these emerged in the first decade of the twentieth century, when US photographer Lewis Hine began including extensive text in his photo-studies documenting immigrants, workers, and child labourers; witnesses were invited to counter-sign Hine's long descriptive captions, which included measurements and statistics. The photographs generated by the New Deal–era Farm Security Administration (FSA) in the 1930s were also supplemented by explanatory captions, sometimes written by the photographers themselves (e.g., Dorothea Lange's text for *Migrant Mother*, 1936).[11] It is telling that these photographs were driven by a strong social conscience and often formed part of a broader campaign for social change. In this tradition, the text anchors the photographic proof, rather than complicating the image with an ambiguous poetic surplus.

In the postwar period, South African photographer David Goldblatt carried forward this baton most poignantly. The extended captions accompanying Goldblatt's photographs from the 1960s onwards incorporate his own research into people and places, together with direct quotations from encyclopaedias or other official documentation, to which his images often serve as a reproach or emotive counter-evidence.[12] The supplementary text seeks to underscore the evidentiary capacity of the photograph while simultaneously casting doubt on its visual potency.[13] A recent example of this double-edged approach, which appears to wilfully embrace the internet phenomenon of the 'research rabbit hole', might be Taryn Simon's installation *A Living Man Declared Dead and Other Chapters I–XVIII* (2008–11): eighteen family trees, each containing three panels (one of portraits, one of text, and one of supplementary images). The entire installation, which fills several galleries when displayed in its entirety, is tellingly described as having 'chapters'; the catalogue weighs twelve pounds and comprises 864 pages.

The second precursor is the film essay, in which a written text is spoken by a narrator and juxtaposed with moving images and music to produce a range of powerful aesthetic and intellectual effects. This genre has been described as 'vococentric', since its soundtracks are dominated and arranged around the voiceover reading a text.[14] Although the genre has existed since 1909, it only gained a name after the publication of Hans Richter's

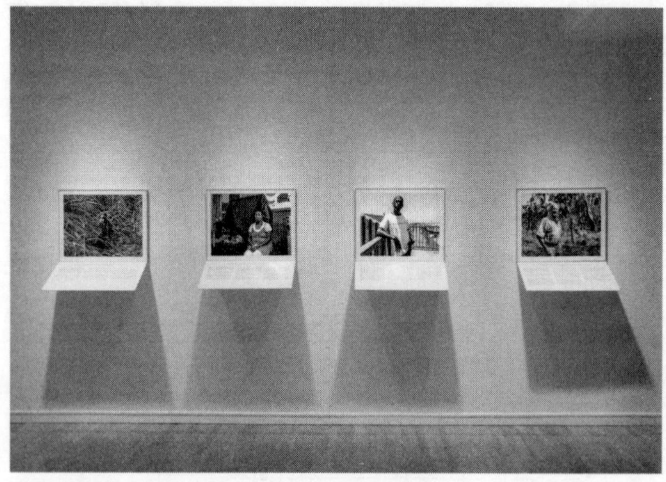

David Goldblatt, *Ex-offenders at the Scene of Crime or Arrest,* 2008–16. Series of forty-eight photographs. Installation view, Pace/MacGill, New York, 2016.

'The Film Essay' in 1940.[15] Richter describes it as a form that makes abstract ideas (like capitalism, or freedom) visible, and which goes beyond documentary in embracing the 'contradictory, irrational, and fantastic'.[16] The film essay was taken up by anticolonial filmmakers in the 1950s, such as Chris Marker and Alain Resnais, and later by exponents of Third Cinema in Latin America. This contestatory, often revolutionary body of work frequently deals with representation's problematic relationship to power and knowledge; in contrast to the evidentiary mode of the photodocumentary tradition, the film essay does not deny a subjective mode of address. The film essay was carried forward in the 1980s by Harun Farocki and the Black Audio Film Collective, among many others; their films, originally made as works for cinema, are now more frequently shown in art galleries for an ambulatory audience. Hito Steyerl, one of the leading contemporary practitioners of this work, has helpfully outlined the relationship between the essay film and artistic research.

The third genealogy is Conceptual art, especially the interdisciplinary work of artists in the 1970s, who worked across psychoanalysis (Mary Kelly), anthropology (Susan Hiller), and sociology (Hans Haacke). Haacke is arguably the paradigmatic artist-researcher of that decade: he drew upon publicly available records to mount exposés of real-estate properties owned by slumlords (*Shapolsky et al. Manhattan Real Estate Holdings*, 1971) and the controversial provenance of works of art in museum collections (*Manet-Projekt*, 1974). Although such projects could be seen as positioning the viewer as an ideologically malleable recipient of the artist's message, Haacke framed his approach through the more neutral, transdisciplinary method of systems theory: his work was an attempt to introduce new information into a gallery or museum where it would be read differently. As Haacke observed, 'Information presented at the right time and in the right place can potentially be very powerful. It can affect the general social fabric.'[17]

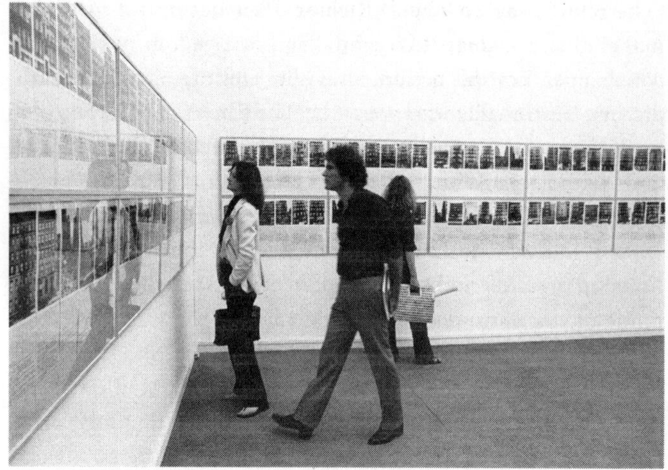

Hans Haacke, *Shapolsky et al. Manhattan Real Estate Holdings, a Real-Time Social System, as of May 1, 1971*, 1971. One hundred and forty-six photographic views of New York apartment buildings, six pictures of transactions, an explanatory wall panel, and maps of Harlem and the Lower East Side. Installation view, Venice Biennale, 1978.

Photodocumentary captions, the film essay, and Conceptual art share an interdisciplinary orientation, and a tendency to edit and present research sequentially – as a series of images (on the wall or in books), as a time-based narrative, or as an installation with a serial arrangement. This linear logic has dominated information systems since the invention of alphanumeric writing and was consolidated by the printing press. In the late 1980s, media theorist Vilém Flusser, detecting a change of paradigm on the horizon, described linear thinking as process-oriented and historical. The lines of a text are causal, he argued, creating vectors of meaning not just on the page but between humans and their reality: 'We are "Western people" because our "forma mentis" has been shaped by the linearity of the alphanumeric code.'[18] Flusser cautioned that linear thinking was about to be surpassed by what he called 'technical images' – his term for a range of media including photographs, film, video, television screens, and computer terminals, that have a 'circular' logic and a bias towards the visual that he found incompatible with the construction of history.[19] Other thinkers of this period, like Gilles Deleuze and Félix Guattari, enthusiastically endorsed the non-linear, upholding the centreless rhizome as an alternative to the hierarchical tree. Partly as a result of their vivid writing in *A Thousand Plateaus* (1980), the non-linear began to hold great appeal for artists – bolstered by the arrival of the ultimate tool of non-linear communication, the internet.[20] As Flusser intuited, a new relationship between technology and knowledge was on the horizon.

Research Rhizomes

The first phase of research-based art in the 1990s demonstrates a conscious break with narrative linearity. Materials migrated from the walls, where they were placed in a specific sequence, and onto shelves and tables where they could be read in any particular order. This break reconceptualizes the viewer: from being a recipient of a message – or a subject to be enlightened, or a spectator to be activated – to being a *fellow researcher*. Renée Green's installation *Import/Export Funk Office* (1992–93) is an early example of this genre. Thematically, it explores African diasporic culture, bohemia, and subculture, with a focus on the reception of African American hip-hop culture in Germany. Formally, it comprises metal shelving units filled with publications and photographs borrowed from the artist's own collection and that of German music critic Diedrich Diedrichsen. Viewers can consult the books, magazines, music and audio recording, as well as over twenty-six hours of video documenting an ongoing conversation between Green and Diedrichsen, who are occasionally joined by other participants (including Greg Tate and Arthur Jafa).

Part archive, part installation, part exhibition display, *Import/Export* introduces the new hybrid category that is research-based art – albeit as a bridge between previous models of artistic research in the 1970s and the emergent model of research-based

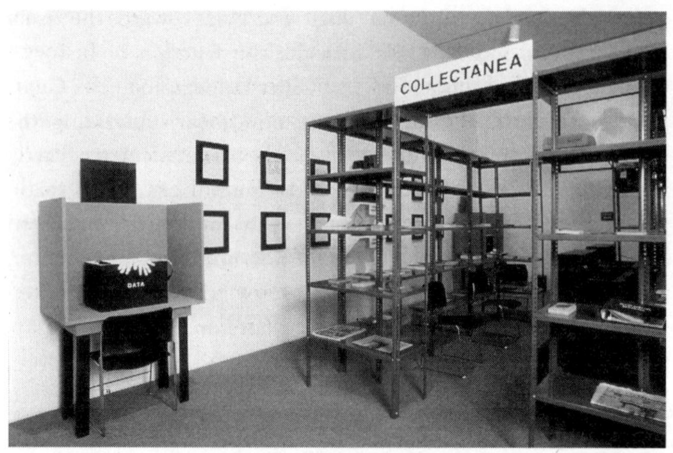

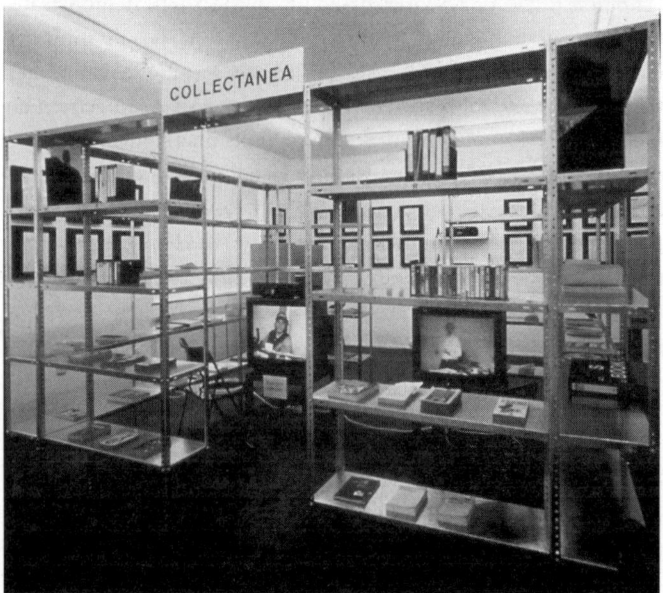

Renée Green, *Import/Export Funk Office*, 1992. Mixed-media installation with metal shelf structure, books, magazines, newspapers, ephemera, BETA video cases, twenty-five hours of digitized video, two monitors, one video projection, cassette cases, sound, acrylic signs, four wooden structures, acrylic signs on four shelves, four cassette players, and thirty wooden plaques with rubber-stamped text. Installation view, Galerie Christian Nagel, Cologne, 1992.

art in the 1990s. With the former it shares an engagement with contemporary culture (rather than a historical topic) and includes the artist's own primary research. It nevertheless augurs later work in its aggregation of pre-existing materials (books, texts, newspapers, photographs) and in leaving the viewer to decide what conclusions to draw.[21] Its most significant break with preceding modes of artistic research is that it invites the viewer to be a *user*, someone who can explore the fragments, synthesize them, and potentially even mobilize the material for his or her own research (or at least perform that role – notice the white gloves placed on top of a box marked 'Data').[22] Green's installation is post-hermeneutic, placing the interpretational onus on the viewer.

Import/Export offers a particularly clear case study because of its explicit relationship to digital technology. In 1995, Green launched a version of *Import/Export* as a CD-ROM, arguing that the spatialization of research implicit in the installation could be more easily consumed via digital hyperlinks on a home computer than in a gallery where viewers never seem to have enough time. This insight, made in advance of widespread use of the internet, points to a distributed model of knowledge that has since become the norm. Rather than using an authorial voice to publicize information (as had Hans Haacke), Green suggests that knowledge is networked, collaborative, and in process. Significantly, her model is not the Web (which in the early 1990s was still not widely used) but *hypertext*: a form of nonsequential writing based on links between verbal and visual information that went on to become the key structural protocol of the internet. Permitting readers to navigate their own paths through masses of information, hypertext was heralded by literary critics like George Landow as a realization of poststructuralist theories of authorship, a virtual instantiation of Deleuze and Guattari's centreless rhizome. The user could follow different paths, disrupting the distinction between text and annotation, and thus between reader and writer.[23] Essays on hypertext are striking in their delirium at the new possibilities of accessing vast amounts of information; the idea that we might feel incapacitated by such quantity and availability was not yet countenanced.

In an essay reflecting on the *Import/Export* CD-ROM, Green approvingly quotes Landow: 'Quantity removes mastery and authority, for one can only sample, not master, a text.'[24] In other words, masses of information offer a compelling alternative to an authoritative model of authorship, and its association with a centred sovereign subject in command of its ideas. Hypertext was championed as opening the door to a more diffuse and participatory mode of reading that signalled both the decisive end to master narratives and the inauguration of a more individual readership, 'since each reader establishes his or her own line of reading'.[25] Accordingly, while *Import/Export* assembles an original constellation of ideas, no overarching narrative is offered – only the raw materials that can be used for building an argument. Nizan Shaked efficiently conveys this when she describes *Import/Export*'s list of materials as a 'syllabus for a humanities course about the 1960s, race relations in the United States, or countercultures. It extended a bibliography rather than a political program, refusing to interpret for the viewer.'[26] Like so much art of this period, ambivalence is permitted, and the artist's own ideological stance is deferred. Back in 1993, Green described her strategy as deliberately avoiding a simple takeaway: the installation 'mocks didacticism', she wrote, and demonstrates 'the complexity of things' rather than making 'any one kind of authoritative statement about the way things are'.[27]

In addition to Green, other pioneers of research-based art include interdisciplinary collectives like the Center for Land Use Interpretation (Los Angeles, formed in 1994), MAP Office (Hong Kong, 1997), Multiplicity (Milan, 2000), and an older generation of artists like Antoni Muntadas (Spain, b. 1942). These first-phase artists undertook their own primary investigations of a topic, often in the form of interviews, critical mapping, or digital archives. Treating research as a public resource, they disseminated their fieldwork on new media interfaces including interactive monitors and websites, transposing materials from walls to shelves and tables where they could be read in any order, creating multi-directional audio-visual environments that pointedly refrained from directing readers along a particular path or providing an overarching narrative.[28]

It's important to stress that for Green and her generation, this aversion to authorial mastery was a response not just to post-structuralism, but also to feminist and postcolonial theory, which variously critiqued linear history as evolutionary, univocal, masculinist, and imperial. To a degree, this rejection of mastery can be seen as a particularly North American response to post-structuralist theory. Humanities scholars fused aspects of Derridean *différance* and Lyotard's end of grand narratives with Frankfurt School critical theory, feminism, and identity politics.[29] In both academia and art schools, poststructuralism's anti-foundationalism (including the 'death of the author') was shifted onto the category of *identity* as the new basis for critique. The situatedness of the authorial subject, manifest as a sensitivity for stating the artist's own 'positionality', came to assume a new importance, resulting in an explanatory excess about the difficulty, contingency, or impossibility of an authoritative position from which to speak (all of which had the effect of asserting another kind of authority, that of the legitimate critical position). The work of graduates of the Whitney Independent Study Program (ISP) and other theory-oriented MFA programmes in the US reflects this academic confluence of deconstruction, critical theory, and postmodernism.[30]

Swiss-born artist and ISP alum Ursula Biemann, for example, offers a particularly clear rationale for open-endedness. The convergence of feminism and postcolonial theory can be seen in her choice of research topics, which focus on the position of working women – in *maquiladoras* on the US–Mexico border, in the global sex trade, and as *domesticas* on the Spain–Morocco border, as well as in the theorists she cites. In the mid-2000s, her work shifted from single-screen video essays to the more dispersed form of multi-screen installations. *Sahara Chronicles* (2006–9), an 'open anthology of videos' about migration in North Africa, has a multi-perspective structure that aims to mirror the migration network itself.[31] The installation comprises an undefined number of videos, which are never all on display when the work is exhibited, in order to keep some out of sight, thereby allegorizing clandestine migration. These are projected on the monitors and walls, and accompanied by wall texts and captioned images. The sheer quantity of information (audio-visual, textual, photographic) is positioned against the streamlining of mainstream news reporting, which reduces complex social relations to a consumable image rather than elaborating a situation.[32] The installation refuses simple messaging in favour of spending time with an issue. Yet, faced with so many hours of video, the viewer is left with the disquieting feeling of only being able to surf these issues. Quantity removes mastery, but sampling turns out to be equally uneasy.

When the rejection of linear argumentation and an authorial voice converged with a restructuring of information and the promise of a collectivized knowledge through new digital technologies, a decisive reorganization of artistic form was accomplished. Information began to be spatialized and networked, leaving behind the seriality that had dominated art of the 1960s and 1970s. Consciously or unconsciously, these new theoretical horizons led to a post-hermeneutic position – in other words, to hesitation over forceful interpretation. A project was said to 'ask questions about' or 'draw attention to' a topic, without any obligation to formulate conclusions or provide an easily digestible message. With hindsight, we can now see that the non-linearity of digital hypertext and poststructuralism cut two ways: on the one hand, it helped to dismantle master narratives; on the other, it produced an excess of information that was difficult, if not impossible, to meaningfully grasp.

Digital to Analogue Conversion

The second phase of research-based art overlaps chronologically with the first but is characterized by an inverse relationship to new technology: rather than embracing digital technology, it is rejected in favour of older apparatuses. Once VHS was replaced by DVD in 1997, obsolete 'dead tech' (35mm slides, celluloid film, record players, overhead projectors) attained a new lease of life – rapidly followed by an enthusiasm for archival ephemera like analogue photographs, postcards, typewritten letters, and eventually even faxes.[33]

The rejection of high-definition video and plasma screens in favour of obsolete technology was accompanied by another unexpected regression – towards narrative. In works by this cohort – Matthew Buckingham, Tacita Dean, Mario García Torres, and others – information confronts the viewer in fragmentary arrays. Yet the rhizomatic structure is reined in by a more conventional mode of storytelling that, while often highly elliptical and subjective, does *not* invite viewers to choose their own adventure. Instead, elements are presented in particular sequences (a row of captioned images, a series of slides, a film with a narrated soundtrack). The seriality that dominated the art of the 1960s and '70s stages a partial return. In some examples, there is a return to subjective interiority; at times, the mode of enquiry can be solipsistic. The issues addressed tended to exist in the past rather than in the present, and interdisciplinarity is rejected in favour of connections to art history.

The Mexican artist Mario García Torres, for example, has consistently deployed outmoded interfaces to present his research since the mid-2000s, when he began a group of works about the Italian artist Alighiero e Boetti. These include nineteen faxes that García Torres 'sent' to the deceased artist (*A Film Treatment [Share-e-Nau Wanderings]*, 2006); ninety slides, accompanied by a fifty-minute-long audio recording in which García Torres recounts his attempts to locate the site of the hotel Boetti established in Kabul in 1971 (*Have You Ever Seen the Snow Coming Down?*, 2010); and a seventy-four-minute 35mm film (transferred to HD video) that chronicles his discovery of the hotel and its subsequent refurbishment as an off-site commission for Documenta 12 (*Tea*, 2012). These works were all shown in Kassel, alongside Boetti's first *Mappa* tapestry (1971), originally destined to be exhibited in Documenta 5 in 1972, and archival correspondence between Boetti and the curator of that exhibition, Harald Szeemann.

Fiction is central to García Torres's work, even though the subjects of his research and documentation are real – usually a well-known cultural protagonist, always male. The artist underscores the instability of history, allowing his subjectivity to enter

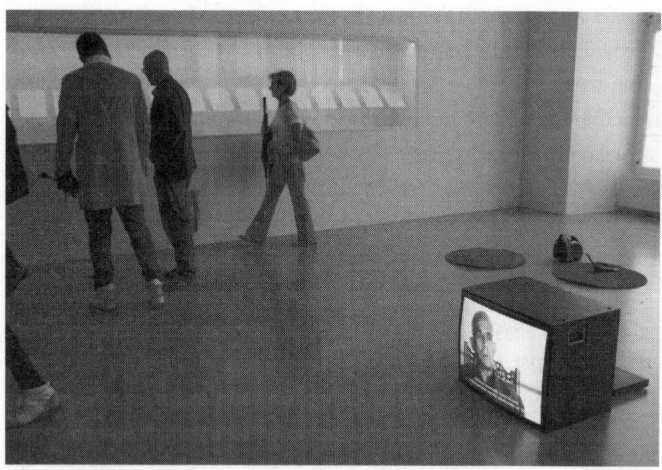

Mario García Torres, *A Film Treatment (Share-e-Nau Wanderings)* (2006) and *After many casual and unscripted talks with Sher Agha, current care taker of Alighiero Boetti's One Hotel site, I asked Aman Mojadidi to formally interview him in Dari and tape his answers. A great talker, Agha went on deep about his childhood in the Share Naw neighborhood of Kabul, the people who inhabited it, their traditions and about his sporadic working relationship with the house occupants since his teens. He chatted about taking care of the house through the last few tenants and about the raise of prices of real estate in the area during the last decade. He finished by saying he had no personal recollection of a hotel being run by Italian twins* (1391, Iranian calendar). Installation view, Documenta 13, Kassel, Germany, 2012.

the frame, less as an autobiographical detail than as a self-reflexive musing on his research process. Each step is laid out like a detective story in which he also confesses his doubts, obsessions, hurdles, and ongoing questions.[34] The text is read slowly, or appears as hypnotically paced subtitles. Because the narrative tends to be arcane and is presented in outmoded media, the results tend to be oneiric, melancholy, and demanding in terms of attention. An overlooked past is brought back into view, but remains forever elusive, clouded with unknowability and obscured by the artist's presence as intermediary. Around 2015, the artist stopped dating his works, in a further effort to undermine the historical fixity of his own career.

Like many of his contemporaries, García Torres presents overlooked histories as fragments, and seems reluctant to extrapolate a bigger point from the shards of information presented to the viewer – but for completely different reasons than the 1990s generation. If the first phase of research-based art was steered by a theoretically informed refusal of master narratives, then the second phase is governed by a desire to show the multiple ways in which individual micronarratives jostle and intersect with History.[35] The self becomes a glue that enables the debris of history to stick together, at least temporarily.

In 2004, art historian Hal Foster took a psychoanalytic approach to this tendency, describing such work as having an 'archival impulse': the artist demonstrates a will to 'connect what cannot be connected', akin to the paranoiac's ability to make connections between disparate points, always with him or herself at the centre.[36] Foster refers to the internet, but primarily to oppose its digital interface with the tactility of archival art; he doesn't mention the fact that the internet had become the technological enabler of this art's connectionist mentality. I would thus revise Foster's argument: the links made by artists are less the result of an unconscious pathological response to social conditions (in Foster's telling, a will to relate at a time of disconnected social order) than an effect of internalizing the apparatus through which their research is increasingly conducted. The new attitude can be evidenced in the following observations by García Torres:

> Obviously [the internet] is always my first point of contact with a subject and many times it leads me to investigate things in a less methodological way, a richer way. It situates normal people, everyday people, at the same level as books and official sources. [The] internet is present all the time, and I don't blame it for often being wrong. I like it. What better way to divert an investigation towards something contradictory or further from the truth. It is there that one finds relations that potentially become something interesting, in the weaving of a new way of telling a story.[37]

In other words, the internet liberates the artist-researcher from academic protocols, and a different type of research becomes possible and validated – a line of thinking governed by drift rather than depth, creative inaccuracy rather than expertise, and accessibility rather than the ivory tower. Nicolas Bourriaud's term *semionaut* might be the best description of this tendency: drifting from signifier to signifier, the artist invents meandering trajectories between cultural signs.[38] In contrast to the first phase, which used a digital logic (the hyperlink) to structure the presentation of primary research, this second phase presents a digital *dérive* as an analogue display. The cold uniformity of the plasma screen is discarded in favour of a more auratic interface and array of objects. Yet artists have already incorporated the search engine and the hyperlink as a method of research. Foster's will to 'connect what cannot be connected' is less a paranoiac symptom than a definition of surfing, updating a trajectory of chance encounters that goes back to the nineteenth-century *flâneur* through to Surrealism and the Situationists – but now with a technological substrate in place of the unconscious.

The second phase of research-based art pries open a gap between *research* and *truth*: rather than being grounded in social themes (migration, sexualized female labour, environmental damage), the work of art pulls disparate strands together through fiction and subjective speculation about history. García Torres has made 'subjective' works about the artists Vito Acconci, Robert Barry, Martin Kippenberger, and Robert Rauschenberg.[39] Here, artistic research opens avenues overlooked by hegemonic historical narratives but tends to shore up a canon of white male protagonists, effectively consolidating received history rather than contesting it.[40] Compare this with the most powerful and radical engagement with micronarrative during the same period, Saidiya Hartman's method of 'critical fabulation'. Her 2008 essay 'Venus in Two Acts' wrestles with the ethical obligations of the researcher, and the necessity of invention in the face of an archive's limitations, exclusions, and deletions.[41] The gap, in her case, concerns the lives of two young women aboard an eighteenth-century slave ship who did not survive the Middle Passage, and the fraught question of how to grant them historical visibility. For fabulation to have critical currency, it matters which histories are being retrieved and why.

Search as Research

The third phase of research-based art can be characterized as fully post-internet, by which I mean not an embrace of, nor a reaction to, but a complete inhabitation of digital logic. It abandons the desire to find connections between links in favour of what art historian David Joselit has described as 'aggregation': the selection and configuration of relatively autonomous elements that signify entirely different values or epistemologies.[42] Joselit argues that aggregation captures the asynchrony of globalization, while also reflecting an 'epistemology of search': in his words, 'what matters more in our contemporary digital world is not making content, but configuring it, searching for it, finding what you need and making meaning from it'.[43] Artists no longer undertake their own research, but download, assemble, and recontextualize existing materials in a desultory updating of appropriation and the ready-made.

What results is a conflation: *search* becomes *research*. The difference is subtle but important. Searching is the preliminary stage of looking for something via a search engine, 'Googling'. Research proper involves analysis, evaluation, and a new way of approaching a problem. Search involves the adaptation of one's ideas to the language of 'search terms' – pre-existing concepts most likely to throw up results – whereas research (both online and offline) involves asking fresh questions and elaborating new terminologies yet to be recognized by the algorithm.

One manifestation of aggregative search-as-research is the propensity to show pre-existing image archives: think of Akram Zaatari's re-presentation of Hashem el Madani's mid-century studio portraiture (*Objects of Study/The Archive of Studio Shehrazade/Hashem el Madani/Studio Practices*, 2007) or Taryn Simon's photographs of folders from the New York Public Library's image archive ('The Color of a Flea's Eye: The Picture Collection', 2013). Other artists aggregate particular types of images: Zoe Leonard's collection of several thousand postcards of Niagara Falls (*You See I Am Here After All*, 2008), or Maryam Jafri's collection of photographs of postcolonial celebration (*Independence Day 1934–1975*, 2009–), both of which are arranged on the wall in grids that evoke a half-loaded page of image-search results. Other artists take aspects of curatorial practice into their own hands by producing lengthy, meandering, or quasi-academic captions to accompany the presentation of their sculptures (e.g., Simon Starling, Danh Vo, Cameron Rowland).

It's rare to find artists who aggregate with an original voice. *Some Gay-Lesbian Artists and/or Artists Relevant to Homo-Social Culture Born between c. 1300–1870* (2007) by Danish artist Henrik Olesen is one refreshing example. Olesen (mis)reads art history through a blatantly anachronistic queer lens, organizing digital copies of paintings and prints and excerpts of pre-existing scholarship (highlighted with a yellow marker) into themes like 'Lesbian Visibility', 'Some Faggy Gestures', and 'Anal Sex in England'. Mounted on freestanding black fabric boards, the display is a conscious reference to Aby Warburg's *Mnemosyne Atlas* (1924–29), in which the German art historian traced the continuation of expressive gestures from antiquity to the Renaissance. Olesen finds a similar persistence of queerness through the centuries. The result is an amusing romp through art history that uses accumulation and juxtaposition to reread works like Gustave Caillebotte's *plein air* paintings of men, now wryly recategorized as 'cruising'.

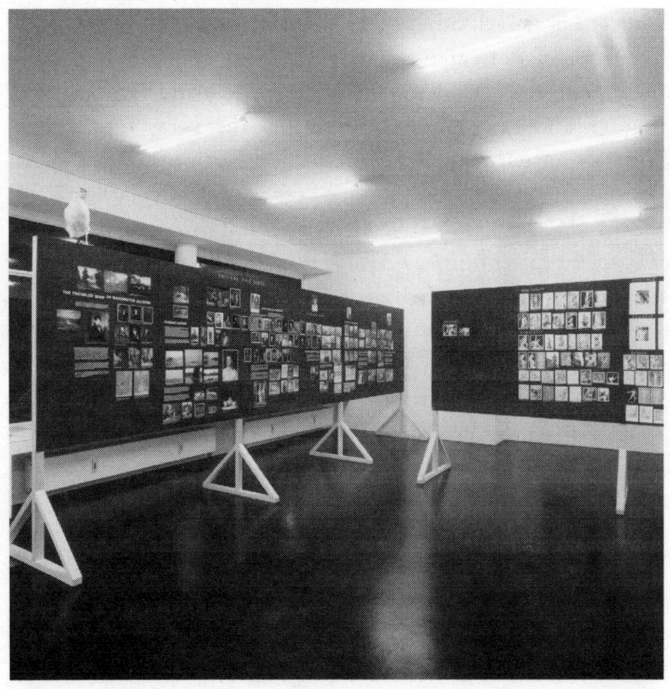

Henrik Olesen, *Some Gay-Lesbian Artists and/or Artists Relevant to Homo-Social Culture I–VII*, 2007. Collage, computer printouts on wooden boards. Installation view, Galerie Buchholz, Cologne, 2007.

More typical, however, is the open-ended aggregation of German photographer Wolfgang Tillmans's 'Truth Study Centre' (2005–). The installation changes from exhibition to exhibition but always consists of many slim wooden tables on which are displayed articles printed out from a range of online media sources. These are placed next to ephemera, the occasional photo by Tillmans, and texts that locate the present moment in relation to a historical event (e.g., 'Now 1993 is as long ago as the Civil Rights Act was in 1993'). In its predominance of text, the installation is a departure from the visuality of Tillmans's wide-ranging photographic practice. It nevertheless shares continuities with his distinctive approach to display: there is an orderliness but no apparent hierarchy between journalism, abstraction, and everyday items like lottery tickets, leaflets, bus tickets, currency, and food wrappers.[44]

'Truth Study Centre' began with sixteen tables (in London in 2005), but some installations have as many as thirty-seven, with

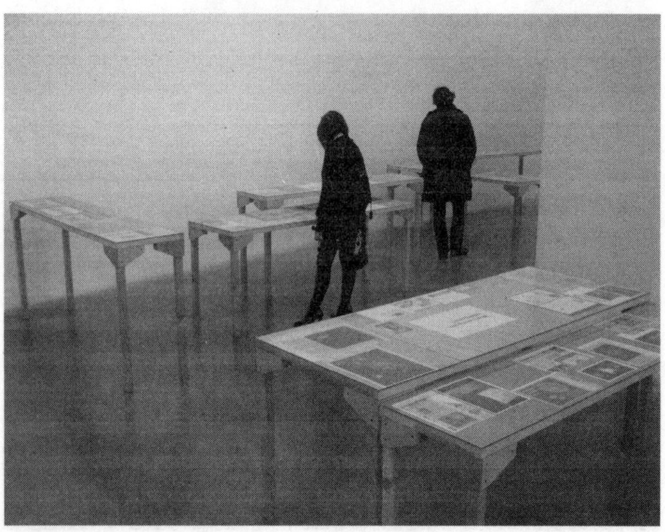

Wolfgang Tillmans, 'Truth Study Center', 2005–. Installation with wooden tables, digital prints on paper, C-print photographs, graphite on paper, and other materials. Installation view, *The Last Newspaper*, New Museum, New York, 2010.

items being swapped in and out according to changes in current affairs. 'There is one table about soldiers and war, one about religion, another about the depiction of war, games and violence on the Internet', observed Tillmans in 2010; 'I also have some images of airlines and the experience of flying and there is one about Americans' attitudes to food.'[45] The most recent iteration, at MoMA in 2022, included newspaper articles dealing with political misperceptions and prejudice, capital punishment, the colonial bias of world maps, the Iraq War, customs and borders, gay rights, and evolution.

An online visualizer of a single table in a 2017 version is hosted on the Tate website, which enables the viewer to zoom in and peruse its content.[46] Cuttings from scientific journals and newspapers – primarily liberal-left ones like *The Guardian* – sit next to photographs of nature (dew drops on a green leaf, an oceanscape, the sea swallowing up a sinking container ship), abstract forms made by running a blank sheet through a printer, and an empty packet of crisps. In an earnest voiceover, Tillmans elucidates connections between the items that would otherwise be difficult to grasp. He makes the oft-repeated point that nowadays we can pick news sources that tell us what we want to hear – to the point

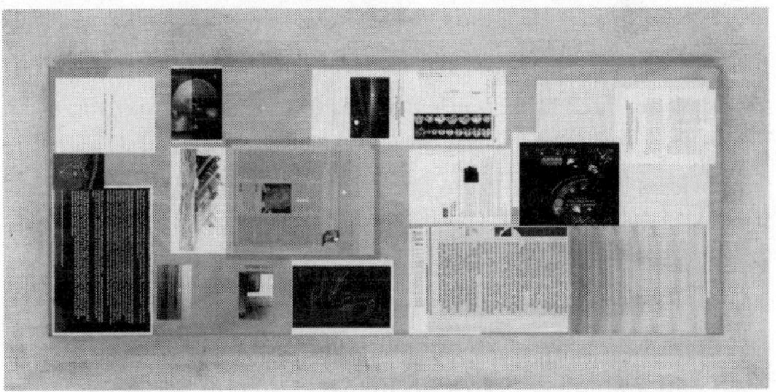

'Studying Truth with Wolfgang Tillmans', 2017. Online visualizer by Nate van der Ende and Johanna Lundberg, created for the exhibition *Wolfgang Tillmans: 2017*, Tate Modern, London.

that even scientific evidence to the contrary has the unfortunate effect of only entrenching beliefs more deeply.

In a telling shift of mood from the early 1990s, Tillmans's commentary invokes research as a matter of authority and truth. The poststructuralist project to dismantle these terms has been completely reframed by the rise of 'post-truth' and 'fake news'. Accordingly, the free library aesthetic of the first phase of research-based art has been replaced by a more careful, even precious approach to composition. In 'Truth Study Centre', we can only read the information through glass, not handle it. The formalism of the artist's arrangement implies that there *are* connections to grasp between the materials – that the truth is out there. But because the arrangements aren't linear, taxonomic, or particularly distinctive, the materials on each table form the visual analogue of a word cloud, conveying a general impression rather than set of specific arguments.[47] The fact that the installation comes across as *data* rather than language in a number of registers is revealing: in a review of Tillmans's installation at MoMA, Peter Schjeldahl confessed to 'only quickly scanning the complicated table works, which smartly anticipated today's torrent of information via institutional and social media – and its numbing effect . . . Any one person's sorting of the data seems essentially interchangeable with anyone else's'.[48]

'Truth Study Centre' reflects on post-truth and the end of an authoritative news media but equally seems to be a symptom of this demise. Each table is effectively a material reformatting of an internet search: the links between the items on display read like a hybrid of subjective curiosity and the algorithmic. With print-outs neatly arranged beneath the glass like files on a tidy computer desktop, the tables even replicate the aesthetics of reading on a monitor; the glass vitrine is like a touchscreen, but one with which we can't interact. The sheer quantity of tables, each containing twenty or so items, promotes a type of rapid reading familiar to us from the daily activity of online browsing. Because of this, and the work's instability of content – 'refreshed' for every exhibition – 'Truth Study Centre' seems paradigmatically to inhabit a post-internet consciousness.

Skimming and Sampling

Each phase of research-based art presents a different understanding of what constitutes knowledge, and a different approach to spectatorial labour. In the first phase, the artist invites the viewer to piece together parts from the materials provided to form their own historical narrative and to experience in their bodies and minds the complexity of a given (usually counter-hegemonic) topic. Knowledge aspires to be new knowledge. In the second phase, the viewer listens to (or reads) a narrative crafted or delivered by the artist. Facts may be partly fictionalized, but there remains a sense of correcting or enhancing history, often through a counter- or micronarrative. The third phase returns the viewer to sifting through information, albeit now in a formal, less interactive mode. Knowledge is the aggregation of pre-existing data, and the work accordingly invites meta-reflection on the production of knowledge as truth. In each case, though, despite creating the look or *atmosphere* of research, artists are hesitant to draw conclusions. Many of these pieces convey a sense of being immersed – even lost – in data, and unable (or unwilling) to get on top of it, even if this were possible.

The trajectory of research-based art since the early 1990s thus tracks and illuminates a subtle restructuring of what constitutes knowledge and how we are expected to attend to it. This impacts both the artists who make this work and the publics who view it. As audience members, we have felt the difficulty of seeing ever larger exhibitions since the contemporary art biennial boom of the '90s. The need for attention triage in such exhibitions became particularly endemic after the turn of the millennium. Documenta 11 in 2002 famously included more than 600 hours of video, to watch all of which would have required the viewer to stay for the full duration of the 100-day exhibition. Documenta

14 in 2017 dumped numerous historical archives into vitrines, without any apparent narrative – or even a basic chronology – to guide us through the near-identical displays.

Of course, the larger context for such visual saturation lies beyond exhibition culture. The pressure placed upon the human capacity to digest information is an inevitable outcome of the attention economy, in which businesses compete for consumers' consideration, as measured by clicks on pop-ups, sponsored posts, personalized offers, etc. In this marketplace, the supply of information isn't lacking; what's scarce is the limited reserve of human attention. It is hard to pinpoint exactly when the effects of an attention economy on day-to-day literacy began to be felt. The first wave of social media platforms (Facebook in 2004, YouTube in 2005, Twitter in 2006) did not affect things too greatly. Nor did the shift to smartphones, which enabled ubiquitous access to the internet. It was only when advertising encroached upon these applications that the pressure began to increase. Facebook began targeted adverts in 2009, with sponsored stories appearing in users' news feeds in 2010. That year, online news sources overtook print media for the first time (at least in the US), and digital advertising soared.[49] Promoted accounts and sponsored posts became rife after Facebook (2012), Twitter (2013), and Instagram (2013) went public and needed to create opportunities for investors. Online advertising has become increasingly personalized, aggregating data from your search history, your social media accounts, your location, your friends, your demographic, and what your phone overhears you talking about.[50]

My concern here is less with the ethics of unsolicited advertising than with the visual and semiotic interference to which we have become habituated and the perceptual routines that have formed and hardened in response. We have learned to recognize and scroll past interruptions, resulting in a style of reading that jumps rather than flows. Block it out, resume reading, scroll down, repeat. We have developed new forms of focus, from the selective blinkering of vision (being able to read a text despite the flashing banner next to it) to enhanced peripheral attention (reading our phones while walking down the street).[51] We have trained ourselves to switch quickly between focal points and to recover more rapidly after interruptions, although sensory onslaught can still produce a degree of panic. At times, this shuttling of attention strikes me as a useful new skill; at others, I wish I hadn't needed to acquire it.

These attentional transitions have been gradual but are now at a point where the effects of online literacy are directly bleeding into our spectatorship of art. When I enter an exhibition, the perceptual exertions that I experience online – the intensification of effort to read while deflecting my eyes from interruptions – do not go away but impact my capacity for consuming text. I find myself reading at high speed for information extraction rather than enjoyment. When an installation deploys large amounts of text, I am now likely to experience it as data overload. This is not to say that text can't be pleasurable. My point is that the craft of assembling language, and how it is presented, need to transcend quotidian communicational efficiency. This is partly why research-based art has come to feel onerous for the viewer – a labour, rather than a joy. Text is never neutral or disembodied but shaped by the mode of its delivery.

Two key rubrics for the new styles of literacy and spectatorship that have emerged in the last two decades are *skimming* and *sampling*. When *skimming*, we accelerate our reading to get the gist. On the average webpage, one study reports, users read about 20 per cent of the words.[52] The more text there is to process, the less we absorb, and the faster we hit our attention ceiling. Studies using eye-tracking technology have noticed that webpages are typically read in an F-pattern:

> A person reads the first two or three lines across the page, but as the eye travels down the screen, the scanned length gets smaller, and, by the time the bottom of the page is reached, the eye is traveling in a vertical line aligned with the left margin. (Therefore, the

> worst location for important information on a Web page is on the bottom right corner.)[53]

When faced with multiple wall texts and vitrines of paperwork in the gallery, we end up reading in the same F-pattern, our eyes scanning vertically down the left margin. Our eyes are scanning the text, but our brains just aren't taking it in.

The second mode is that of *sampling*: we dip into one vitrine, table, or web archive, studying it in the hope that a fragment will offer sufficient understanding of the whole. Sampling is what a scientist does when a dataset is too large to be analysed in full. A subset is selected for analysis, results are inferred, and then generalized back to the larger unit, such as the population. This is arguably the best way to experience research-heavy installations within a reasonable time frame, and perhaps explains why so much of this art is based on modular units (like Tillmans's tables). We have to assume that the artist doesn't expect us to digest all the material on display, but just to taste a few dishes. Time-pressured curators and art-world professionals have long preferred this option.[54]

Of course, there are always visitors who will dutifully read the entirety of the text in an installation (even if this comes at the expense of seeing the rest of the exhibition). But this type of immersion comes with its own contemporary corollaries: exhaustion and alienation. A review of Renée Green's exhibition at MAK in Los Angeles in 2015 is notable for containing sentiments not found in criticism of her work twenty years earlier. Tellingly, it is couched in the vocabulary of post-digital fatigue:

> This abundance of information – of content – displayed with clinical restraint is difficult to absorb and easiest to conceive of as a grouping of thoughts whose relationship belonged primarily to the artist herself . . . [T]he viewer browsed around, forever waiting for the artist to arrive in some authorial form to tell her how it fit together. This is what it feels like to be alone with information:

> awash in abundance, forever waiting for the connection to go through, confronted with the generous and endlessly frustrating opportunity to make sense of matter.[55]

It's not that Green has significantly changed her artistic methods since *Import/Export*. What has changed is the viewer's ability and desire to put in the effort of looking. An abundance of information without authorial pointers now feels unwelcome, plunging us into intellectual uncertainty, 'waiting for the connection to go through'. The existential limbo of buffering signals the degree to which certain artistic strategies from the '90s are no longer reaching their audience, who seem less and less willing to take up the baton of co-researcher. Such exhibitions seem to demand a kind of reading that is no longer pleasurable or innovative but echoes the all too quotidian experience of frantically trying to synthesize a morass of conflicting opinions online (about medical conditions, hotels, recipes). Renouncing the authorial rudder is no longer a subversive gift but experienced as frustrating, burdensome, and opaque.

Faced with this situation, some formal strategies might need to be rethought. This is not to invalidate the experiments of the 1990s – spatialized materials, a fragmented authorial voice, and information as public resource. In their moment, these were necessary alternatives to the hegemony of white male voices and offered crucial opportunities for transversal, cross-disciplinary research that had not yet found a place within academia. Today, however, the stakes have changed. As digital-media theorist Geert Lovink observes, 'A century ago, the "destruction of coherence" was experienced as a shock. Today it's the new normal.'[56] Immersion in information no longer feels liberatory when we spend our lives adrift in data. On the other side of aggregation and fragmentation, I find myself yearning for selection and synthesis – a directed set of connections that go beyond the subjective, contingent, and accumulative – and for ideas that don't feel like a chore. In the strongest examples of research-based art, the viewer is offered a signal rather than noise – an original proposition founded on a clear research question, rather than inchoate proliferating curiosity. If this sounds like a crypto-academic call to apply traditional research criteria to works of art, then it is, to an extent. Earlier, I differentiated between *search* and *research*, and I unabashedly prefer the latter.

But art can also become academic. The practice that best represents the vanguard of research-based art, and a possible fourth phase, is housed at a university and is organized precisely around the refutation of neutrality. Forensic Architecture, an interdisciplinary group of academics based at Goldsmiths, University of London, since 2010, did not begin as an artistic collective but is now recognized as such by museums globally. Although their research has been used in international courtrooms, United Nations assemblies, parliamentary inquiries, citizens' tribunals, and truth commissions, it makes more frequent appearances in art institutions, where the group's audio-visual installations elegantly present video, architectural models, maps, timelines, wall texts, and diagrams. The group's interests are multiple but centre on state and corporate violations of human rights; past projects have included studies of chemical attacks, detention centres, migration, heritage, land rights, and police killings. New technology plays a large role in their research and its presentation. Through 3D modelling, pattern analysis, geolocation, remote sensing, and virtual reality, among many other methods, Forensic Architecture uncover counter-evidence to the established narrative, often reframing who or what is culpable. For example, their Turner Prize presentation at Tate Britain in 2018, *The Long Duration of a Split Second*, was based on ninety-five blurry and chaotic mobile phone videos of the Israeli police's nocturnal raid of a Bedouin village the previous year, which had destroyed buildings and killed two people. Forensic Architecture analyse the time-stamp metadata and sounds of gunfire – along with eyewitness accounts, autopsy reports, wind direction, police aerial footage, and news materials from

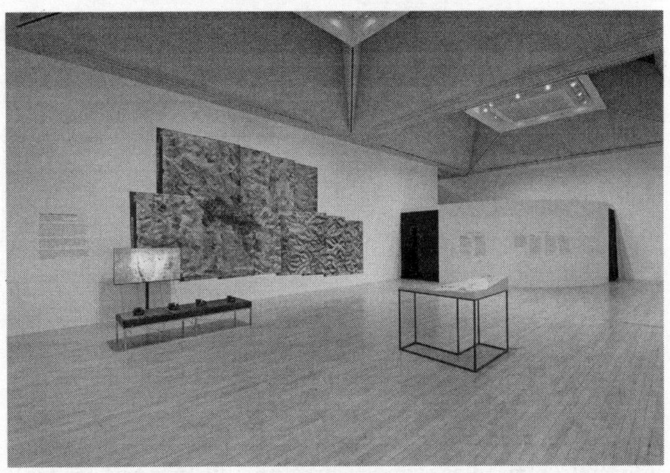

Forensic Architecture, *The Long Duration of a Split Second*, 2018. Mixed-media installation. Installation view, *Turner Prize 2018*, Tate Britain, London.

Al Jazeera – to reconstruct a sequence of events that disproved the police's version of what occurred.[57]

In their interdisciplinarity and technophilia, Forensic Architecture have much in common with the first phase of research-based art. Formally, the aesthetic is informational and high-tech. The content is counter-hegemonic, in opposition not just to mainstream media but also state officials and corporations. The group insist on the value of their work as a public resource. Rather than being noncommittal to avoid didacticism or authoritarianism, however, Forensic Architecture believe that 'having an axe to grind should sharpen the quality of one's data rather than blunt one's argument'.[58] Accordingly, viewers are carefully taken along the process of the group's research method, which they call 'forensis'.[59] Their video *Triple Chaser* (2019) is a case in point: it proves that tear-gas canisters used in the Occupied Territories were manufactured by US company Safariland, whose CEO Warren Kanders sat on the board of the Whitney Museum of American Art, where the work was first exhibited. The video doesn't focus on the connection between Kanders and the

Whitney (which by that point was widely known), nor what should be done about this, but offers a bravura presentation of forensis as method. The spectator is no longer expected to formulate their own arguments (as in phase one), or to question the artist's narrative (as in phase two), or to second-guess the artist's connections (as in phase three), but to follow the forensic method to its logical, parcelled conclusion. There is no room for ambiguity or contestation.

My point is not to disparage Forensic Architecture's highly original practice and often dazzlingly inventive research, but to draw attention to how the relationship to knowledge has changed once more in this genre of art. After two decades of right-wing falsification, truth is back in fashion. Data produces information, information produces knowledge, and knowledge produces 'public truth' – now in the service of explicitly ethical claims. Yet the viewer's experience of this in a gallery still feels like an exercise in processing and visualizing a surfeit of information. That Forensic Architecture hold our hand throughout only reinforces the sense of monodirectionality.

Metabolizing Knowledge

We need to be careful what we wish for: at one pole, the presentation of information without an authorial voice or position; at the other, a position that can't be contested, only agreed with. Despite these risks, artistic research can push against the limits of academic research in two ways: first, by allowing personal narrative and challenging an objective relationship to truth via fiction and fabulation (a tendency already present in academia via feminism and Black studies); and second, by presenting research in aesthetic forms that exceed the merely informative (the pleasure of a well-crafted story; connections and juxtapositions that surprise and delight).

The work of the Lebanese artist Walid Raad provides a vivid counterpoint to the information overload described above. Raad has pioneered the use of fiction to trouble documentary since the late 1990s, when he began making work in response to the absence of official histories of the Lebanese Civil War (1975–90).[60] His next project, begun in 2007, was to research the history of modern and contemporary art in the Arab world and the proliferation of new museums in the Gulf region. An installation of his findings, gathered under the title *Scratching on Things I Could Disavow* (2012), formed the basis of his contribution to Documenta 13 that year. This was accompanied by a live talk by the artist – or to use Raad's preferred term, a 'walkthrough' – also available as a recorded audio guide. Part of this research comprises an investigation into the Artist Pension Trust (APT), whose owner, Raad uncovered, is connected to military intelligence in Israel. This revelation is not delivered as a scandalous denunciation (in the manner of 1970s art) but as part of a parable that reflects on the impossibility of political purity today.

Standing before a flickering network diagram projected onto a free-standing wall, Raad's *Walkthrough* unfurls a tale of

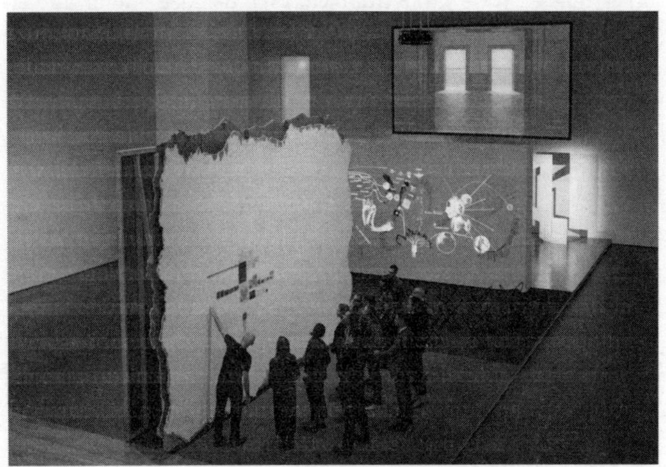

Walid Raad, *Scratching on Things I Could Disavow: Walkthrough*, 2007–. Performance view, Museum of Modern Art, New York, 5 October 2015.

neoliberal finance (APT's application of risk-management strategies to the art world), paranoid internet research (his own over-Googling of the Israeli owner and his employees), and how he finally met the owner (and was disarmed by his good looks and charm). During this meeting, Raad is embarrassed to be told by the subject of his investigation: 'Please don't tell me that you are one of those naive left-wing, head-in-the-sand pontificators who actually think that the cultural, technological, financial, and military sectors are not, and have not always been, intimately linked?'[61] The artist concludes by accepting this critique and admitting that his research conclusions are so banal and expected that they're ultimately undeserving of anyone's attention.

Raad's narrative seems to perform the full range of positions one can occupy as a researcher: suspicion, curiosity, investigation, confrontation, humiliation, disappointment, and self-doubt. Or, in the artist's own words, 'Sometimes I may come across as sober, as a rational political economist; at other times, I seem rational but borderline conspiracy-minded, maybe as some much-too-committed-almost-over-the edge investigative journalist; and at other times, I seem quite troubled, even deluded and/or a lunatic.'[62] By the end of the lecture-performance, we are unsure if the narrator's resignation really does reflect the actual beliefs of Raad, or whether his apparently apolitical submission is in fact a symptomatic 'withdrawal' of the kind explored elsewhere in *Walkthrough*.[63]

The use of fiction by Raad makes clear that art and performance are realms in which licence can be taken to depart from objective truth in a way that investigative journalism, for example, may not. It also acknowledges that art can do more than disperse and reassemble information – precisely because these are everyday operations in the hyper-capitalized space of the internet. Raad's *Walkthrough* manages to foreground the poetic surplus of research by drawing attention to the researcher's affective investment in their subject, as well as the psychic consequences of thinking against the grain. It's not unimportant that his mode of delivery privileges listening over reading. Even when performed live, as at MoMA in 2015, Raad's voice enters our bodies through the intimacy of headphones and holds our attention through his beguiling, confidential tone.

Lest Raad – so beloved by academics – seem too obvious an example, I will end with a figure from an older generation, Egyptian artist Anna Boghiguian. Since the 1970s, Boghiguian has produced small-scale paintings, collages, and books that reflect her itinerant lifestyle – travels across the Middle East, the Mediterranean, Southeast Asia, and farther afield. She sketches the locals she meets and the contemporary bustle of street life, but also investigates the past, charting the complex and intertwining paths that have led to the current moment. Her works on paper and canvas are often overlaid with near-illegible handwritten text that elliptically condenses these narratives. In the past decade, she has incorporated these two-dimensional works into installations, such as *The Salt Traders* (2015), in which drawings that incorporate painting, photography, collage, and handwritten text are displayed on a grid of 144 frames arranged like a large folding screen. The work weaves together a range of global histories in which salt plays a role: from Alexander the Great discovering salt mines in Pakistan, to ancient Rome (where salt gave its name to 'salary'), to its centrality to the transatlantic slave trade, to Gandhi's pacifist Salt March in 1930, to the recent economic crisis in Greece (known as the 'collapse of bread and salt').

While Boghiguian undertakes research online as well as offline, the more significant point is that it is embodied and durational: all her literary, historical, and philosophical reading is grounded in time spent on the sites where these events took place. Her paintings and drawings are made on location or from her own photographs of each site; past and present events are visualized in sketched portraits, jittery lines, bursts of text, and pools of colour. The viewer's mode of reception is equally somatic. *The Salt Traders* evidences research on the part of the artist, but

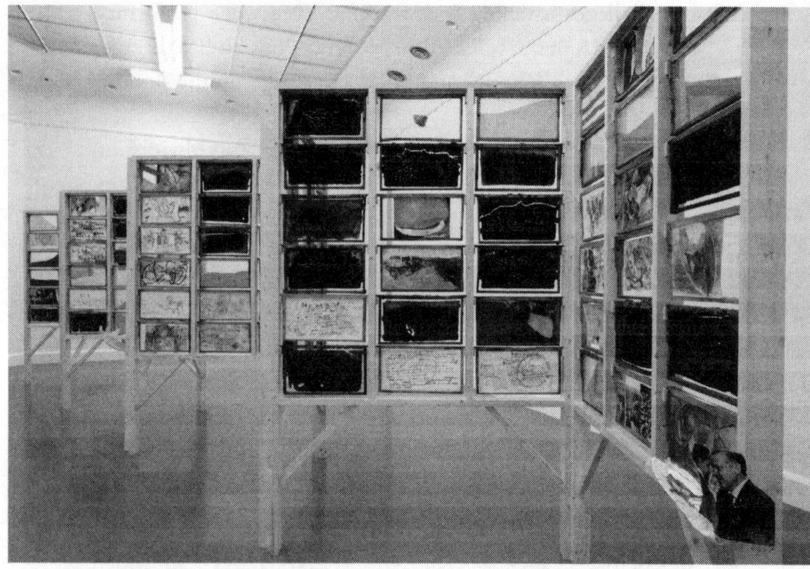

Anna Boghiguian, *The Salt Traders*, 2015. Mixed-media installation. Installation view, Stedelijk Van Abbemuseum, Eindhoven.

synthesizes this into a richly sensorial, partisan overview that is sculptural and olfactory. Throughout the grids, images and texts are intertwined, but also punctuated by empty frames filled with organic materials – sand, salt, and honeycombs – that offer moments of silence and opacity, and a chance to pause, inhale, and reflect.

Boghiguian's internalization and processing of history is thus not the outcome of digital meandering (although that inevitably plays a role). It is a lived, sensuous encounter that has been digested – in marked opposition to the more usual signalling of 'research' by presenting books and archives as ready-mades. The format of the grid enables a line of thinking that is non-linear but not unstructured, while the honeycomb frames anchor the research in a non-digital apparatus of communication that nevertheless evokes pages or screens. Nor is it an unmediated truth-claim: *The Salt Traders* is a poetic and critical journey of

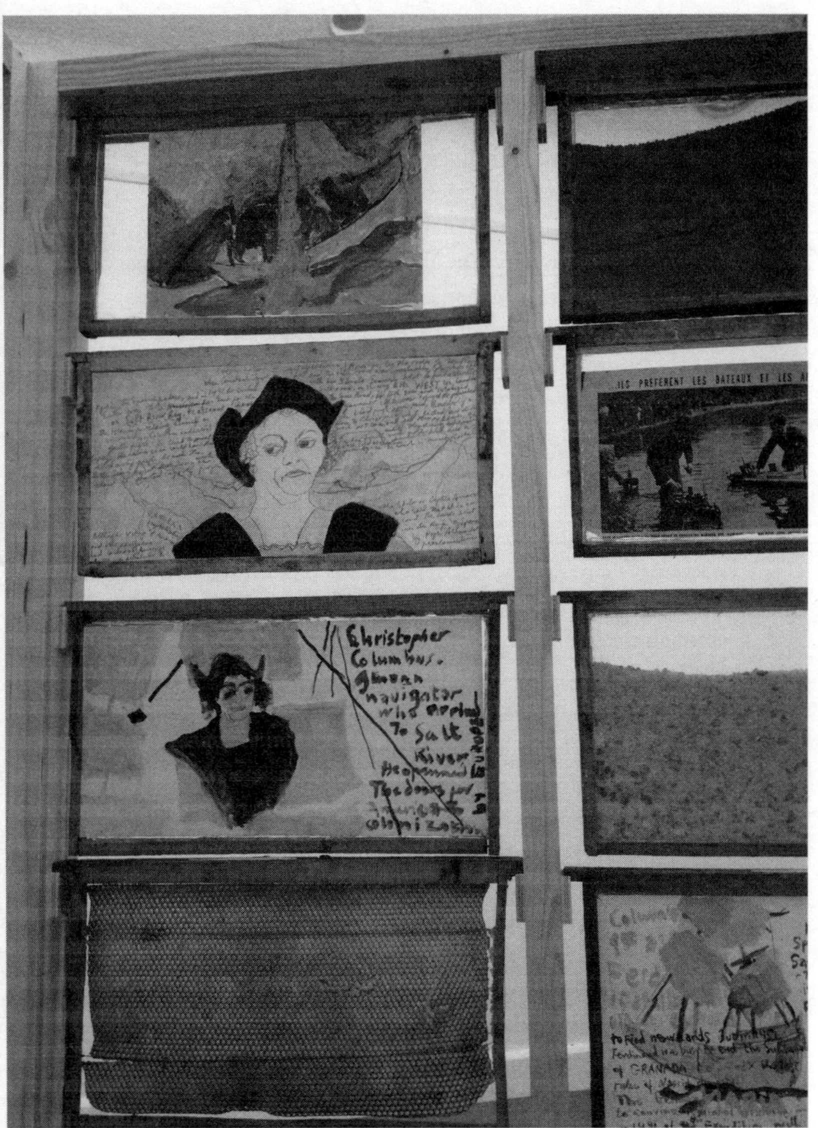

Anna Boghiguian, *The Salt Traders*, 2015 (detail).

visualized connections between the past and today – one in which history is presented as a messy, unfinished business.

The works of Raad and Boghiguian point to some of the differences between search and research, and between information aggregation and original lines of enquiry. They don't drag us back to academic criteria of rigour, but assert and embrace artistic mediation – a difference that seems particularly pressing when faced with the development of new AI search engines, image generators, and GTPs (generative pre-trained transformers). As British artist Mark Leckey observed over a decade ago, 'Research has to go through a body; it has to be lived in some sense – transformed into some sort of lived experience – in order to become whatever we might call art . . . A lot of art now just points at things. Merely the transfer of something into a gallery is enough to bracket it as art.'[64] The richest possibilities for research-based installation art emerge when pre-existing information is not simply cut-and-pasted, aggregated, and arranged in a vitrine but *metabolized* by an idiosyncratic thinker who feels their way through the world. Such artists show that interpretative syntheses need not be incompatible with a decentred subject, and that an unforgettable story-image can also be a subversive counter-history – packing all the more punch because artfully and engagingly presented.

This chapter has tried to show how the use of text in research-based installation art has been tied to digital literacy at every stage of its development. In the early 1990s, artists forged a break with conceptualist precedents of the 1960s and 1970s by changing the mode of display from the walls to vitrines and screens, and from linear seriality to rhizomatic arrangements. In tandem with emergent models of hypertext, the viewer was positioned as co-researcher, navigating material with agency and autonomy; interpretation was rejected in favour of the post-hermeneutic. Over the following decade, however, there was a shift in tandem with the growth of the internet: a method of working that espoused drift rather than proposition, the aleatory over the anchored, the individual narrative over the (counter-)public resource, and the (art) historical over the transdisciplinary. Surfing, as a mode of research, was in part a rebellion against the perceived authority of academia and the archive, and in part a capitulation to the new digital logic. As Web 2.0 became hegemonic, and information began to circulate with ever greater intensity, aggregating pre-existing image collections and archives became viable new artistic strategies of appropriation and the ready-made. During the 2010s, the right began to mobilize social media and online news channels to produce its own versions of fictional history. The idea of universal and objective 'truth' that had been shattered by poststructuralism was now, much more dangerously, under attack from the right.

A shift in spectatorship can be mapped onto this trajectory: from the viewer as co-researcher (with the promise of empowered agency), to a subject overwhelmed by information, to one who need not contest, only appreciate and consume what they see. Yet in mapping all these changes, my account has presupposed a solitary viewer. This is not always our experience of art. Exhibitions are also social spaces, and my most rewarding experiences of research-based installations have been in the company of friends and colleagues. Sometimes a shared spectatorship is necessary: another person's eyes to make me look more closely and to encourage me to be less lazy and dismissive. Together we divide and conquer the job of reading, and fathom what's going on. This sociality is rarely structured into most forms of text-heavy installation, which often skew towards isolated or intimate spectatorship (small-scale ephemera within a vitrine, books on a shelf, or a video monitor with headphones). For a more overt sociality to emerge and flourish, we must now switch genres and turn to performance.

2

Black Box, White Cube, Grey Zone: Performance Exhibitions and Hybrid Spectatorship

Midway through the 2010s, contemporary etiquette reached a peak of anxiety over the incursion of mobile phones into theatres. Numerous high-profile actors on Broadway and in the West End voiced complaints – sometimes mid-performance – about audience members using mobile phones.[1] Anonymous theatre fans set up campaigns to bring public attention to the problems of phone use: rings and pings, addictive checking, and photography/filming.[2] Theatre ushers in Shanghai and Beijing have resorted to 'laser shaming', pointing lasers at unruly theatregoers.[3] Onstage dialogue can trigger digital assistants such as Siri, leading some theatres to lock up patrons' mobile phones until the end of the show.[4]

By contrast, museums and galleries have loosened their restrictions on mobile phone use, especially the use of these devices for photography. It used to be the case that visitors wishing to take (analog or digital) photographs in a museum had to sign a special form and wear a sticker with a camera logo indicating that they had been given permission. By 2010, just three years after the introduction of the iPhone, these rules were almost entirely dropped, and smartphone technology was embraced. Museums now frequently suggest hashtags for uploading photos to social media and provide QR codes to access additional information on works, audio-guide streaming, and even to hear video soundtracks. Some museums, like Brooklyn Museum of Art, have experimented with participatory tagging (to crowd-source statistics on the collection) and a special app called 'ask' that enables one-on-one texting with a team of in-house experts that includes an archaeologist, an anthropologist, and art historians.

These contrasting approaches to smartphones and spectatorship have collided in the abundant performances that have proliferated in art institutions over the last fifteen years – in museums, biennials, art fairs, and new venues dedicated to hybridizing art and performance. During these events, photography has become a central aspect of spectatorship: smartphones and tablets are held aloft, at times discreetly, more often flagrantly. A lean dancer moving fluidly in a brightly lit white gallery is seemingly irresistible to photographic capture. My own phone contains many such clips. Yet it is precisely this connection to photography and social media that has led critics to disparage live art in the gallery as a misguided fad.[5] Some writers go even further to make an implicit equation between performance as a category and the idea of social media. *New York* magazine critic Jerry Saltz, for example, was outspoken in his distaste for MoMA's extension plan in 2014 because it 'privileges live-action events, performance, entertainment, and almost anything that doesn't just sit still to be looked at . . . The new MoMA is designed to allow for an ever-increasing number of events whose primary purpose is to produce little hits of serotonin and dopamine.'[6] His comments were echoed a year later by German critic Sven Lütticken, who writes that the work of artist Tino Sehgal exhibits a 'perfect compatibility with the temporalized and *eventized* museum, in which something (anything) must happen almost all the time'. When dance is brought into the museum, he argues, 'the visitors effectively become co-performers in . . . the museum as three-dimensional Facebook'.[7] A Canadian critic lamented that Anne Imhof's gallery performance *Angst* (2017) was just a 'supremely Instagrammable spectacle': a 'repertoire of images drawn at random' in which performers labour four hours a night to produce carefully choreographed images that are ultimately 'as fleeting as the Snapchats documenting it'.[8]

This disdain is echoed in more scholarly publications. In his 2016 book *Singularities*, dance theorist André Lepecki argues for a distinction between the *spectator* and the *witness*. The spectator is someone who watches passively, Instagramming clichéd poses that 'coldly disseminate the coordinates of presence'.[9] The witness, by contrast, takes responsibility for the performance by transmitting it to future audiences, translating their experience into 'storytelling' (his reference is to Walter Benjamin). Only the witness sees the whole performance and is embodied and emotionally in touch with what they are experiencing – or in Lepecki's words, is properly 'subjective-corporeal-affective-historical'.[10] Two different models of sharing thus emerge: a bad one (Googling, taking photos, and texting *during* the event) and a good one (storytelling as an 'affective-political task' assumed *after* the event). Instagram, for Lepecki, amounts to 'anti-witnessing'. Art historian Hal Foster, by contrast, focuses on performance rather than audiences, but has a similar suspicion of social media dissemination. Referring to the trend for 'activating' museums through live art, he disparages the 'zombie time' that results from the restaging of historical dance and performance, since it virtualizes (rather than actualizes) time: 'what is staged is less a historical performance than an image of that performance; the performance appears as a simulation, one designed to produce more images for circulation in the media'.[11] Seemingly oblivious to the skill and labour of the performers, not to mention the entire history of scored works that are always iterations without an original, Foster is able to appreciate the multiple temporalities of visual art objects but misses their coexistence in performance. In calling for greater actuality, Foster overlooks the continual presence of the virtual, both as photographic mediation and as the presence of the past in historical performances. The coexistence of these two 'actual-virtuals' is one of the hallmarks of contemporary performance in museums.

Embedded within some of these dismissive comments about performance and its photographic circulation as 'Instagram fodder' is a latent snobbery – one that objects to people taking their own pictures and interpreting them by adding their own captions.[12] Critics look down on this vernacular practice because they can't shake the idea that it's *déclassé* to take photographs rather than to commune deeply and be in the moment with art. Yet the relationship between viewing art and taking photographs has changed drastically in the last fifteen years. What used to be synonymous with tourist behaviour – cameras swinging around the neck, eager to prove they were there – is now something that museums (and even some artists) encourage in order to obtain free publicity. Yet the idea of instrumentalization by museum marketing bothers critics much less than evidence of partial or intermittent attention. An outmoded distinction between high and low culture persists: slow absorptive looking is held up as the high cultural ideal, while live forms of mass entertainment (music concerts, sports events) can be consumed with a camera phone in hand.

In this chapter, I want to complicate such binaries of presence/absence and actual/virtual, arguing that smartphones produce a new form of hybrid looking – and moreover herald the return of a long-repressed social spectatorship. To do this, I will focus on a relatively recent genre of work that I call the *performance exhibition*. This genre is characterized by the adaptation and prolongation of performance to fill museum spaces and opening hours.[13] It is a genre used both by visual artists who hire professional dancers, singers, and actors to undertake their works (think of Pablo Bronstein, Cally Spooner, Alexandra Pirici, Anne Imhof) and by choreographers willing to adjust their stage works to gallery spaces in order to reach bigger, more diverse audiences (such as Anne Teresa De Keersmaeker, Xavier Le Roy, Maria Hassabi). Occasionally, the performance exhibition has been used by musicians and theatre artists: think of playwright and director Richard Maxwell staging open rehearsals for a week during the Whitney Biennial (2012), sound artist Tarek Atoui staging daily improvised performances for three weeks at Tate Modern (*The Reverse Collection*, 2016), or composer Ari Benjamin Meyers's various efforts to fuse the concert and exhibition (e.g., *Kunsthalle for Music*, 2017 onwards, and *In Concert*, 2019). Despite the breadth of this phenomenon, the present chapter will focus on the relationship between visual art and dance, because it represents one of the most notable curatorial developments of the 2010s, and because it offers the most conspicuous nexus of contemporary anxieties around attention, technology, labour, and mediation.

Performance exhibitions began to appear in Europe around 2008, directly influenced by the precedent of German artist Tino Sehgal.[14] Their emergence has produced a particular assemblage of effects that I call the 'grey zone'. The grey zone results from the convergence of experimental theatre's 'black box' and the art gallery's 'white cube' and gives rise to a new set of spectatorial protocols, at the centre of which is networked technology. While Sehgal can be said to have devised the protocols for sustaining performance continually in an exhibition space in 2000, it is telling that he prohibited photography of his work. Sehgal thought that mystique and rumour were key to the value of his ephemeral situations, and for a while that was true. By the time of his high-profile solo exhibition at the Guggenheim Museum, New York in 2010, however, it was no longer possible to control the photographic circulation of his works. The iPhone enabled a more discreet, rapid, and silent type of digital photography that was nearly impossible to monitor.

The iPhone could be said to have consolidated the emergence of this new exhibition format. A symbiotic relationship ensued between performance, the exhibition, and new technology that has been fundamental to the production, consumption, and flourishing of this genre. Emerging from this synergy is a new type of attention, a new type of spectator, and a new type of liveness, to which the camera phone is central. In what follows, I will trace the emergence of the grey zone as a meeting of the black box and white cube, not in order to reinforce Foster's grey zone of virtual 'spectrality' but rather to assert the grey zone's intrinsic relation to performance in a digital era. Three aspects of technology will then be explored through performance exhibitions from the past decade by Maria Hassabi, Xavier LeRoy, and Anne Imhof.

A Prehistory

How did we arrive at a moment when so many visual artists are moved to hire dancers, and so many choreographers are drawn to performing in museums? There seem to be three clear waves of overlap between visual art and dance: the late 1930s to 1940s, the

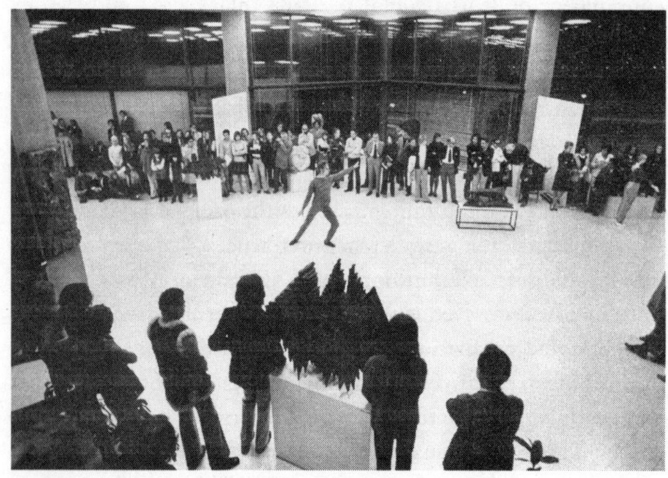

Merce Cunningham, *Event #45*, 1972. Performance view, Museum of Modern Art, Belgrade, 17 September 1972. Performer: Merce Cunningham.

late 1960s to 1970s, and the late 2000s to 2010s. The first wave was the acquisition and exhibition of ephemera relating to dance, spearheaded by Lincoln Kerstein at MoMA in the 1930s, but which rarely included live performance.[15] The second wave is where we find the historical blueprints for performance exhibitions: Merce Cunningham's 'Events' from 1964 onwards and the postmodern choreography associated with Judson Dance Theatre (1962–64). It is not coincidental that both precursors arose in tandem with rich interdisciplinary collaborations with visual artists.[16]

Cunningham's Events were ninety-minute performances that recombined elements of his pre-existing repertory into virtuosic new arrangements without intermission. The sequence of excerpts differed for every performance, as did the sets (if any were used) and accompanying music. The first was held in the Museum der 20. Jahrhunderts in Vienna in 1964 and was an impromptu solution to discovering, upon arrival at the venue, that the building was a modernist glass box without a clearly demarcated stage area. In the ensuing forty-five years until Cunningham's death in 2009, more than 800 Events were performed, many in non-theatrical venues such as museums, gymnasiums, amphitheatres, armouries, and city plazas. The early Events share with performance exhibitions an embrace of duration without intermission, a rejection of frontality (the performance can theoretically be seen from any angle), and an experimental attitude that pushes the capacity of the dancer (who must perform excerpts in new sequences, with new facings, and on a hard, unsprung floor).

The best-known dancers and performers associated with Judson, by contrast, were interested in a more deskilled approach: a non-expressive, desubjectivized aesthetics of the everyday (in part as a reaction to Cunningham's virtuosity). They used scores, task-based exercises, chance procedures, and pedestrian movements like walking, leaning, and running. This deskilling was a rejection of the conformity of body types (and training) in ballet, as well as of the expressive interiority of modern dance. Performances took place in the gymnasium and sanctuary of Judson Memorial Church and occasionally outdoors. In 1968, choreographer and dancer Deborah Hay wrote to the Whitney Museum of American Art to ask permission to use the third-floor galleries, arguing that the work of her contemporaries 'has found its greatest support from the art audience, patrons and artists'.[17] Hay's work, together with that of her Judson contemporaries (including Trisha Brown, Lucinda Childs, Meredith Monk, Steve Paxton, and Yvonne Rainer), was subsequently shown as part of the Whitney's long-running series 'Composers' Showcase', which usually presented musicians and composers. Audiences sat close to the performers, often on floor cushions, in an arrangement that continues in many performance exhibitions.

Yet for all their interest in and affinities with visual art, neither Cunningham nor the Judson generation were interested in engaging with the exhibition as an apparatus. Duration was never extended to fill museum opening hours; instead, the exhibition

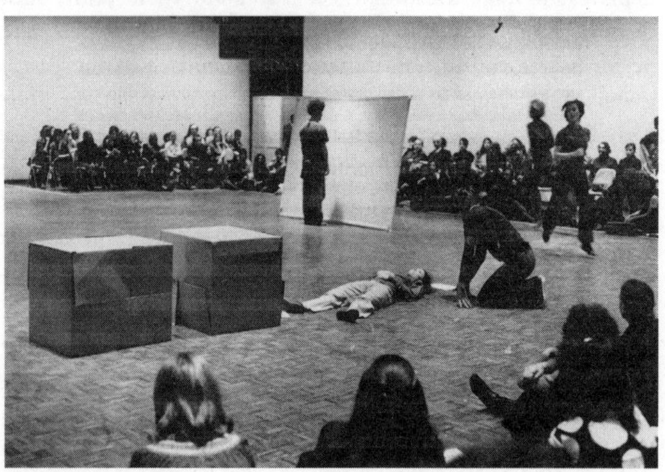

Yvonne Rainer, *Continuous Project Altered Daily*, 1970. Performance view, Whitney Museum of American Art, New York, 1970. Performers: Steve Paxton, Barbara Dilley, David Gordon, Yvonne Rainer.

was just one of many expanded sites for performance as a one-off, ticketed event. The default mode for the presentation of dance was not the exhibition but the 'concert'. Trisha Brown's *Walking on the Wall* (1971), for example, was presented at the Whitney as part of *Another Fearless Dance Concert*. Nobody thought to do things differently, presumably because contemporary art museums were not yet economic powerhouses, able to lure performers with larger fees and bigger, more diverse audiences than would attend a limited theatrical run.

The event that opened up the possibility of duration for artists across all media was John Cage's all-night restaging of Erik Satie's *Vexations* (1893) at the Pocket Theatre in Manhattan, in 1963. The temporal experiments that followed in its wake tended to involve film (e.g., Andy Warhol's six-hour movie *Sleep*, 1964; Jack Smith's drug-fuelled all-night screenings-cum-improvisatory performances in his loft) or music (e.g., LaMonte Young's group, the Theatre of Eternal Music, who performed drone-like music of extreme length, often with no beginning or end). In both instances, drugs assisted duration. It was not until the 1970s that avant-garde theatre began to experiment with looser, longer, episodic structures over an extended period, with less stringent rules about spectatorship that permitted the audience to come and go.[18] In visual art, the closest analogy was durational body art by male artists who occupied the gallery during exhibition opening hours: Chris Burden spending twenty-two days in bed (*Bed Piece*), Vito Acconci masturbating daily beneath a raised gallery floor (*Seedbed*), and Stuart Brisley sitting in a bath of black paint for two weeks (*And for Today . . . Nothing*), all 1972. The enthusiasm for this way of working did not last into the 1980s. It was only in the 1990s that visual art performance made a concerted return to duration, and with it a decisive shift to the *dispositif* of the exhibition.

The convergence of performance and exhibition can be traced in two developments during this decade: delegated performance and re-enactment. In both instances, the central point of reference was labour (working/not working) rather than the concerns of the 1960s and '70s (Eastern religions, queer sociality, intoxication). In delegated performance, visual artists hired performers to do the work on their behalf – unlike the 1970s body art model in which the artist used his or her own body as primary material. Informed by Fluxus and Conceptual art instruction-based works, delegated performance de-linked durational art from the singular charismatic artist and instead prioritized the bodies of amateurs, non-professionals, or everyday subjects hired to perform their demographic identity or subject position. Notable early examples include the display of young gay men in Elmgreen and Dragset's *Try* (1996), two labourers hired to paint walls all day in Nedko Solokov's *A Life (Black and White)* (1998) and Santiago Sierra hiring low-paid Latin Americans to do menial tasks (or simply show up and stand still) from 1998 onwards. As soon as the individual artist was replaced by a hired workforce, a new relationship to duration became possible. A performance could persist in a space for days, weeks, or even months. Performers were paid by the hour and organized by rota – and thus became replaceable and interchangeable.[19]

On the one hand, delegated performance has more in common with sculpture and live installation than with the temporality of dance. It tended to be shown alongside works in more traditional media, contributing texture to larger exhibitions or collection hangs rather than being an exhibition in its own right. On the other hand, it enabled visual art performance to become subject to the same division of roles found in music, dance, and theatre, in which the composer, choreographer, or director occupies a separate role to the performers. The works tended to be score- or instruction-based, and thus readily re-performable, since there was no original to speak of. The instructions could even be acquired by museums, as evidenced in the meteoric rise of Tino Sehgal; it is telling that it took an artist trained in choreography and economics to hybridize performance and exhibition and turn the result into transferable property. Not long thereafter, instruction-based works by older generations became newly available for acquisition. The event score, whose open-ended iterability was so radical and noncommodifiable in the 1960s – because anyone and everyone could fulfil the work – became, after 2000, a stabilizing force: a way to enter the marketplace, guarantee aesthetic continuity between different versions, and ground meaning and value in a secure authorial gesture.[20]

Re-enactment was the second development that paved the way for the performance exhibition. For artists, this became a method for revisiting previous works (and even historical events) without a score, and to explore difference through repetition.[21] Re-enactment loosened the relationship between authoritative original and contemporary iteration, and thereby allowed a palimpsest of two temporalities (or in Foster's terms, the actual/virtual). For a handful of curators, re-enactment became a way to think through the historical presentation of performance art in an exhibition context: what if an older generation of artists were invited to *re-present* their performances and events, rather than simply *represent* them through objects and photographs in the gallery? Early examples invited the original artist to return and remake their own works – for example in 'Out of Actions' at the Los Angeles Museum of Contemporary Art (1998, which included re-enactments by John Latham, Raphael Montañez Ortiz, and Wolf Vostell) and 'A Short History of Performance Art' at the Whitechapel Art Gallery (2002–6). For the latter, artists of the 1960s and 1970s – including Robert Morris, Martha Rosler, and Carolee Schneemann – were invited to revisit and restage their own (now historic) works, sometimes with the assistance of young performers. Marina Abramović's *Seven Easy Pieces* (2005), in which the artist re-performed canonical works of body art by her contemporaries over seven nights at the Guggenheim Museum, is regularly cited as a high watermark of re-enactment, but the more important example for this chapter is her 2010 retrospective at MoMA: all the re-enactments were extended to fill exhibition hours and outsourced to a team of dancers. In the last decade, the idea of re-enacting an 'original' work seems to have entirely disappeared from discourse and been replaced by various forms of re-performable score, usually executed by dancers.[22] Trained dancers have been central to re-enactment, and more generally to the performance work of visual artists, precisely because the labour of dancing is traditionally tied to the execution of another artist's work. Unlike the general public, or the transgressive performance artist, the dancer is professional, reliable, and obedient.

The dance world had already wrestled with re-enactment. The late 1980s saw the academic reconstruction of canonical works, the most contentious being Millicent Hodson and Ken Archer's recovery of Vaslav Nijinsky's *Le Sacre du Printemps* (1913) for the Joffrey Ballet in 1987. In reaction to this development, the Paris-based collective Quatuor Albrecht Knust – named after the German ballet master and first professional notator in the Laban system – turned to works of the historical avant-garde by Kurt Jooss and Doris Humphrey, and to the second wave of avant-garde experimentation associated with Judson: Steve Paxton's *Satisfyin' Lover* (1967) and Yvonne Rainer's *Continuous Project Altered Daily* (1970). Quatuor Albrecht Knust preferred the phrase 'historical investigation' to re-enactment or reconstruction, precisely in order to avoid any claims to authenticity. They preferred a post-structuralist emphasis on conflicting interpretations, emphasizing the power of institutions and education to form canons, and 'the possible resistance of choreographic works to the historical model'.[23] As with re-enactment in visual art, the Quatuor's performances were palimpsests: at once historical and contemporary, actual and virtual, doubling both time and authorship.

Quatuor Albrecht Knust was instrumental for the revival of an intellectual and theoretical approach to dance not seen since the 1960s. It influenced a generation of choreographers whose work came to be labelled as 'conceptual' or 'contemporary' rather than 'postmodern' (the term most frequently used to describe Judson). Conceptual dance in Europe denoted an ideas-led practice that took its lead from the objectivity of Cunningham and Judson but also reflected on theatre as an institution. In the words of dance theorist Bojana Cvejič, conceptual dance 'arose from a critique of representation in theatre, taking Rainer's debunking of spectacle further into a deconstruction of theatricality in self-referential speech acts and procedures with readymade, citation, and collage'.[24] As Cvejič's references imply, this generation of choreographers were conversant with contemporary art and identified with the *auteur* model of the solitary visual artist, rather than working with a company to generate a performance through rehearsals.[25] In the 2010s, it was these 'conceptual' choreographers who were most frequently invited to perform in museums and galleries. They followed developments in contemporary art, attempted to bring a degree of institutional critique to dance and theatre, and increasingly paid attention to the exhibition itself as a display device.[26]

This chiasmic move, from choreography towards visual art, and from visual art towards dance, enabled a common set of problems to emerge around the exhibition as a container for performance. Performa, the New York-based performance biennial that began in 2005, provided further points of connection, as did the daily performances of Trisha Brown's *Floor of the Forest* (1970) at Documenta 12 (2007). Yet the disciplinary and economic differences between visual art and dance caused unease. The fact that an artist like Sehgal was reluctant to use the word *performance*, despite hiring professional dancers to do his work, seemed symptomatic. He argued instead that his 'situations', as he called them, were best thought of as sculpture – an analogy best seen in his early works like *Kiss* (2004), which directly references historical works of art that depict embracing couples.[27] Discussing Abramović's landmark retrospective at MoMA, curator Klaus Biesenbach similarly observed that the performers re-enacting her works 'will be present as if they were sculpture'.[28] This insistence on rebranding performance as sculpture could be seen as a way of dissociating it from a feminist history of performance and body art, and locating it more squarely within a visual art discourse of timelessness, mastery, and singular authorship that undergirds the art market.[29] Several journals felt the need to publish special issues on the intersections of dance, visual art, and curating in order to work through heated debates about differing economies and aesthetics.[30] In one of them, dance scholars Mark Franko and André Lepecki express this interdisciplinary anxiety in a discussion of Sehgal's prize-winning contribution to the Venice Biennale in 2013: 'dance attempts to rewrite performance as exhibition', they write, but 'what could it mean to *exhibit movement*, rather than to dance it?'[31] For choreographers, by contrast, this question – and the resulting tension between spaces and audiences, economies and traditions, temporalities and attention spans – offered a new set of challenges and was precisely what attracted them to the grey zone.[32]

Event Time, Exhibition Time

When the performing arts migrate into the museum space, they shift from one temporal regime to another: from *event time* to *exhibition time*. I use the phrase *event time* to refer to a set of theatrical conventions that are not just temporal but also behavioural and economic: arriving at a designated venue at a set time, usually in the evening, for a seat at a ticketed performance, which one watches with others, from beginning to end.[33] The term *black box* designates the spatial equivalent of this temporal convention and its mode of attention.[34] *Exhibition time*, by contrast, is linked to museum opening hours, typically 10:00am to 6:00pm. It is governed by self-directed viewing, desynchronized timing, and physical mobility rather than stasis: one can move in, around, and out of the exhibition at any time. This mode of attention is housed in the *white cube*, which I will use as shorthand for all modern gallery contexts, regardless of their actual architecture and décor. The result is a shift from *choreographing* dance (which is temporal, guiding our attention as to what unfolds on stage in a particular sequence) to *exhibiting* dance (which is more spatial, and allows for self-guided viewing on the part of visitors, who might also go in reverse or skip ahead).

The white cube aspires to be a blend of objectivity, timelessness, and sanctity: a paradoxical combination that makes claims to rationality and detachment while also conferring a quasi-mystical value and significance upon the work.[35] It is the archetypal modern exhibition space, appearing in Europe in the first decade of the twentieth century, and then gradually becoming the norm for galleries worldwide. As Mary-Anne Staniszewski has influentially argued with reference to MoMA in the 1930s, modern exhibition display unconsciously produces ideological effects. With paintings hung on neutral walls, at the height of the average viewer's eye, and with ample space between each work, MoMA's installations created a one-to-one relationship with the viewer that reinforced the ideal of the autonomous individual with free will so foundational to the American dream.[36] Although there are alternatives to the white cube, it remains the global standard for art fairs, museums, and alternative spaces alike.

The black box, by contrast, denotes a small flexible theatre for experimental productions, more empty studio than proscenium theatre. It gained popularity in the 1960s, especially on university campuses, where it could draw upon a low- or no-cost student workforce.[37] Although its architecture was an outgrowth of 'flexible theatre' and 'modular theatre' in the 1950s, the black box was not ideologically crystallized until the publication of two books in 1968: Jerzy Grotowski's *Towards a Poor Theatre* and Peter Brook's *The Empty Space*.[38] Both directors sought to eliminate theatrical trappings, stripping away elaborate sets and effects in order to expose the actor–audience relationship that they perceived to be the essence of theatre (in the words of Grotowski: 'Let the most dramatic scenes happen face to face with the spectator so that he is within arm's reach of the actor, can feel his breathing and smell the perspiration').[39] This encouraged smaller, more intimate performances: in Grotowski's *Dr Faustus* (1962), the audience was seated around a large table on which the action takes place; in *Kordian* (1962), set in a mental asylum, they sat among the actors on bunkbeds. For both Grotowski and Brook, what motivated the new desire for proximity was technology: theatre was unable to compete with the seductions of cinema and television, but what it could offer was immediacy, proximity, and communion. The parallel with our screen-saturated lives seems obvious: today, the performance exhibition is where you go to see performers sweat.

Both the white cube and the black box are purportedly neutral frames that steer and hierarchize attention, and thus construct viewing subjects. Even when the black box presents works of a longer duration and for a mobile audience – as in Ralph Lemon's reworking (or to use his term, 'refraction') of *Scaffold Room* (2014) for an ambulatory audience in exhibition time – the dark walls and theatrical setting still tacitly enforce a protocol of rapt attention that disincentivizes photography, talking, and texting. The white cube, meanwhile, under the pressure of digital technology, has been recalibrated as a space for unlimited documentation: taking installation shots of (and selfies with) the work, and posting them on social media platforms. Following Giorgio Agamben's broad definition, both black box and white cube are apparatuses: 'anything that has in some way the capacity to capture, orient, determine, intercept, model, control, or secure the gestures, behaviours, opinions, or discourses of living beings'.[40] His examples include not just the usual Foucauldian suspects (panopticon prisons, asylums, schools, factories) but also 'the pen, writing, literature, philosophy, agriculture, cigarettes, navigation, computers, cellular telephones and – why not – language itself'. Apparatuses generate a repertoire of conventional behaviours. Both the white cube and black box shape and discipline a bourgeois model of the subject – one that monitors their neighbours for indications of nonconformist behaviour.[41] Hence the disapproval of mobile phones, and the need for etiquette manifestos.

When dance is inserted into an exhibition, the viewing conventions of both the black box and the white cube are disrupted: a single-point perspective (seating in the theatre, standing before a painting or sculpture) is replaced by the absence of an ideal viewing position. Lighting rarely directs our attention; more often than not, it is still directed towards art on the walls, leaving the performer in less than brilliantly lit conditions. Sound, if employed at all, tends to bounce horribly around the space. An infrastructure designed to deny time (by displaying inanimate objects in pristine condition for as long as possible) now needs to confront a living body that must be fed, clothed, sheltered, medicated, and paid. The care of art objects comes into direct conflict with care for performers, especially when the latter need hydrating.[42] The audience, meanwhile, changes its character: from sedentary, self-selecting theatre goers to multiple mobile publics – or occasionally, no audience at all.[43] Photography, which remains largely frowned upon in theatre, is now explicitly encouraged by museums. The hashtag '#dancingmuseum' was put into circulation by Tate Modern's marketing department during choreographer Boris Charmatz's two-day takeover of the institution in 2015, while the Centre Pompidou promoted '#worktravailarbeid' for Anne Teresa De Keersmaeker's eponymous performance exhibition in 2016.

The movement from black box to white cube thus brings two distinct spatial ideologies, apparatuses, and sets of behavioural conventions into tension. When a performance exhibition occupies museum opening hours, there is little to no expectation that viewers will watch the performance in its entirety. Instead, audiences come and go, drifting from room to room, talking, watching, participating, taking photographs. The sense of only ever glimpsing a partial view is exacerbated when the exhibition occupies several galleries simultaneously, with a more or less improvisational structure (as in Charmatz's *expo zéro* and *20 Dancers for the XX Century*). When artists use a short live loop, by contrast, at least some sense of the entirety can be grasped (as in Obrist and Biesenbach's '11 Rooms'), since the scores/scripts are repeated for the duration of the working day.

Because of the centrality of photography to this genre of exhibition, the grey zone combines physical presence and virtual space into a new way of looking with camera in hand. The contiguity between actual and virtual spectatorship has been reinforced in recent years by the aesthetic slippage between the white cube and the white webpage. As Michael Sanchez has observed, galleries today 'employ a large number of high-wattage fluorescent-light fixtures, as opposed to more traditional spot lighting, making their walls pulsate like a white IPS screen (the now-ubiquitous LCD technology introduced by Apple in 2010)'.[44] Today, the white cube can seem less of a space for welcoming physical visitors than a stage set for taking photographs that circulate digitally on the clean white interfaces of Instagram, Twitter (now X), or the gallery's own website. Some artists even acknowledge that they now install exhibitions with the installation shot in mind.[45] The exhibition has become just an ephemeral moment en route to its afterlife – if not its real life – as an online jpeg. But if hybrid looking already exists in the gallery, how does this differ when the photographed work happens to be a performance, rather than an object?

Hybrid Looking, Hybrid Structures

Choreographer Maria Hassabi has long specialized in extremely slow dances presented as hour-long theatrical performances. Around 2013, she began to receive invitations to work in museums and in outdoor public spaces, as seen in her striking contribution to the Lithuanian Pavilion at the Venice Biennale that year. She refers to the extended temporality of her work as 'live installation'. *PLASTIC* (2015) marks her most ambitious realization of this genre to date, as it occupied several spaces at each of the three museums where it was performed, turning dance into an exhibition, albeit one that appeared in transitional areas like lobbies and staircases.[46] At MoMA, where I saw the work, there were seventeen dancers in total, including Hassabi. Their decelerated movements formed a counterpoint composition to the crowds of museum visitors. At moments – as the dancers crawled across the floor, arched over a couch, or inched down the

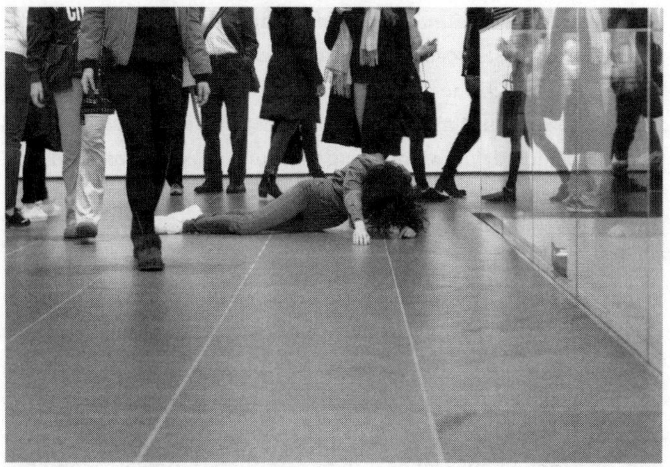

Maria Hassabi, *PLASTIC*, 2015. Performance view, Museum of Modern Art, New York, 2016. Performer: Maria Hassabi.

stairs – they even resembled lifeless corpses, as if recently shot or felled by hazardous gas, an impression that was particularly striking when viewed from a balcony above. This abject horizontality contrasted with the vertical visitors, who either stepped over the dancers as if nothing were happening, or stared at them, moved closer, and reached automatically for their camera phones. The dancers' proximity to objecthood, due largely to their extremely slow movements, seemed to encourage audiences to photograph them, even to the point of being intrusive.[47] To a degree, Hassabi and her dancers welcomed this.[48]

Like most performance exhibitions, *PLASTIC* was disarmingly low-tech and embraced immediacy: no stage, no seating, no special lighting to demarcate the performance area, and no props or special effects.[49] Nor was there an official beginning or end to the work, just a continual performance from the moment the museum opened its doors until it closed. By the time the public had made its way past the ticket desk and coat check, the performance was already underway, even if the movement was so incremental that is was barely visible. It took two hours, for example, for Hassabi to descend the twenty-four steps of MoMA's main staircase while streams of visitors trudged past her.

How to organize a continuous dance performance to last the whole working day is an ongoing problem. Hassabi resolved this through the structural device of the live loop – a device that takes its lead from reproductive technologies of film, video, and DVD.[50] As Hassabi explains: 'because we need to sustain the "loop", which is essentially the structure of the work, counting becomes very important. Each performer counts everything we do, and we synchronize our rhythm of counting with the iPhone timer in the morning – like little machines'.[51] Dancing to clock time rather than to a metric pulse is not new. In the 1950s, Merce Cunningham abandoned musical beat in favour of the stopwatch, and his dancers developed an internal sense of rhythm in order to stay in unison. Hassabi's comment updates his choreographic precision by identifying the dancer with the iPhone, both as little machines.

PLASTIC thus hybridizes the dancer and digital technology, while its photogenic slowness stakes out a tension between the physical and the virtual. The title suggests artificiality, but also a visual art discourse of form and materiality (in French, *les arts plastiques*): the dancers' movements pass through, and fleetingly evoke, Western classical sculpture – from figures standing contrapposto to the trope of the fallen warrior.[52] The performance continually foregrounds embodiment and confrontation with physical materiality as the dancers press themselves against and into the building. Warm fingers stretch over the cold floor; a supple torso sinks uncomfortably into the hard staircase; a soft face pushes awkwardly into a leather sofa. In a certain sense, these movements could not be *less* virtual; the dancers do not exhibit the gravity-defying verticality of ballet (or for that matter, the weightlessness of CGI animation) but instead appear as vulnerable organisms prostrate on a range of unforgiving surfaces.

At the same time, *PLASTIC* appeared ready-made for photographic capture and circulation on social media apps like Instagram.

The dancers paid attention to this circulation and, for the most part, treated it as a guilty pleasure ('The piece ends, I'm sweaty, back in the green room, and within eleven minutes everyone's on social media. What have I been subjected to? Everyone wants to see, especially with durational work').[53] Dancers observe how the images are edited to approximate an ideal viewing situation: they are sanitized ('photographers wait for the audience or the old man to get out of the way'), conventional ('certain patterns appear and you understand what provided the best image'), and repetitive (e.g., the popularity of time lapse) – in part because Hassabi's work offers no arc or climax that can be captured in a fifteen- to thirty-second video. Since the image is pivotal to Hassabi's method, it is no surprise that photography has accordingly become central to the audience reception of her performance exhibitions – for better and worse.[54]

PLASTIC thus exemplifies, in a particularly concise way, how the hybrid looking experienced today in any gallery space becomes most explicit in the grey zone of the performance exhibition. In keeping with the black box tradition, the theatrical apparatus is stripped back to expose the degree zero of performance as sheer presence: bodies in space and time, without lighting, props, or other special effects. Embracing the protocols of the white cube, loops and slow movement are mobilized to organize experience for a mobile audience with camera phones. *PLASTIC* both reasserts the actuality of the live body and encourages its virtual mediation through the apparatus of digital technology. It is not coincidental that Hassabi and her dancers were clad in grey denim, and that the walls of MoMA's atrium were painted grey – underscoring how the space and time of the work was neither black box nor white cube, but the new interstitial apparatus of the grey zone.

A similarly hybrid relationship between choreographer, dancer, audience, and camera phone can be evidenced in Xavier Le Roy's *'Retrospective'* (2012), in which a rotating cast of sixteen dancers present their own versions of Le Roy's solo works originally produced for theatres. As implied by the title, which places 'retrospective' in inverted commas, Le Roy's work is self-consciously an exhibition and spans six to eight weeks in duration; all the works are presented in one space and time, rather than as eight consecutive solos every night.[55] Central to the choreographer's conceptual schema is the use of three different display structures to present fragments of his solo performances – the sculpture, the loop, and the narrative.[56] Sculpture is exemplified by the reduction of Le Roy's fifty-minute piece *Self-Unfinished* (1998) to one particularly iconic pose, in which the performers fold themselves over with arms outstretched (sometimes referred to as 'the chicken'). Meanwhile, short excerpts (between two and five minutes) of *Sacre de Printemps* (2007) and *Giszelle* (2001), among other works, are repeated on a loop. The narrative contribution is a lecture-performance, scripted by each performer, that recounts his or her own path to dance, after the fashion of Le Roy's sixty-five-minute-long autobiographical lecture-performance, *Product of Circumstances* (1999).[57] This section can last up to thirty minutes.

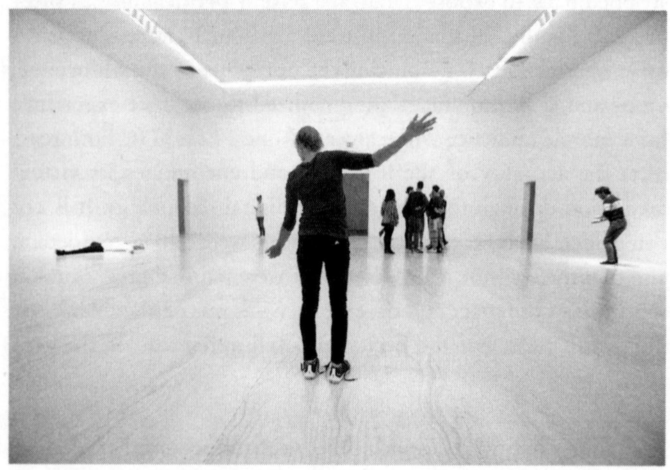

Xavier Le Roy, *'Retrospective'*, 2012. Performance view, MoMA PS1, Queens, New York, 2014. Performers: Oisín Monaghan, K J Holmes, Eleanor Bauer, Michael Helland.

Yet the unfolding of time in *'Retrospective'* is more complicated and heterochronic than this description. While all three modes are presented simultaneously, in the same space, there are four performers. The one who is stationed nearest the entrance to the exhibition space begins their own lecture but never finishes, because every time a new visitor enters the gallery, they emit a shrill buzzing sound that signals to the dancers performing the 'sculpture' and 'loop' to scamper out of view. All three then return to a different 'station' and resume their activity.[58] Only the performer delivering a lecture-performance in its entirety remains in the same position and ignores the reset. As a result of this sequence remaining uninterrupted, the majority of visitors end up spending most of their time at this station. The exhibition as a whole thus exceeds the logic of the loop: the audience watches the different sequences by the four performers, but three of these sequences are regularly reset every time a new visitor enters the gallery.[59] Cvejič has described *'Retrospective'* as a 'choreographic machine' that restarts every time someone presses the reset button.[60] An explicitly digital analogy might be the 'refresh' button on a web browser – or a webpage where headlines, stories, videos, ads, banners, and pop-ups are all updated at different speeds. *'Retrospective'* effectively amounts to a live browser containing multiple temporalities that the audience can surf – walk away from (or click off) – at will.

Since all the performers in *'Retrospective'* tend to wear plain block colours, their activity is highly photogenic. Le Roy is interested in his dancers having agency (hence the emphasis on creating their own versions of his lecture-performances) and so – unlike *PLASTIC* – objectification via the image is not part of his work's conceptual apparatus. As *'Retrospective'* has toured globally since 2012, the dancers have noted an increase in camera phone usage, resulting in the feeling of performing more for these devices than for people.[61] This is an inevitable consequence of tarrying in the grey zone. Like *PLASTIC*, *'Retrospective'* is doubly hybrid, doubly grey: in its vehicle of display (the convergence of black box and white cube), in its structure (sculpture, loops, and resets), and in its modes of soliciting attention (photogenic poses, direct interpellation).

The pose as a base unit of performance is central to the work of German visual artist Anne Imhof, who constructs her partly improvised durational performances in terms of mental images. In her 'exhibition-as-opera' *Angst* (2016), for example, dancers move from one 'scripted image' to another, dissolving and reconstituting each image according to their own entirely personal criteria ('hold a pose until you are bored with it, or move in a certain way until it feels like the appearance of the gesture is pathetic or ridiculous and then push on further past that point').[62] *Faust* (2017), as a six-month-long production for the German Pavilion at that year's Venice Biennale, marked a new level of commitment to the performance exhibition. Visitors entered the pavilion on a highly reflective glass surface, raised about four feet above the existing floor, beneath which one could see a cast of ten dancers engaged in a range of affectless poses and desultory activities, which included checking their phones. Occasionally the performers emerged from under the glass floor to share the viewer's space, or to perch on protruding shelves, or stand behind glass partitions. Although the performers were all trained dancers, held poses were more important than movement; this rendered the work self-consciously photogenic, exuding an attitude and sensibility familiar from fashion magazines and advertising.[63]

When I visited *Faust* during the preview days, the public's desire to capture it on their phones was frenetic and overwhelming. Watching the audiences on their devices, I had the impression of the pavilion as a mise-en-abyme of screens. The central component of the installation – the glass floor and walls – became the central interface between the performers and viewers, who clamoured to take photographs – as if physical proximity could only be registered through photographic capture. In turn, the dancers pushed up against the barrier between themselves and the

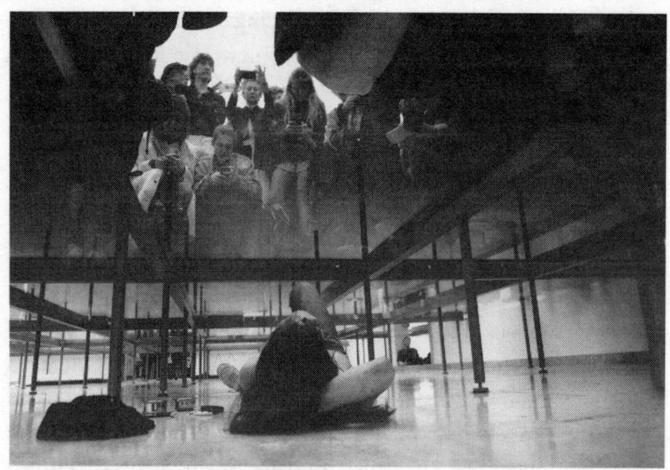

Anne Imhof, *FAUST*, 2017. Performance view, German Pavilion, Fifty-Seventh Venice Biennale, 2017. Performer: Eliza Douglas.

audience by breathing onto or licking the glass, or pressing their heads and torsos against its surface. The entire pavilion became a post-digital apparatus for capturing and circulating corporeality as image. The live body, pinned behind or beneath glass – I am tempted to describe the dancers as 'interfaced' – epitomized the hybrid status of presence in the grey zone: part physically immediate, part screened and distanciated; part virtual and ready for circulation, part unforgettably present in the here and now.

The coolness, popularity, and authoritarian frisson of Imhof's work has led to abundant critical frowning. But the tension it stages between photogenic liveness and collective fervour is emblematic of contemporary attention as a collective phenomenon. With all three works discussed above, the simultaneity of watching and documenting makes explicit the photographic condition of spectatorship today. Unlike the traditional theatre model of performance–intermission–performance, these dance exhibitions are more akin to the museum blockbuster with its photographing crowds. They nevertheless differ in their internalization of digital technology as a means to structure the work – through looping, resetting, posing, and interfacing. Willingly and unwillingly, the camera phone is accorded a new role as a ubiquitous prosthesis for viewing.

Sociable Spectatorship

At stake here is not just the competing discourses of black box and white cube, the virtual and the actual, but the centrality of technology for structuring contemporary attention. Earlier I mentioned Lepecki's dismissive characterization of the phone-in-hand, fact-checking spectator who 'hovers between being a consumer and broadcaster of dis-experience'.[64] Technology, in his reading, is not a human prosthesis, but a 'coldness', an alienation from embodiment and presence. In place of the witness's 'corporeal affirmation', Lepecki writes, the spectator 'chooses to check his iPhone or to Google the last blog on the piece he is presently (non)watching, so as to be (forensically) assured of the *facts*'.[65] Curiously, Lepecki doesn't discuss the spectator's return to watching after this screen moment – perhaps now able to see the work in a new way, or with a richer sense of the artist's agenda. Yet this continual oscillation between watching and being online feels like a more accurate description of how we watch today, even in theatres, especially now that printed programmes have been reduced, post-pandemic, to QR codes.

We also need to recall that fully focused attention is a relatively recent phenomenon. Before the 1850s, theatre had been replete with peripheral distractions, primarily social, but also sexual and political, which were among the main reasons why people attended theatre in the first place. Prints of eighteenth- and nineteenth-century theatres hardly ever show captivated audiences: instead, people turn to converse with each other or look across the orchestra stalls to scrutinize their counterparts in the boxes opposite. During performances in eighteenth-century London, 'fruit women' moved among the audience selling refreshments, playbills, and songbooks (which were needed to understand what was happening on stage, so loud was the peripheral chatter).[66] In Paris, the crowds were mobile, especially in the *parterre*, and did not necessarily focus their undivided attention on the stage for three hours. Instead, writes Jeffrey Ravel, 'it appears that they milled about the parterre, interacting with each other and with spectators in other parts of the hall, all the while keeping track of the onstage performance'.[67] Ravel draws on French philosophers Abbé de Condillac and Denis Diderot to suggest that eighteenth-century attention was *co-constituted* rather than monodirectional: the tumultuous crowd and the physical stimulus of a full theatre, he writes, even helped to focus attention.[68] For Diderot, attention was infectious: 'The play commenced with difficulty and was interrupted often, but when a good part was reached . . . The enthusiasm went from the parterre to the loges, and from the loges to the boxes.'[69]

Taming rowdy audiences through the construction of undivided attention took place gradually over the course of the late eighteenth and early nineteenth centuries. The privatization of theatre and increased ticket prices began this domestication and disciplining; it was finally accomplished through technology, above all lighting, which changed from gas to electric over the course of the nineteenth century, enabling the introduction of almost entirely dark spaces. It was only in 1876, when Richard Wagner designed the theatre at Bayreuth to remove lateral views and boxes, provide a frontal perspective for everyone in the audience, conceal the orchestra, and plunge the audience into near-complete darkness, that the ideal of immersive plenitude and concentration began to be realized with any consistency.

In this long perspective, the hybrid spectatorship of performance exhibitions does not represent a dilution of attention, but a return to an oscillating focus. It evokes a pre-modern model of sociable spectatorship, and reminds us of the degree to which attention is always collectively constructed as a field of dynamic relationships. In a performance exhibition, our attention can be oriented towards the performance, but not exclusively; we participate in a collective experience and its documentation, but selectively turn away from the performers to converse with our friends, whether online or sitting next to us; we look at the work together, compare thoughts, report to friends who aren't there. We are present for the work, but we are also networked to many elsewheres. Professional critics perform a version of this oscillation whenever they take notes during a performance. My equivalent is photography: images have become indispensable to my thinking about performance exhibitions, and I end up relying on my own documentation whenever the artist's official publicity shots fail to correspond to my experience.

Over the last decade, sociable spectatorship has been explored in dances that do not assume an exhibition format but nevertheless emphasize duration. Mårten Spångberg's *La Substance, but in English* (2014, four hours and twenty minutes) and *The Internet* (2015, three and a half hours) both take place against a backdrop of brightly coloured fabric backcloth, piles of clothes, bags, and bottles – more installation than set. Both are propelled by pop music: in the last hour of *The Internet*, Lil Wayne's *I'm Single* is played on a loop for fifty-seven minutes. The audience is given permission to be 'part of a landscape' – in other words, to chat, drink beer, check email, take photographs, and so on.[70] The performers continually talk to each other (but in voices too low for the audience to hear) and receive any changes Spångberg makes to the performance in real time via text message or Facebook.[71] There are numerous costume changes; unremarkable activities; phases with clearly choreographed movement, and others where nothing much seems to be going on. In Spångberg's words, 'something has started but nothing has yet happened'.[72] The installation and the dance slip in and out of our attention; in person presence coexists with online experience to simultaneously construct a shared landscape.

Sociable spectatorship, then, can signal conversation and appreciation alongside the act of watching. Richard Schechner's term 'selective inattention' is crucial here: rather than describing audiences as 'distracted' (an adjective that carries moralizing connotations), the word 'inattention' suggests a mode of spectatorship untethered from normative expectations of full attention.[73] Yet Schechner only describes inattention twice. The first is in reference to the behaviour of insiders and professionals who ignore something as a way of showing off that they know what's going on. The second definition is more interesting. He describes alternating swells of attention and inattention at a music concert in Madras in 1971: 'There was no pressure to maintain, or appear to maintain, a single focus high-tension attention. But at the same time the use of selective inattention led not to a feeling of laxness or "I don't care", but to a greater discipline on the part of the audience.' Schechner continues:

> The audience isn't quiet. I mean they not only accompany the music, they talk to each other – not loudly, but there's always a buzz. Also the 'tsk-tsk', the 'ooos', the slapping of hands on the thighs keeping the rhythms, the bursts of applause (always selective, that is, always just a portion of the audience), the low talking. Somehow the collective effect of all this is not distracting – it is natural, business like – like eating hot dogs at a ballgame.[74]

Or, we could add, like taking photographs in a gallery. In the three performance exhibitions I described above, the mix of live performance, watching, and discussion, combined with the opportunities for digital photography and its circulation, was a way to look more closely. My enduring memory of seeing *'Retrospective'* for the first time was standing in the space and trying to fathom its structure – first by myself and then by talking to friends. We went on to compare the individual performers and their iterations, pausing to take photographs throughout.

Repetition through looping, if pitched at the right level of complexity and for a suitable duration, can thus facilitate greater understanding of the work. The performance exhibition *Work/*

Travail/Arbeid (2015), by Belgian choreographer Anne Teresa De Keersmaeker, is perhaps one of the most virtuosic and challenging of the last decade. It comprises a restructuring of *Vortex Temporum*, De Keersmaeker's sixty-five-minute stage work first performed in 2013 by her company Rosas and the music ensemble Ictus. The components of the original piece – which features seven dancers alongside six musicians – are fragmented and transformed into a nine-hour cycle of roughly one-hour phases, performed in a different sequence each day. Gérard Grisey's 1996 music composition, after which De Keersmaeker's original dance is named, is also split into its constitutive parts, performed by just one or two musicians, who move around the space with the dancers. Every nine hours, the entire dance company and full cohort of musicians come together. The first version I saw was at Wiels, in De Keersmaeker's home city of Brussels, and lasted nine weeks.[75]

By segmenting the choreography and music, and encouraging our proximity to the performers, De Keersmaeker enabled us to become attuned to subtleties of composition that would be

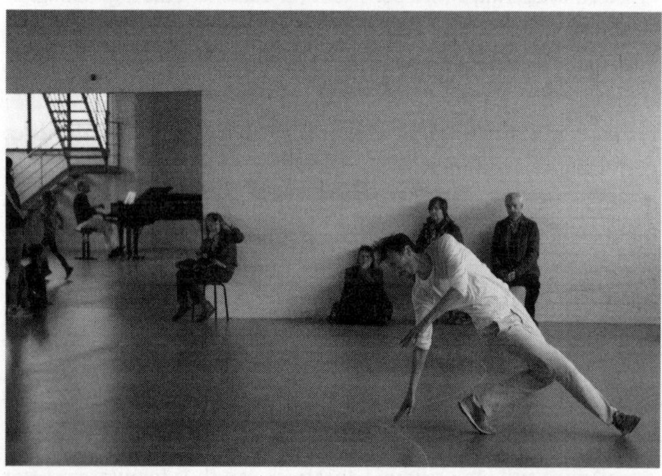

Anne Teresa De Keersmaeker/Rosas, *Work/Travail/Arbeid*, 2015. Performance view, Wiels, Brussels, 2015. Performers: Jean-Luc Plovier (piano), Igor Shyshko.

difficult for anyone but a seasoned professional to grasp in a single theatrical presentation: the overall choreographic structure, the movement vocabulary, the occupation of space, the complexity of the music. I came to anticipate certain sequences, to recognize phrases, and to respond to the dance more profoundly. When it was time for the *tutti*, I was ready, all sensors on high alert, to integrate the separate sections I had seen previously. This preparation had been laid in multiple ways: on my own, by talking with my viewing companions, and through taking photographs and video.

Conventional theatre spectatorship has long been celebrated as collective, on the basis that we sit among dozens or hundreds of others, most of whom we don't know, sharing the same cultural experience. Yet we often find ourselves disciplined by these neighbours if we talk or text. Performance exhibitions permit a freer flow of communication with and about the work. They are closer to the 'relaxed performances' that have arisen over the same period for neurodiverse audiences, especially adults and children with learning difficulties and autism.[76] Even when we are policed (or self-police) and conditions seem ideal for maximum focus, our attention drifts. Watching a performance exists on a continuum of other states not necessarily attached to the optical, including trance, reverie, daydream, hypnosis, meditation, and dissociation. Durational forms of performance have traditionally provided a rich space for such internal meditation. Philip Glass has observed that it is perfectly acceptable for audiences to nod off during his four-and-a-half-hour opera *Einstein on the Beach* (1976), and quotes the director, Robert Wilson: 'Well, you know, if you fall asleep, when you wake up it'll still be going on.'[77]

The difference between duration in the 1970s and the duration of performance exhibitions in the 2010s is that the two-way oscillation between watching a performance and the mind's own internal journey is now multidirectional and explicitly social – attention drifts from the performance, to inner reverie, to conversation with fellow viewers, to taking photographs, to texting

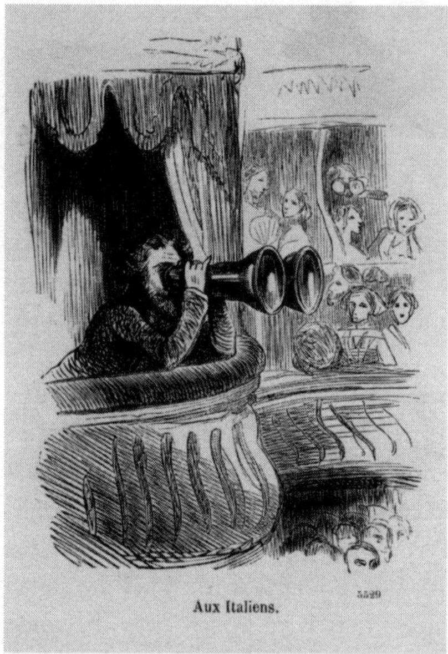

'Stop' (Louis Morel-Retz), *Aux Italiens* (At the Italian Theatre), 1857. Engraving published in *Le Petit Journal pour Rire*, 1857.

friends, to being present again. Rather than denigrating smartphone use as the foreclosure of focused attention, we should recall that *all* performances prior to the 1870s were social occasions with an expansive, multidirectional understanding of attention. Today, the technological prosthesis has simply changed – we no longer wield opera glasses but tablets and smartphones.

Grey Zone

Critical scepticism about performance in museums is the latest iteration of longstanding anxieties about technology's detrimental effect upon attention, and it places pressure on the debate about liveness and mediation that dominated performance studies in the 1990s. Mediation today is less a question of 'live performance' followed by 'documentation' than fully anticipated to the point of being a compositional strategy: Hassabi holding poses that invite photographic capture; Le Roy deploying a

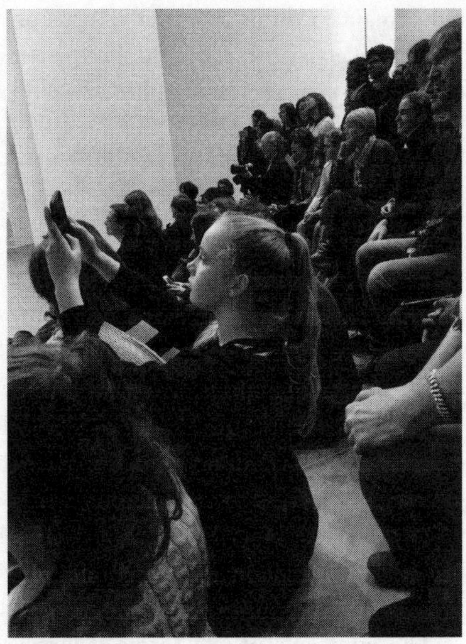

Audience members watch Jérôme Bel, *MoMA Dance Company*, Museum of Modern Art, New York, 2016.

'refresh' structure; or Imhof constructing a work on what is effectively a vast glass screen. In other words, spectatorship isn't something that happens prior to mediation; it is constructed through the artist's decisions about how to engage with the exhibition as a mediating apparatus itself.

This, then, is the grey zone. For the audience, it's not knowing where to sit, whether you should take photographs, or how close to get to the performers. For artists, it's an uncertainty about sightlines, audience, and gallery guards. For institutions, it's the uneasy accommodation of human needs (a place to change and hydrate; cushioned flooring) to a building designed to preserve objects. It melds two earlier *dispositifs*, the white cube and the black box, with a third apparatus, the smartphone, which enables a continual shuttling between physical presence and online viewing. That the grey zone emerged so soon after the introduction of Web 2.0 and the iPhone is symptomatic: it is both an extension of the daily virtualization of our perception and its compensation.

Performance exhibitions offer a locus of temporal deceleration, shared collective presence, physical proximity, and sense of place, even while they encourage photography and digital circulation. This knot of contradictions defines spectatorship today.

Admittedly, qualities have been lost as well as gained in the emergence of the performance exhibition. It has allowed choreographers to reach broader audiences, but viewing conditions are not always ideal, and there is often a tension between devoted fans and casual passersby. When dance moves into the museum, it almost guarantees a lack of institutional critique, because its home institution is elsewhere – the theatre.[78] The curatorial interest in dance and the performing arts has prompted a certain de-fanging of visual art performance, which has largely abandoned its historical investment in transgression and protest. That said, activist groups like Liberate Tate and P.A.I.N. have leveraged the photographic conditions of the grey zone to generate attention for their causes.[79]

The emergence of new forms of virtuosity that conform readily to a neoliberal economy is another change difficult to map as a loss or a gain. For the choreographer, it's the flexibility to make project-based, site-specific work rather than developing repertoire; the ability to adapt existing pieces to museum conditions; the production of choreography that can operate in a continual flow without beginning, middle, or end; a willingness to exhibit not just one's work, but also one's labour (for example, by putting rehearsals on display); and a disposition that welcomes not just greater proximity to the audience but also its diverging (and sometimes non-existent) levels of attention. The last applies to the performer too, who must develop new skills and abilities: to respond judiciously to unpredictable and inappropriate audience behaviour, to recombine different performance skills and dance techniques, and to mobilize and perform a distinctive subjectivity onstage as a version of themselves.[80] At its worst, the performance exhibition continues the white cube's reputation for autonomy and detachment; dance historian Thomas DeFrantz has lamented Sehgal's suppression of 'vibrational connection' between dancers and the audience: a certain imperviousness to viewers, 'dancing as if they were not really there in the museum gallery'.[81]

For a small sector of choreographers, the tyranny of the smartphone and social media is something to be resisted. Alternatives to a perceived excess of mediation have begun to emerge: strategies to disincentivize photographic circulation by organizing performances late at night, in intimate surroundings or interstitial spaces, and restricting the public's access to work through carefully controlled dissemination. Choreographer Faustin Linyekula gave a 'performative lecture-demonstration' in and around an elevator at the Walker Arts Center (*Artist Talk*, 2011) while Trajal Harrell performed at MoMA late at night, by the escalator and with reduced lighting (*In the Mood for Frankie*, 2016). Ralph Lemon tightly controls the images that circulate of his performances, while Sarah Michelson, like many experimental choreographers, expressly forbids photography even when she performs in a gallery.

Now we have emerged from the COVID-19 pandemic, performance exhibitions have resumed to a degree in Europe, but not in the US. Most of what I have been discussing now exists as bittersweet memories. In March 2020, live performance ground to a halt; when it reappeared, it was cautiously – most often outdoors – where proximity was less of an issue. Some of these performances interpellated random publics as occasions for informal assembly: Kevin Beasley's embodied sonic animation of a street intersection (*The Sound of Morning*, 2021) or Moriah Evans's punctuation of a long beachfront with dancers in lime green (*Repose*, 2021). The same grey zone of hybridized spectatorship was created, but now without the behavioural restrictions and policing of the museum. These were 'relaxed performances' in a new sense: events where multiple forms of spectatorship could coexist (the passerby, the casual onlooker, the devoted fan), that interpellated multiple audiences (different classes, ages, family units), and where the sociality of spectatorship could be given full rein (there was little to no expectation of fully focused attention).

What happens, though, when the circulation of performance documentation outpaces the experience of live spectators? In the works described above, the online circulation of photographs and video is important but never overshadows the physical experience of the performance. Sometimes, however, a work takes place so quickly that there are no viewers to speak of, only documentation, the circulation of which then goes viral. To this work, interventions, I now turn.

3

Seizing the Moment: Interventions

The scope of this chapter is more geographically and temporally expansive than the preceding two. It begins in Brazil, in the late 1970s. During the night of 27 April 1979, members of the artist group 3Nós3 placed garbage bags on the heads of public statues in the city of São Paulo, tying them closed with a rope around the neck. Their carefully created itinerary began with the Monument to Independence and continued on to statues around the city – celebrated writers and intellectuals, neoclassical nymphs, military generals, and the well-known Monument to the Bandeiras at the entrance to Ibirapuera Park. Although the figures were diverse, as a group they represented what monumental statuary represents everywhere: national identity, authority, and political and artistic conservatism. Aware that their gesture might not last long, and thus not be seen by many, the artists anonymously called journalists and alerted them to the fact that 'something strange' had happened to monuments across the city.[1] Photographs of the intervention, called *Ensacamento* – roughly translatable as 'bagging' or 'hooding' – appeared in several newspapers the next day, including the *Diário de São Paulo* and the front page of the *Diário da Noite*, accompanied by reports of officials' confusion over the gesture.

A year later, when 3Nós3 were invited to exhibit in Porto Alegre, they pinned all the press coverage to the wall, forming a

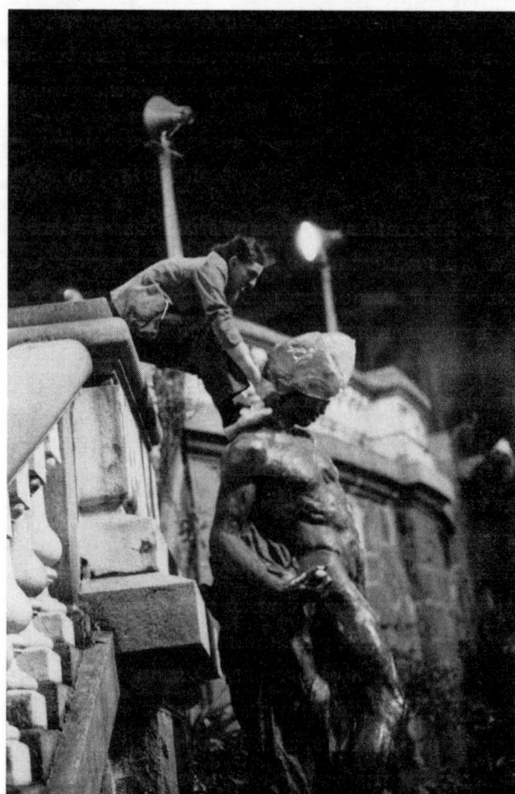

3Nós3, *Ensacamento*, 1979. São Paulo, 27 April 1979.

long horizontal line. Below this was installed a black band showing a strip of photographs of the intervention: creating two strips of information, visual and textual, black and white. Later, an edition of *Ensacamento* press cuttings and photographs was available to purchase as a limited edition. As the group continued to make interventions into the early 1980s, securing media exposure became increasingly important, despite the work becoming more abstract and playful. Aspiring to occupy the maximum number of media channels, especially newspapers and television, they took on the task of press promotion – writing press releases, contacting photographers in advance, and regularly

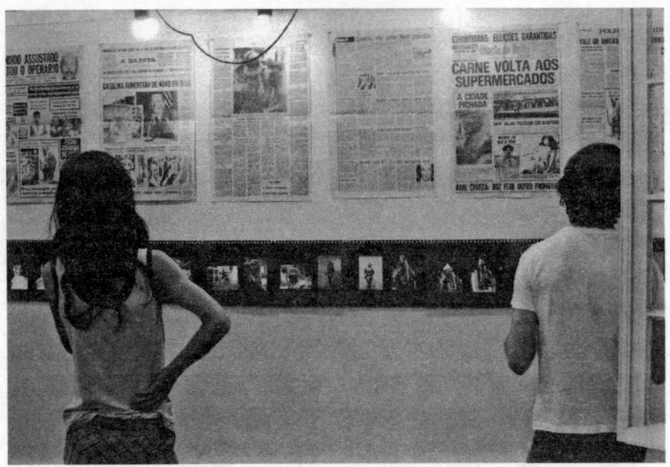

View of 3Nós3 exhibition, Espaço Nervo Óptico, Porto Alegre, 1980. Installation includes photographs and press cuttings about the group's interventions.

appearing on television. As a result, group member Mario Ramiro has argued that 3Nós3's urban interventions are less installations or performances than 'television or print media stories'.[2] The actions of 3Nós3 thus have a double or hybrid identity: occupying a physical location in the city but also circulating virtually, in the media.

Ensacamento is typical of a mode of working that I want to elaborate in this chapter: fast, unauthorized, and politically timed interventions. This is a crucial category of art making (and culture more broadly) that has, to my knowledge, never been historicized or theorized. I define interventions as self-initiated actions that address the *polis* through the use of public space, employing an everyday visual language, and harnessing the media to force an issue into public consciousness and spark debate. Interventions, I argue, seek out the attention economy of their moment – be this print media, television, or social media. As an artistic strategy, the intervention has changed in tandem with developments in technology, resulting in today's viral methods of circulation: think of Alexandre Vogler's *Tridente de Nova Iguaçu* (2006) on the slope of Morro do Cruzeiro in Rio de Janeiro, Pussy Riot's *Punk Prayer* (2012) in Moscow's Cathedral of Christ the Saviour, or the 'standing man' protest of Erdem Gündüz in Istanbul's Taksim Square (2013–14).

Interventions are predicated on the peak-and-decay model of viral attention. This has been described by information scientists as the sigmoid curve, or s-curve, that is characteristic of epidemics: a slow start, followed by a huge acceleration, which reaches a tipping point, after which there is inertia and eventually a precipitous drop (no more new bodies to infect, no more new readers to reach).[3] Best exemplified by the meme, viral attention is an infectious proliferation specific to digital networks: collective focus is produced and spread like a pathogen in the body, through sharing. Being the object of viral attention however, is a double-edged condition: either the dream of mass approval or the nightmare of mass condemnation and disgust; usually it's a lot of both.

Interventions offer a foil to the types of work discussed in previous chapters: their temporality is fast, compared to the sustained effort of reading in a research-based installation (Chapter 1) or the sociable duration of performance exhibitions (Chapter 2). The brief intensity of debate they catalyse can prompt overfamiliarity, eye-rolling, and fatigue ('not *that* again'). The intervention thus rubs against a depth model of culture bolstered by the slow work of academic attention. Instead of gaining in profundity of meaning over time, it rapidly comes to seem exhausted. In the chapter below, I aim to provide a history and theory of this way of working, to explore some recent examples (by Voina, Pussy Riot, and Tania Bruguera), and to offer some reservations about interventions at a time when disruption – the central strategy of this genre – has been co-opted by the alt-right.

A Quick and Dirty History

As an artistic strategy, interventions continue the historical avant-garde's investment in disruption and transgression. The Futurist group, founded in 1909, were described by their leader Filippo Tommaso Marinetti as the 'Primi Interventisti' (First Interventionists) – in fact a reference to the group's political sympathies, not to their artistic strategies. At that moment, Italy was debating whether or not to enter the First World War, and the Futurists aggressively took the side of military engagement ('intervention') as a way to assert a strong national identity. On 15 September 1914, Futurist artists attended a crowded Puccini opera at Teatro dal Verme in Milan, unrolling an Italian flag from the balcony at the end of the first act; from another, they burnt an Austrian flag, which, as Marinetti later relished, fell 'onto the creamy bosoms in the stalls'.[4] The following evening, the artists repeated the action at the Galerie Vittorio Emanuele and nearby Piazza del Duomo, pulling 'black-and-yellow flags out of their underwear' and setting fire to them, creating chaos and starting fights.[5] All eleven of the group were arrested for this disruption, and spent five days in San Vittore prison. Their actions and the aftermath were covered in at least three articles in the evening newspaper, the *Corriere della Sera*.

Russian Futurists, inspired partly by Marinetti's precedent and partly by provincial hooligans going on destructive rampages around Russian cities in the 1910s, similarly mobilized disruption for media purposes.[6] Beginning around 1912, these artists and poets sought to provoke the public via carnivalesque actions. Groups of two or three Futurists wandered through the streets of St Petersburg in outlandish clothes and tattoo-like face-paint, in order to provoke and frighten passersby and generate publicity for their evening performances. Poet David Burliuk – who reportedly strolled around with a radish in his buttonhole, a gilded nose, a powdered face, a lorgnette, and the inscription 'I'm Burliuk' on

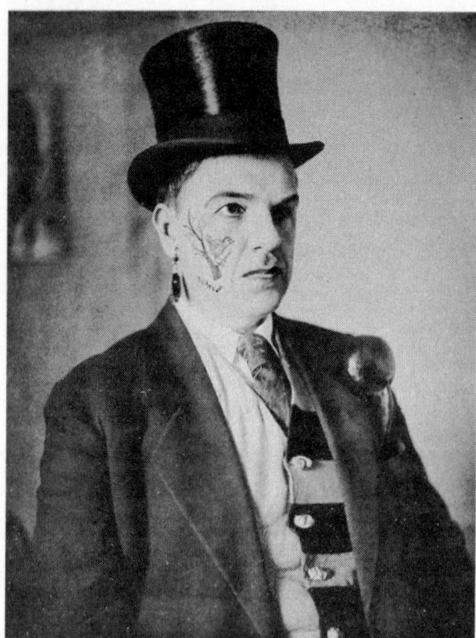

Portrait of David Burliuk, 1928.

his forehead – was a particularly proficient manipulator of the press.[7] He informed journalists about Futurist events and altercations, and created the illusion of a scandal even when these didn't come to pass. The audience for their activities was twofold: both the immediate onlookers and those who read about them the next day in the newspapers.

These actions – as with those of the Paris Dada group in 1921 – cast the historical avant-garde in an attention-seeking light.[8] The historical avant-gardes are conventionally understood in terms of 'negation' (i.e., a hostility towards art institutions, previous forms of art, and the general public's approval), yet they nevertheless sought out and welcomed media coverage. The new possibilities of print media were embraced as a way to attract audiences and stir up public sentiment. In the case of the Italian Futurists, this was explicitly directed towards a nationalist politics; the anarchism of Russian Futurism and Paris Dada were more nonsensical, seeking rupture with the past for rupture's sake. These early examples also tended to be group efforts, rather than individual gestures.

One notable exception to this pattern is the idiosyncratic Brazilian architect Flávio de Carvalho, who referred to his first nonconformist action in 1931 as an *experiência* (in Portuguese, the word connotes both 'experience' and 'experiment'). In *Experiência no. 3* (1956), he debuted a skirt and blouse he had designed as a two-piece suit for male office workers. Walking prominently through the streets of São Paulo, he attracted a crowd of bemused onlookers. Upon arriving at the headquarters of the media company Diários Associados, he stood on a table and gave a press conference, explaining the benefits of his design, which was titled – with a nod to Christian Dior – *New Look: Summer Fashion for a New Man of the Tropics*. The event, as he hoped, was well covered in the press, propelled him to notoriety, and secured his position as a precursor of Brazilian performance art.[9]

Contemporary interventions, as performative provocations that exist simultaneously in public space and in the media, continue the efforts of the historical avant-garde. They also owe something to the terminology assigned to describe art since the 1960s. Much of what I will be discussing as interventions has previously fallen under the rubric of *actions*, the most widely used term before 'performance art' became dominant in the late 1970s.[10] If *performance art* has historically skewed towards the visual (in part due to the earliest and still dominant account by art historian RoseLee Goldberg), then the term *action* always seems to have more neutral connotations; from the 1960s onwards, it was the category of choice to describe embodied gestures throughout Eastern and Western Europe, Russia, and much of South America.[11] Another closely related term is *site-specificity*, a way of working in which the art object is understood as inseparable from its location. Interventionists choose their sites carefully – although, as I will argue, they place as much, if not more, emphasis on timing. A final term, which has emerged more recently, is *artivism* or *art activism*, a label for practices that seek to bring about social change. Art activism can take the form of interventions, but it often relies upon a textual supplement to clarify intention, rather than allowing for the controversial polysemy of the image or action alone. I will return to the fine line between interventions and activism below.

The Invention of Intervention

Outside art history, the word *intervention* (from the Latin *inter* + *venire*, 'between' + 'to come') was originally used in a religious context to describe intercession or prayer. In the mid-nineteenth century, it took on a secular political meaning as a military occupation or invasion, and this is the sense in which Marinetti refers to the Futurists as interventionists.[12] By the postwar period, the word acquired the connotations of covert political manoeuvring, particularly on the part of the US's Central Intelligence Agency (CIA) and National Security Council (NSC). These agencies repeatedly sought to quash governments considered a threat to US interests, and supported or engineered anti-democratic coups throughout South and Central America; one estimate tallies forty-one US interventions in Latin America between 1898 and 1994.[13] In the late 1960s and early 1970s, after the catastrophic failures of the US war in Vietnam and the 1973 assassination of President Salvador Allende in Chile, interventions began to acquire connotations of extralegal interference. By 1981, the United Nations had passed a 'Declaration on the Inadmissibility of Intervention and Interference in the Internal Affairs of States' and the term acquired unequivocally negative associations.[14]

In response to the US-supported military dictatorships in the 1960s, leftists across Latin America turned to guerrilla tactics – the key elements of which are speed, surprise, and improvisation.[15] By the late 1960s, there was a growing body of literature on the necessity of reframing cultural practice as 'guerrilla'. Brazilian poet Décio Pignatari, for example, published 'Teoria da Guerrilha Artística' in 1967, drawing an equation between the guerrilla and the cultural avant-garde, while Argentinian artist Julio le Parc (then living in Paris) brought out '¿Cultural Guerrilla?' a year later.[16] In 1970, the influential Brazilian critic Frederico Morais built on Pignatari's article to advocate an *arte guerrilheira*, which he characterizes as 'open situations, projects, processes, play-books, inventions, ideas' rather than objects for contemplation.[17] Morais outlines a 'counter-history' of guerrilla art: from Marinetti and the Futurists, through Dada and Constructivism, to the Brazilian neoconcretists (Hélio Oiticica, Lygia Clark) and younger artists such as Cildo Meireles and Antonio Manuel. Morais alludes to the importance of speed and surprise: '[Guerrilla] art is like an ambush. It acts abruptly, in places and moments when it is less expected, in uncommon ways (because everything today can be transformed into an art weapon or art warfare), the artist creates a permanent state of tension, a constant expectation.'[18]

Around 1978, a shift in terminology took place and the guerrilla dropped out of fashion. The Brazilian theatre collective Viajou Sem Passaporte began using the term *intervençao* to describe their actions in public space. They focused their efforts on small dislocations of behaviour: situations constructed to test audience reactions rather than being announced as theatre.[19] They did not make an explicit connection to political interventions, but the term was already in use by Brazilian media throughout the 1970s in reference to US intervention in Latin America – *intervenção Americana*, *intervenção da CIA*, and *intervenção Norte-Americana*.[20] Other groups followed the lead of Viajou Sem Passaporte, referring to their own activities as *intervenções urbanas* (urban interventions) and *intervenções criativas* (creative interventions). Grupo Manga Rosa (1978–82) created billboards and erected sculptures in the city, while the first street art collective in Brazil, Tupi Não Dá (1983–91), sought to valorize neglected urban spaces through graffiti and dancing. The group 3Nós3, discussed above, referred to their activities as *interversões*, which puns on *intervenção* but carries the connotations of an inversion or subversion – in their mind, a shift of everyday perception. By the end of the 1970s, *intervenção* had systematically replaced the rhetoric of the *guerrilheiro*. It conveyed a way of working in public space that was rapid and disruptive – like Morais's guerrilla artist – but without the militant political connotations.

The two uses of *intervention*, military and artistic, are thus dialectically intertwined in Latin America in the 1970s. They share many formal characteristics: both are unsolicited, rapidly executed, manipulate the media, are politically timed, and have little regard for consequences or legality. Yet they operate from different positions of power. That intervention as an artistic term emerges at the high point of US military intervention in Latin America – a systematic attempt to crush democratically elected leftist governments – signals an ambition to speak back to power, but to do so, perhaps, more covertly and ambiguously than the revolutionary leftist guerrilla.

In US art criticism, the first uses of *intervention* in art date from slightly later, in the 1980s. The term slowly gained currency to cover a wide range of practices – from performances and gallery installations to any type of art in public space. It was applied equally to the conceptual outdoor installations of Daniel Buren, to the slide projections of Krzysztof Wodiczko, and to the wheatpasted posters of the Guerrilla Girls (who also issued handbills in museums denouncing art-world misogyny). In 1990, Mira Schor noted that intervention had become 'the buzzword that defined and prescribed the kind of political act considered effective and correct during the 1980s', of which the Guerrilla Girls were exemplary: 'brief, site- and instant-specific'.[21]

During the same decade, the concept of an 'artistic intervention' slowly started to change its meaning as it entered institutional settings. The first shift was the merging of 'urban interventions' with the North American discourse of site-specificity, public art, and installation.[22] The publication of Erika Suderberg's anthology *Space, Site, Intervention: Situating Installation Art* (2000) consolidated this conflation. Given the municipal and corporate investment that poured into biennials as a function of city branding, works labelled as interventions rapidly lost their disruptive quality and drifted in the direction of sanctioned spectacle. In 2005, the biennial InSITE (1992–) took interventions as its theme, promising 'uncontrollable experiences and continuous challenges' – even while many of its projects were so modest and dispersed as to be near invisible to the public.[23] The second change was the neutralization of intervention by museums. This accelerated during the 1990s as an outgrowth of artist-curated exhibitions that questioned museum display conventions, particularly in relation to anthropological artifacts.[24] Working alongside a curator, artists were invited to 'intervene' in a collection and reorganize the institution's displays. The canonical example is Fred Wilson's *Mining the Museum* (1992–93), for which he rehung several rooms of the Maryland Historical Society with objects from the collection evidencing the state's history of slavery. But what should have led to a thoroughgoing revision of museum practices simply gave rise to a glut of compensatory invitations.[25] Institutions preferred to delegate critical gestures to the artist rather than rethinking their own curatorial strategy when hanging their collections.

Curiously enough, in the mid-1990s, the military intervention also underwent a domestication and rebranding. The magic word that accomplished this transformation was the prefatory adjective *humanitarian*, first used during the Balkan Wars. Interventions could now be perceived as alleviating suffering and protecting minority groups – in short, as altruistic and universalist.[26] In both artistic practice and foreign policy, then, postwar interventions changed from covert and extralegal to officially sanctioned, ostensibly benign, and minimally disruptive. This model of the intervention has little to do with the unsanctioned, unruly, and polemical interventions whose genealogy I want to foreground here.

Some Guerrilla Definitions

An obvious problem with the term *intervention*, as we can see above, is its expansiveness and overuse. Instead, I want to narrow down the characteristics of an artistic intervention in ways that return us to spirit of 3Nós3's *Ensacamento* in 1979. This is not simply a matter of academic policing. My goal is to retrieve and interpret a way of working that is urgent, nimble, low-budget, inventive, polemical, and reaches a broad audience, with a view to making a range of historical examples available to contemporary artists.

Interventions have several characteristics, and successful ones hit most (if not all) of the following. The first is the use of *public space*. Interventions are executed in locations that are understood to be public-facing (even if privately owned by a corporation) and are thus often outdoors. Artists are particularly drawn to reaching random passersby because the norm is a privatized gallery system or museum with a self-selecting audience. Outdoor locations raise questions of property, ownership, and the right to the city. The artist William Pope.L, who crawled around Manhattan on his hands and knees dressed in a business suit multiple times beginning in 1978, observed that making work in public immediately prompts the issue of propriety: 'as soon as you go outside, there's this issue of where are you in space . . . how you're supposed to behave in that space, who can own that space, and how you can own it'.[27] The sight of a well-dressed African-American man crawling through Times Square (in 1979) or around Tompkins Square Park (1991), wearing a hi-visibility yellow square stitched onto his back, was a startling provocation. (Pope.L noted that viewers of colour were particularly annoyed; one passerby complained, 'I wear a suit like that to work . . . You make me look like a jerk.'[28]) Yet Pope.L's gesture was triggered by another horizontal population – the homeless – and implicitly drew attention to them by exaggerating their disruption of the urban flow. The differences are nevertheless important: the image he generates

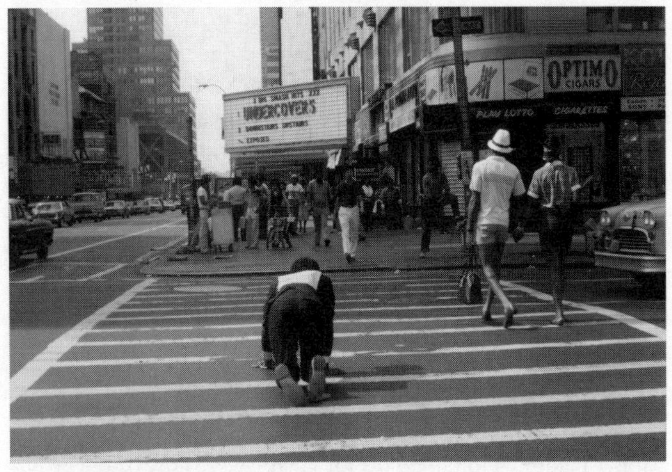

Pope.L, *Times Square Crawl a.k.a. Meditation Square Pieces*, 1978. Digital colour photograph on gold-fiber silk paper.

is tight, punchy, and out of place (the business suit, the high-vis square); his crawls are anti-heroic, amusing, and chilling. It's an intervention that foregrounds public space, its users, and their reactions. Pope.L's crawls could *only* take place outdoors, in the city, because he sought to force an image or idea into public consciousness – and because the stakes (whose streets? whose body?) are collective.

Second, interventions are *unauthorized* and lack official permission; they are self-initiated rather than commissioned. This is because they respond to an urgency, seek to focus attention quickly, and cannot wait for an invitation in order to trigger a debate. Sometimes there is no institution willing to support such gestures anyway, especially if their spirit is oppositional or provocative. Seizing public space without permission is a time-honoured way to speak back to power, even or especially when anonymous. Colectivo Acciones de Arte (CADA), for example, working in Chile from 1979 to 1985, intervened with graffiti, tagging *No+* (*no más*, no more) at night across the walls of Santiago. Initiated to mark the tenth year of Pinochet's coup, the phrase *No+* could be completed by the public adding a word to the slogan, indicating what they wished to see eradicated (no more . . . torture, disappearances, fear, etc.). Since then, the *No+* tag has been used in protests all over Latin America – by Indigenous peoples objecting to the quincentennial celebrations of Columbus in 1992, by Cuban citizens protesting against violence in 2009, and by Mexican women denouncing femicide over the last decade.

Sometimes the self-initiated gesture can be less anonymous, even flamboyant. In August 1989, also in Santiago, as the transition to democracy was underway, the artist duo Las Yeguas del Apocalipsis intervened during a ceremony to officially nominate the presidential candidate of the democratic opposition. The pair stormed the stage wearing coats, heels, and tutus, and unfurled a banner reading 'Homosexuals for Change'.[29] Many of the prominent political figures against Pinochet were present, and the event received wide coverage in the national and international media. Las Yeguas pointed up the absence of public debate about gay issues and the AIDS crisis through a hyperbolic assertion of their own homosexual and lower-class alterity, setting in motion a new phase of queer presence in the Chilean public arena.[30]

It should be clear from the above examples why commissioned interventions in a museum or biennial are not part of the genealogy I am tracing. Consider the difference between an artist being invited to intervene in a museum collection and those groups or individuals who enter the institution uninvited to make their own impromptu gesture – like Alexander Brener spray-painting a dollar sign on a Malevich painting at the Stedelijk Museum in 1997 (for which he went to prison for ten months); Liberate Tate's numerous actions at UK museums in protest of British Petroleum sponsorship (2010–16); or the recent surge of climate activism in museums, in which food has been thrown at popular paintings (2022). The temporality of museum and biennial commissions is entirely antithetical to the radical agency of self-initiated interventions – for what could be less disruptive than being invited to make a disruption? You can't curate *carpe diem*.

Third, interventions tend to employ a *vernacular* visual language, rather than academic references to the history of art or performance. They harness a set of familiar images or behaviours – hooding, crawling, tagging, defacing – that are widely understood by the public in that place and time, and that do not rely upon an elite artistic vocabulary. In keeping with this accessibility, speed, and urgency, interventions often make use of everyday, inexpensive materials, working with what is readily available. Disruption can take the form of transgression: defiling space through graffiti, trash, plastic bags, bodies lying on the floor, foodstuffs, or vulgar words. Brazilian artist Artur Barrio deposited abject 'bloody bundles' made of fabric, blood, and meat in a park in Belo Horizonte (*Situação T/T1*, 1970) and on the sidewalk in downtown Rio (*DEFL . . . Situação +s+ . . . Ruas . . . Abril . . .*, 1971). The ominous, red-smeared bundles were both a rethinking of sculpture outside conventional forms and materials but also quietly alluded to the political violence of the dictatorship. Ten years later, US artist David Hammons urinated against Richard Serra's enormous COR-TEN steel sculpture in downtown Manhattan (*Pissed Off*, 1981). As with Barrio, the intervention was both a contestation of existing art norms (macho, austere postminimalism) and a political reference to racialized homelessness and spatial exclusion.[31] In 1991, members of the group known as 'ETI' (*экспроприация территории искусства*, or Expropriation of Art's Territory) took advantage of Russia's political chaos to make transgressive and visceral bodily gestures in symbolically charged locations. On 18 April 1991, the group lay on the ground outside Lenin's mausoleum on Red Square, the most revered site in communist ideology, where they spelled out the word 'dick' (ХУЙ, pronounced *huì*) – an expletive that frequently appeared in graffiti to express political dissatisfaction. The action was a direct response to a law that had been passed three days earlier prohibiting foul language in public. The performance lasted less than a minute before being broken up by the police, but was photographed by members of the press and

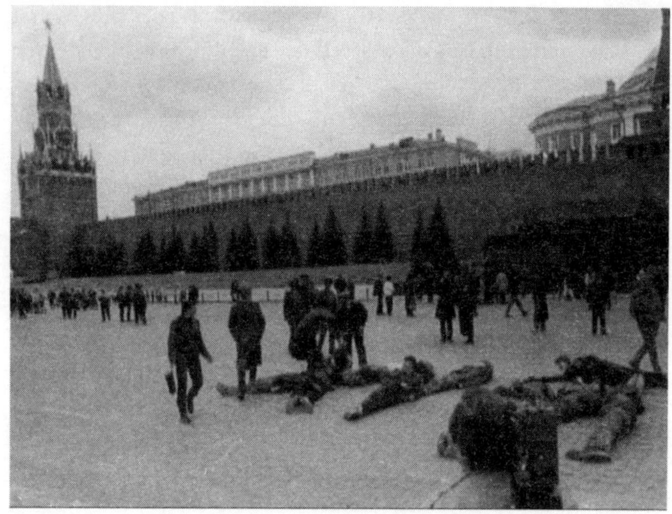

ETI, *TEXT*, 1991. Red Square, Moscow, 18 April 1991.

reproduced in newspapers the next morning.[32] ETI's gesture was crude and impromptu, combining the highest communist symbolism (Lenin) and the lowest vulgarity (a swear word).[33] Their intervention set the tone for much Russian Actionism that followed – from Oleg Kulik's naked impersonations of a wild dog in the 1990s to Voina and Pussy Riot in the 2010s.

Because interventions make use of an everyday visual language, they tend not to need anchoring in text or explanation – but this also opens up the work to *polysemy*, a fourth characteristic. In this, interventions differ from forms of art activism that seek to produce an unequivocal message.[34] Because visual form tends to be more ambiguous than language, interventions can polarize the public and force a debate precisely because of their semiotic equivocation. Take for example the Chicano collective Asco, working in East Los Angeles in the early 1970s, who created outdoor actions on the streets, traffic islands, and building façades, often using traditional Chicano imagery. Inflected with a sensibility equal parts rock star and carnivalesque, the group's urban performances, graffiti, media interventions, and 'walking murals' were both antagonistic and celebratory – in keeping with their name, which suggests the Spanish phrase *me da asco* ('it disgusts me'), as well as 'fiasco'.[35] In *Decoy Gang War Victim* (1974), a male member of the group lay on the streets pretending to be a victim of Chicano gang violence; the image was taken up by the media and reported as further evidence of the city in decay. Saturated in blue and punctuated with pink lights, the photograph is striking but remains politically undecidable: does it reinforce and glamorize gang violence, or bitingly satirize the media perception of Chicanos as violent and disposable?

During the 1990s, the intervention moved from outdoor action to online communication, where the term *tactical media* emerged to describe 'quick and dirty' interventions in the new public sphere of the internet.[36] While some tactical-media groups produced apolitical hoaxes, hacks, and pranks, others developed new forms of digital activism as 'electronic civil disobedience'.[37] Electronic Disturbance Theatre (EDT) and The Yes Men used

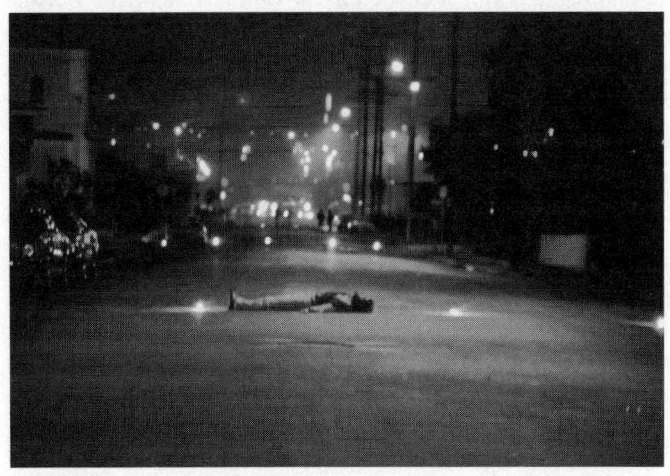

Harry Gamboa Jr., *Decoy Gang War Victim*, 1974. Colour photograph of Asco intervention.

guerrilla tactics to interfere with brand identities, jam websites, and slow down servers. EDT's *FloodNet* (1998), for example, was a virtual sit-in of the Mexican government's website in support of the Zapatistas and marked a new level of distributed civil disobedience; it even made the front page of the *New York Times*.[38] On 3 December 2004, one of The Yes Men appeared on a BBC news broadcast as a representative of Dow Chemicals, the company responsible for the 1984 chemical disaster in Bhopal that killed 3,800 people. In a live television interview, he apologized for the accident, promising to pay damages and dissolve the company – and, as a consequence, sent the company's stocks into freefall.[39] The intervention has been widely celebrated as an example of subversive affirmation, but has equally been critiqued for its limitations: drawing more attention to The Yes Men than to Bhopal.

A fifth point: the *media*, then, is central to the publicness of interventions. Whether it's Asco in East LA newspapers or The Yes Men on live television, interventions reach their biggest audience through mediation, and have a co-dependent relationship with it. This is not to say that all interventions *must* be captured in photographs and circulated in the media. Cuban artist Tania Bruguera cites as formative her experience in the years between 1986 and 1989, when a flurry of young Cuban artist collectives arose in the wake of Fidel Castro's Rectification of Errors policy (which in turn was a response to the new Soviet programme of *glasnost* and *perestroika*). Groups like Arte Calle, Grupo Pure, and Grupo Provisional were made up of young artists, many still only teenagers, who undertook daring, irreverent actions in public space, and with huge popular support. Most of their interventions weren't photographed – the artists were unable to obtain cameras, and were anyway uninterested in documentation (since this presupposes a relationship to posterity but also the possibility of media transmission).[40] Circulating by word of mouth instead, their actions drew a large following in Havana and paved the way for public discussion of then-taboo subjects ('corruption, dogmatism, cult of personality, lack of democracy').[41] In a country without a free press, the very fact that a large sector of the public knew of them was enough to threaten order and stability.[42] In contemporary Cuba, however, the mobilization of media has been central to interventions. As Bruguera notes, the media is 'respected and feared by politicians; it is the medium they use to communicate and by which we communicate back to them . . . Using the media is necessary to distort their voice and create an alternative narrative.'[43]

A sixth and final characteristic is *timing* – not just the rapidity of an intervention's execution, but the artist's intuition that history is (or should be) changing. Interventions often take the form of rapid, ad hoc gestures at moments of political or economic instability. Bruguera coined the term *political timing specificity* to note this shift of emphasis from site to temporality. She opposes this term to art that comments on a political issue after the fact, from a safe distance. Instead, she argues, political-timing-specific art seeks to *generate* a political situation – entering a debate, controversy, or firestorm. It goes beyond raising awareness to creating a shift on a given issue. The artist manipulates the mood around current affairs, and thus renders art 'a player in the political landscape'.[44] Bruguera's definition is informed by day-to-day life in Cuba, where a single state-owned media creates a clear binary between those with power on one side and the people on the other, without the confusion of a free press catering to multiple demographics in various shades of grey.[45] The chain of artistic gesture and political response that she describes is arguably less easy to achieve in a neoliberal context that neutralizes dissent through absorption. Artists in the global north rarely make interventions with politicians in mind as the primary audience. Even fewer politicians care what artists are up to. Their disinterest is crucial to art's impotence.

Cultural theorist Raymond Williams devised the term 'structure of feeling' to describe a mentality that exists 'in an embryonic phase before it can become fully articulated' – a qualitative sense of the present shifting from one set of discursive terms to another.[46] The conditions for an intervention often arise at moments of political uncertainty: the *abertura* in Brazil, *rectificación* in Cuba, the transition to democracy in Chile, the disintegration of the Soviet Union . . . But they also arise at moments of more localized crisis: a new level of repression, state-sanctioned violence, or authoritarianism; a sharp uptick in homelessness, race riots, or gender anxiety. So although site is essential to an intervention's construction of meaning, speed and timing are equally if not more important factors. The artist Aldo Damian Menendez, describing Arte Calle's artistic actions of the late 1980s, vividly captures this way of working. The group's performances, which occurred on a weekly basis, 'slipped between the legs' of the Cuban government and were 'working against the clock':

> We kept our projects secret, and took advantage of any kind of event in the city to make surprise interventions, in the way that one might prepare an assassination. We would study the site, the context, the kind of public, and the risk and implications of what might happen, and on that basis we would plan our strike as a way of manipulating or altering reality violently to give it another meaning.[47]

In this concise account, we find many of the components of an intervention: the use of the public sphere, a guerrilla attitude that deploys secrecy and surprise, the re-semiotization of reality, and an embrace of violence (figured here through words like *strike* and *assassination*). Ernesto Leal, another member of the group, described Arte Calle as 'a catalytic agent, a bomb'.[48]

Stepping back from the artist's perspective, we might draw further conclusions. Interventions tend to foreground a model of authorship that heroicizes the artist (or group) as a daring and rebellious outsider. There is a reason why most of the above examples are male and white – this kind of intrepid assertion of the self in public space (and cyberspace) privileges those who feel secure enough to penetrate that zone and claim it.[49] This is exacerbated by the undercurrent of militarism, evidenced readily enough in a phrase like *avant-garde* (used in the nineteenth-century by the French army to denote a small group that went ahead of the main force) and persisting in some of the adjectives used thus far: hit-and-run, rapid-fire, guerrilla.[50] Two decades after Morais's *arte guerrilheira*, the practitioners of electronic civil disobedience described their operations in a similar fashion: 'PR war', 'guerilla information war', 'information warfare', 'semiotic terrorism', 'communication guerilla'.[51] Critical Art Ensemble referred to themselves as an 'elite force' of 'cells' with diverse expertise.[52] The collectively authored activist manual *Beautiful Trouble*, first published in 2010, presents a wide range of tactics under this rubric: electoral guerrilla theatre, guerrilla projections, guerrilla advertising, guerrilla newspapers, and guerrilla musicals.[53] Voina's name, let us not forget, translates as 'war'. The rhetoric is combative and masculine: fighting power with power's own tools.

The Right Moment

The sense that there is a favourable time for an action evokes the ancient Greek concept of *kairos*. Unlike the word *chronos*, which signifies the duration of time, *kairos* refers to *timing* – a propitious moment, an opportune alignment of circumstances. Its etymological roots are multiple, but the most pertinent is found in archery, where *kairos* first denoted the 'mark' or 'target' – the precise point on the human body where the arrow's entry would be fatal.[54] While this might seem to overemphasize location, the meaning developed with an appreciation of what is required to hit this mark: 'an opening or opportunity' as well as 'due measure', since releasing the arrow 'requires not only accuracy, but also the right amount of power . . . in order to pass successfully through the opening'.[55] An aperture opens up that requires both timing and skill to penetrate. The goddess Occasio, the Roman equivalent of Kairos, shares the same qualities but as a female personification; for both, the right moment can be dangerous or critical, as well as advantageous or favourable. The Renaissance iconography of these figures provides an irresistible image of the artist as interventionist. Both Occasio and Kairos are depicted with wings on their ankles, allowing for a quick escape; they hold scales for judgement, and a razor because they are sharper than a knife. Both have a luxuriant forelock because opportunity must be grasped head on, at the right moment; the backs of their heads, meanwhile, are shaven, so they can't be caught from behind by their hair.[56]

The deities Kairos and Occasio, while vivid points of reference, nevertheless have limitations. They allegorize an agency understood to be external to the subject rather than as a capacity of the individual, and thus have only limited application for thinking civic agency. Renaissance political philosophy provides this transition into a modern authorial framework. Occasio informs the theoretical provocation that is Niccolò Machiavelli's *The Prince*, his treatise on the dark arts of power written for Lorenzo de' Medici in 1513. Machiavelli puts forward the concept of *occasione* as the opportune moment for political action. *Occasione* denotes those rare openings when those who are savvy can seize and

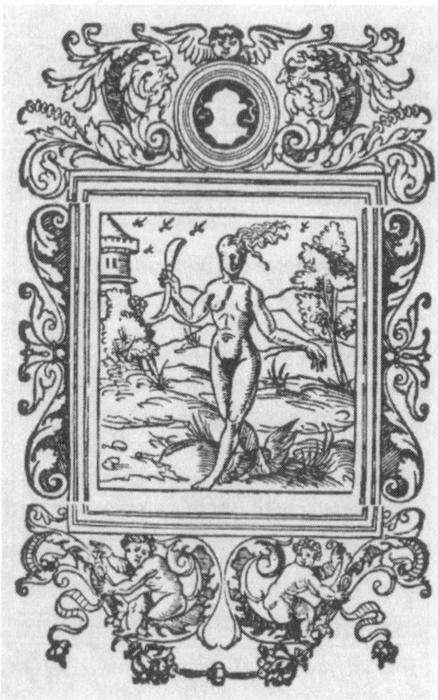

Guillaume de La Perrière, 'Depiction of Occasio', *Le théâtre des bons engins, auquel sont contenuz cent emblèmes*. Paris: Denis Janot, 1539.

take hold of power. It is situated between *fortuna* and *virtù*: the political leader takes advantage of *fortuna* (luck) to use his *virtù* (virtuosity, not virtue). Machiavelli revolutionized political philosophy by encouraging moral relativism: rather than subscribing to a universal code of good and bad (i.e., Christian moralism), he advised that each situation should be taken individually. The prince must be willing to use his *virtù* – understood here as political skill – as necessity and opportunity dictate. Two different and morally opposed actions may both be justifiable, depending on the circumstances.[57]

Artistic interventions continue the legacy of Machiavellian *occasione*: they are an art of propitious timing, and take advantage of disorder and instability to insert themselves into a situation. (Bruguera again: 'Political timing is a window that opens and closes very quickly: it is a space that you have to enter quickly, during a brief moment when political decisions are not yet fixed, implemented, or culturally accepted.') There is also, perhaps, a certain amorality to interventions: the ends justify the means. Rather than making a clearly ameliorative or conciliatory gesture, the interventionist approach prefers provocation, disruption, attention, debate.

The problem of the 'right moment' for political action was a preoccupation for revolutionary thinkers throughout the twentieth century. In classical Marxist theory, the 'right' conditions needed to be in place before a revolution – namely, the readiness of the proletariat (in Lenin's formulation, 'when *"the lower classes" do not want* the old way, and *"the upper classes" cannot carry on* in the old way').[58] Following the Cuban Revolution in 1959, the idea of waiting for these preconditions was challenged by the concept of guerrilla warfare and Foquismo. Elaborated by French intellectual and government official Régis Debray in his influential handbook *Revolution in the Revolution* (1967), the concept of Foquismo or 'foco' theory put forward the idea that small, fast-moving paramilitary cells could provide a focus (in Spanish, *foco*) for political discontent and spearhead rebellion.[59]

Foco theory, like guerrilla warfare, is opposed to the passivity of awaiting the right revolutionary moment. Opportunity isn't just a moment to be seized, but can be instigated by a bold and daring vanguard.

In their emphasis on political timing, interventions produce a new model of artistic virtuosity. This is centred not on the formal skills and technical accomplishments of traditional visual art training, but on the ability to use *timing* as a technique for grasping and shifting public perception. Politicians continually use timing to manipulate public opinion, as satirized in television series like *The Thick of It* (UK, 2005–12) and *Veep* (US, 2012–19).[60] In these shows, politics is the management of media opinion and mass affect, rather than the implementation of a coherent ideological agenda; government policy is depicted as drifting on a whim, according to what is anticipated to read best in the eyes of the media and by extension the public. *When* things are said matters as much as *what* is said. This is a skill that artists can also deploy: the ability to recognize a window of opportunity, the ingenuity to make a gesture, and the mettle to improvise in the moment. Artists can exploit loopholes and take chances. Sometimes their actions aren't deeply considered, because the moment can't wait – the opportunity must be seized, and the idea must be brought to public consciousness.

So how are we to judge the efficacy of an intervention? One thing is clear: it should not be measured by its ability to instigate demonstrable change or to resolve a problem – unlike politics and activism, where these are arguably essential criteria of success. Interventions are designed to make a point quickly, to grab attention, to cultivate a mentality of (and admiration for) rebellion rather than to be an object of contemplation or direct tool for change. Interventions should instead be gauged by their construction and problematization of public feeling. At best, an intervention can seize the public imagination and compel debate, not just in the art world but among a general audience, including those in power. It differs from conventional activism in that the ultimate goal (beyond generating attention to an issue) can be unclear: the gesture itself counts more than the consequences. All the disruption, debate, and protest might turn out to be ambiguous or a political cul-de-sac, because the time frame is short-term rather than the long game. The need to act quickly and seize the moment leaves little time for the consideration of possible outcomes.

Interventions and Social Media

Some concrete examples will help to clarify this distinction, while drawing out the specific relationship between social media and interventions in the twenty-first century. With the rise of Web 2.0, interventions became subject to wider and more complex networks of circulation than in previous decades. The duality that characterized earlier interventions (a physical gesture in space and virtual dissemination in the media) has now fragmented into a kaleidoscopic array of perspectives. Social media modulates the concept of authorship, since its foundational unit is the profile – the self-curated individual – who is positioned in turn within a network of equally presentation-conscious friends and followers. The interventionist as an individual is increasingly foregrounded, rather than – as in the 1970s – the gesture itself, left as an anonymous trace in the city.

The actions of the artist-anarchist group Voina, founded in 2006, coincided with the emergence of social media in Russia in the late 2000s. Although the Moscow-based group undertook a number of transgressive interventions in their home city – in McDonald's, the subway, a department store, and the State Museum of Biology – their best-known action took place in St Petersburg. In the early hours of 14 June 2010 – a date chosen for Che Guevara's birthday – the group daubed the outline of a huge penis on Liteyny Bridge. The group was stopped after just twenty-three seconds, before they managed to complete the left testicle. One person was arrested. Three minutes later, when the drawbridge was raised, it faced the FSB building (the Federal Security Service, formerly the KGB) like a raised middle figure, stripped of any anatomical euphemism. Reports of the intervention immediately circulated on local news media, but because the graffiti was obscene, the image went viral on social media – and not just within Russia.[61] As Slavic scholar Oliver Johnson pithily summarizes: 'The artists only painted the image; the scheduled raising of the bridge brought it to fruition; and the internet laid it bare for all to see and participate in.'[62]

Voina's *Dick Captured by the FSB*, as it has come to be called, has been widely described as a 'protest' or 'stunt' rather than a performance or intervention. But it successfully combines public space, instant legibility, media circulation, and political (not to mention comic) timing. Putin had recently served two terms as president (2000–8) but was blocked by the Constitution from running for a third consecutive term. To get around this, he switched positions with his prime minister, Dmitri Medvedev, taking on the more junior role but essentially maintaining control over the country. In early June 2010, Putin hinted that he would again run for president in 2012, as was already widely

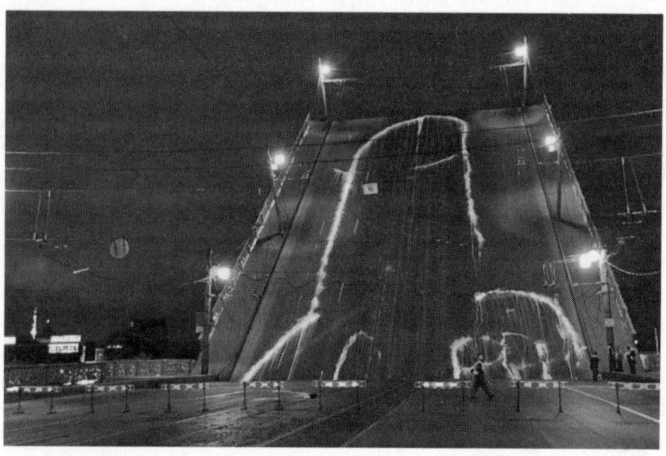

Voina, *Dick Captured by the FSB*, 2010. Liteyny Bridge, St Petersburg, 14 June 2010.

assumed. At the time of Voina's intervention, public anger at the corrupt government and judiciary was at a high, but Russian citizens had 'no constitutional means of escape'.[63] Further, as journalist Masha Gessen suggests, the Putin regime had created a system in which outright opposition was made to look pathetic, laughable, and socially regressive; confrontation had been discredited to the point where 'there were no words left'.[64] Voina responded with a visual action of visceral humour, claiming that the dick was 'turned on not only by the main KGB office, but by the whole hierarchy of power in Russia'.[65] Before their graffiti could be erased, the drawbridge was raised and visible to the city, completing a majestic 'fuck you' to the FSB and by extension to St Petersburg, the hometown of both Medvedev and Putin.

Voina's intervention was well timed not just in the comedy of the raised drawbridge, but time*ly* in seizing the new possibilities of networked social media, which had only just become a tool for activist self-organization in Russia. Two days after the intervention, Alexei Plutser-Sarno (author of the group's written materials and its self-described 'ideologue') published a post about the action on his blog at plucer.livejournal.com, where he framed the intervention as a media action with a tripartite structure ('photo + video + text'), claiming that the blogpost itself should be seen as the artifact.[66] In Russia, reactions were predictably split along political lines: some saw it positively as an act of political commentary, while others saw it as a symptom of moral decline requiring punishment; some saw it as pure vandalism, while other debated its status as art.[67]

Despite harnessing the latest contemporary technology, Voina equally harked backwards: to the *skomorokh* (a harlequin or jester) of Russian medieval carnivals, to the Decembrists (a group of revolutionaries who led an unsuccessful plot to overturn Tsar Nicholas I), and to Russian Futurism.[68] For all the verve and pluck of their action, Voina subscribe to an unabashedly romantic and masculinist outlaw-hero model of the artist.

Furthermore, the group's close identification with social media led to a too-willing conformity to the viral attention span of online discourse; in retrospect, the group's lack of a coherent political viewpoint is one of the central problems for anyone engaging with Voina in writing longer than 140 characters. *Dick Captured by the FSB* is both heroic and juvenile – and can be championed (and denigrated) from a wide range of positions. Social media is a double-edged tool: it helps spread public knowledge of an action but also reduces the level of discussion to the lowest common denominator. The public reaction to *Dick Captured by the FSB* descended into a set of opinions as crass as the gesture itself.

Pussy Riot, a feminist punk band formed a year later as an offshoot of Voina, offer a more substantial (but no less polarizing) example.[69] Having undertaken a number of protest actions following the 2011 elections, including one on Red Square (*de rigueur* for Russian actionists), Pussy Riot decided to storm the dais of the Cathedral of Christ the Saviour – a site so holy that the Orthodox Church regards it as 'theandric' (i.e., both divine and human). There, they performed a punk song calling upon the Virgin Mary to depose Putin and save women from the patriarchy, *Mother of God, Drive Putin Away* (2012). How the action came about, the speed of its undertaking, and the complexities of its filming, have been well described by Gessen.[70] The consequences – the trial, imprisonment in a prison colony, global uproar, eventual release, and celebrity – have also been extensively recounted elsewhere. Here I want to draw attention to the way in which Pussy Riot's use of social media helped to construct a new modality for interventions for the twenty-first century, and how this decision reinforced the opacity of its meaning for a local audience. While Voina's interventions had already shown the problem of polarized debate on social media, the gendered content of Pussy Riot's action, and the ecclesiastical context, exacerbated the divisiveness and legibility of their intervention.

ПАНК-МОЛЕБЕН "БОГОРОДИЦА, ПУТИНА ПРОГОНИ" В ХРАМЕ ХРИСТА СПАСИТЕЛЯ

february 21st, 2012

СЕГОДНЯ В ПОЛДЕНЬ МЫ ОТСЛУЖИЛИ В ХРАМЕ ХРИСТА СПАСИТЕЛЯ ПАНК-МОЛЕБЕН "БОГОРОДИЦА, ПУТИНА ПРОГОНИ"

pussy_riot

1.

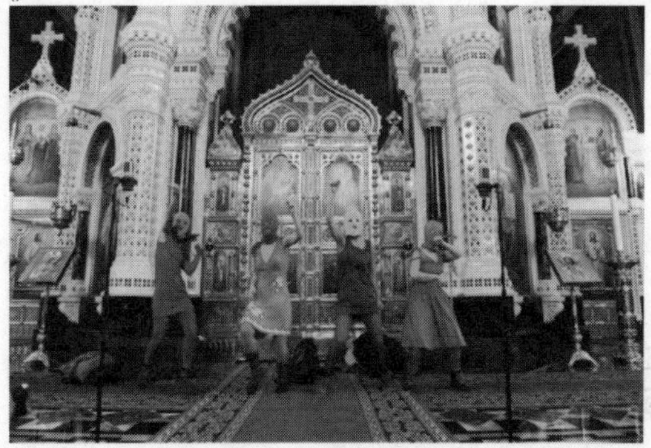

Сегодня, во вторник Масленичной Недели, мы - солистки Pussy Riot Гараджа, Тюря, Шумахер, Серафима и Кот позвали всех самых набожных друзей группы на "панк-молебен" в Храм Христа Спасителя.

Pussy Riot, *Mother of God, Drive Putin Away*, 2012. Cathedral of Christ the Saviour, Moscow, 21 February 2012. Screengrab from livejournal.com where the video was originally posted.

Mother of God, Drive Putin Away was designed from the beginning as an 'offline-online choreography': a two-minute music video to be circulated and disseminated through online networks such as YouTube and LiveJournal (a Russian blogging site), circumventing Russia's state media apparatus to attract international attention.[71] It marked a new level of integration between physical action and virtual dissemination, and tipped the balance towards the latter. While Voina had tried to document their FSB action *in medias res*, the best images of their intervention were captured by the public, standing further back at ground level or on a nearby rooftop as the bridge was slowly raised. Pussy Riot, by contrast, carefully organized their own videographers to be discreetly positioned in the Cathedral and record the action. The need for clear footage meant that half of their performance was pre-recorded at another church (the less symbolically loaded Epiphany Cathedral at Yelokhovo) and spliced together with forty seconds of footage taken at the Cathedral of Christ the Saviour before the group was arrested.

A shift thus takes place: Pussy Riot's intervention was created, published, and circulated by the artists themselves on social media, rather than by the news media. This fact alone is significant, but I also want to flag a further point about social media as the conceptual precondition for their intervention. For women, the very ability to conceive of oneself (and one's group, and one's network) as agents in the public sphere has been boosted through social media. For Russian women, this empowerment was entirely new; prior to Pussy Riot, Russian actionism was almost entirely the terrain of male artists.[72] The introduction of social media enabled the assertion of individual autonomy and provided confirmation that there existed a distributed but sympathetic audience for the group's actions. That this sense of identity is contingent upon social media can be seen in the group's attention to a distinctive visual aesthetic – brightly coloured dresses and tights, neon balaclavas – and the way this both brands them collectively while protecting their individual identities. It is further conveyed in their confident importation of Western feminist views to a post-Soviet culture that was entirely unready for this discourse. In the twenty-first century, the artist-interventionist is no longer an individual or group operating anonymously at the margins of society, unsure if there exists an audience but willing to forge ahead anyway, but a subject assured of the support of a pre-existing online following.

Of course, the possibilities of social media for asserting subjectivity and harnessing international solidarity turned out to be central to the problem of Pussy Riot's contested reception in Russia. To Western eyes, their song was clearly a feminist critique of the Church and Putin: an assertion of women's independence, access to abortion, and LGBTQ rights. To post-Soviet audiences, however, the feminist framework was illegible; instead, reactions centred firstly on the question of blasphemy, and secondly on the threat of pro-Western cosmopolitanism. A 2012 poll revealed that

23 per cent of Russians thought that the performance was against the Russian Orthodox Church and its followers, 19 per cent believed it was anti-Putin, while another 19 per cent 'could not say' who or what the performance targeted.[73] This was not just because Pussy Riot spoke a new language of Westernized feminism, concerned with questions of recognition (individual freedom) rather than tradition. It was also because the intervention exposed a larger fault line between a new class of educated, globally connected, English-speaking elites and the non-technologically dependent, newly subaltern working classes.[74] Social media is thus constitutive of twenty-first-century interventions in ways that concern more than just the material substrate of circulation. It is both the engine that enables the creation of transgressive subjectivity and offline-online action – and what restricts the 'correct' reception of this action to those equally educated, networked, and ready to listen. Occupying the explosive intersection of feminism, faith, and politics, the reception of Pussy Riot's action was so fraught because it exposed these contradictory forces at play in post-Soviet Russia.

My final example is an artist from Havana whose name has already been mentioned several times, and to whom I am indebted for the central ideas motivating this chapter. In the early 1990s, Tania Bruguera illegally issued two newspapers listing the names of cultural producers who had left Cuba, and these remain some of the only examples of a free press on the island since the Revolution (*Postwar Memory*, 1993–4). In 2014, she mobilized social media to even more disruptive ends. Unlike the examples by Voina and Pussy Riot, above, her effort was – by any traditional measures of art history or visual culture – a failed project. It was a proposal for a public gesture: to give members of the public a minute of free speech on Plaza de la Revolución. The call was taken up online but never happened, as the artist was arrested before the performance could even begin.

Bruguera's proposal appeared in an open letter to Raúl Castro, Barack Obama, and Pope Francis, dated 17 December 2014, in direct response to the resumption of diplomatic relations between the US and Cuba, for which the Pope had served as intermediary. In her letter, the artist states that she hopes the détente will lead not just to free markets, but also to a free press and freedom of speech. She concludes by throwing down a gauntlet: inviting Raúl Castro to restage her controversial performance *Tatlin's Whisper #6* from 2009. In this performance, members of the audience are invited onto a podium to speak freely for one minute, flanked by two actors in military dress, who place a white dove on the speaker's shoulder.[75] The setup is a conscious evocation of Fidel Castro's inaugural address to the nation fifty years earlier, when white doves auspiciously landed on his shoulders in the middle of his speech.

Two days after Bruguera's open letter was published online, her challenge was circulated on social media by her sister, Deborah Bruguera, and the curator Clara Astiasarán, under the hashtag #YoTambienExijo (I also demand). They began a Facebook page on 19 December, reposting the open letter, and called for citizens to gather on Plaza de la Revolución for a *micrófono abierto* on 30 December at 3 p.m. T-shirts were printed, press releases were issued, and a Twitter feed was established. Bruguera posted videos on YouTube inviting people to participate, while the Cuban rapper Normi Queen released a song and video titled *Yo Tambien Exijo*.[76] Bruguera was warned by the president of Cuba's National Council for the Arts (CNAP) not to undertake the performance, but she refused to cancel it. On the afternoon of 30 December, a crowd of media gathered on Revolution Square, but the event never took place: Bruguera had been arrested at 5am that morning. Her passport was confiscated for eight months, and during that period she was subject to interrogations two to three times a week.

But I am already getting lured into a narrative of what happened (or didn't happen) and its aftermath – a prolonged drama of move and countermove by the artist and the government.[77] Instead, I want to dwell on Bruguera's notion of political-timing-specificity

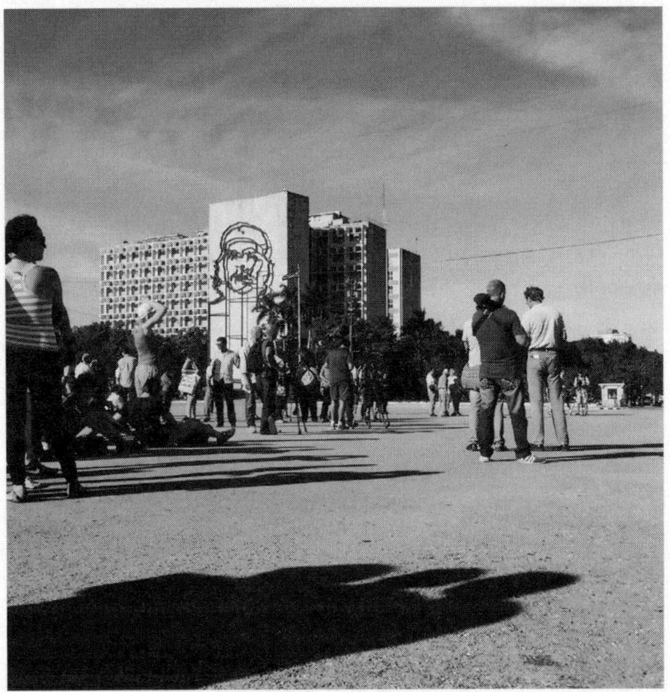

Tania Bruguera, *#YoTambienExijo*, 2014. Reporters wait on Plaza de la Revolución, Havana, 30 December 2014.

that is formative for my definition of interventions, and return to the question of social media. #YoTambienExijo was prompted by the specific moment of a possible thaw in Cuban–American relations. The end of the US embargo (which had been in place since 1958) and resumption of diplomatic relations heralded the possibility of certain freedoms; like many Cubans, Bruguera wanted to be sure that these freedoms were not just the freedom of foreign investment but civic freedoms too – freedom of expression, of the media, and of dissent. Bruguera's open letter and #YoTambien Exijo grasped a new mood, a window of opportunity, contained in this historical conjuncture. The speed and accuracy of her intervention exposed the contradiction of that moment: that being a 'good' revolutionary subject, loyal to the principles of the Cuban Revolution, meant going against the government, which was betraying those principles. To be true to her revolutionary education, she had to dissent.[78]

There are risks to the politically timed intervention, as Bruguera will be the first to attest: such work can be deemed illegal, lead to arrest, divide the public, and invite critical backlash. As with Pussy Riot, there was a disconnect between domestic and international reception. #YoTambienExijo polarized those living on the island because it forced an uncomfortable reckoning with their own silence; Bruguera perceives this as complicity, but it is understandable for the many millions who do not share her global mobility. On top of this, social media proved to be fatal to artistic intentionality. While Facebook enabled the international art world to mobilize around Bruguera's plight, it also pulled the project in unexpected directions, focusing on the artist as an individual rather than on the opposition movement against the government. The complications and possibilities of the détente were quickly cast aside in favour of subjecting Bruguera herself to examination as an attention-seeking individual (a claim, we should note, much less frequently levelled at her male contemporaries like Ai Weiwei, who are more likely to be heroicized as dissidents). Because the structure of social media is built on the individual profile, opportunity can be easily misinterpreted as opportunism: seizing the moment to advance your own career, rather than serving as a portal for what Bruguera calls 'art of the not yet'.[79] By April 2015, #YoTambienExijo had morphed into #freetaniabruguera – even though she wasn't detained in prison, but placed under house arrest. Restagings of #YoTambienExijo sprang up internationally in support of the artist – from Times Square (with which I was involved) to Tate Modern. My point here is not to detract from Bruguera's gesture but to point yet again to the capriciousness of social media. It enabled international solidarity for the artist but exposed the limitations of mobilizing support for her on the island where arguably it mattered most. Bruguera's subsequent efforts, in tandem with the group 27N (formed in 2020), have been more collective, more effective – and even more subject to repression.

The Conjuncture vs the Emergency Present

It's clear that #YoTambienExijo challenges the way in which we usually analyse art, performance, and activism. In conventional art-critical terms, it is barely conceivable as a work; it is a thwarted attempt to restage a performance. It is an extreme example of the degree to which interventions can throw up methodological challenges for art historians. Yet these challenges are also opportunities. 'Social history of art', the influential method put forward by T. J. Clark in the 1970s, has largely devolved into a formulaic description of an object floating nebulously before a background of 'context', without the two ever being intrinsically connected.[80] The concept of the *conjuncture*, by contrast, helps mitigate this effect by entangling the work and its moment: an intervention is always an intervention *into* a particular historical conjuncture; it is an active provocation.

The concept of the conjuncture traverses a long history of leftist political thought – from Marx, to Lenin, to Antonio Gramsci, to Stuart Hall, to Ernesto Laclau and Chantal Mouffe. For Althusser, it is even 'the central concept of the Marxist science of politics'.[81] Identifying a conjuncture is essentially a work of periodization. It can be short, or long, but it is singular and marks transitions between political *durées* in a way that goes beyond facile generalizations like 'the 1960s' or 'the military dictatorships'. When Stuart Hall and his collaborators at the Birmingham School of Cultural Studies developed conjunctural analysis in the late 1970s, it was in reaction to orthodox Marxism's economic determinism and its privileging of the working class.[82] Conjunctural analysis, by contrast, seeks to articulate the present-day reality in greater complexity, and to identify a contradictory system at work. There are many forces, not just one singular logic unfolding through history, and many political actors, not just the proletariat as agents of change. A conjunctural analysis is also forward-looking: whenever political theorists speak of conjunctural analysis, they agree that what lies at stake is finding a path to 'intervention'.[83]

Conjunctural analysis is useful for any discussion of artistic interventions, because the latter tend to occur at moments when history is shifting gears, when there is a new balance of forces, when ideological discourses are being restructured and new elements are emerging. This is why interventions are often undecidable at the moment of their appearance: they frame a situation in new ways. This undecidability is precisely their debatability, and an important part of why they go viral. Artists diagnose the moment, seize a window of opportunity to draw attention to an issue or problem with an action that inhabits a contradiction, and embolden others to do the same.[84]

For art historians, conjunctural analysis offers several possibilities. It expands the field of reference beyond the artist to a host of forces that give rise to the intervention – economic, cultural, political. Each of these has its own affects and associations that both determine the artist's choice of form and how the intervention is received. Clearly, this is very different from the way Hall used conjunctural analysis to analyse Thatcherism; when we mobilize conjunctural analysis to interpret an artistic intervention, we find that the latter is also *performing its own mode of conjunctural analysis*. The interventions by Voina, Pussy Riot, and Bruguera discussed above, for example, all articulate the contradictions of their historical moment: the fact that no effective political protest is possible apart from a twenty-three-second graffiti of a penis; that a forty-second punk song is more blasphemous than ecclesiastical corruption; that the freedoms promised by a diplomatic *détente* will only be economic and not civic. Interventions thus not only require a conjunctural analysis, but perform one – albeit in highly abbreviated form.

A conjunctural analysis might nevertheless place too much value on rupture and change. Some interventions point to an ongoing crisis that occupies a different sense of time. One way of designating this temporality is the 'emergency present'. Geographer Ben Anderson provides a critique of *kairos* and the right moment by criticizing the contemporary use of *emergency* as a technique of extrajudicial control that imposes a state of exception on a population.[85] Emergency is always a sovereign declaration from above, and always arrives too late – after a police murder, or when it's too late to control a pandemic. A state of emergency in this hegemonic sense is never anticipatory, preventative, or constructive. Anderson shows how the term *emergency* has nevertheless been appropriated and retooled by Black Lives Matter in order to point out that states of emergency are not a brief interruption in an otherwise normal state of affairs but endemic and routine for Black subjects in the United States. The same phrase, emergency present, could be used to describe the catastrophe of femicide in Central America. The idea of the emergency present thus contains an acknowledgement of a chronic condition that transcends the conjuncture and summons more forcibly the idea of acting now to change the future.[86]

An artistic intervention that operates within this temporality occurred during the Whitney Biennial in 2017, when a young queer Black artist called Parker Bright decided to stand in protest before Dana Schutz's *Open Casket* (2016), a painting that depicts the corpse of Emmett Till, a Black teenager who had been killed and mutilated by white vigilantes in 1955. Bright picketed Schutz's painting for two days, wearing a T-shirt with 'Black Death Spectacle' handwritten on the back and 'No Lynch Mob' on the front, effectively blocking a clear view of the painting, and inserting a living Black artist before a representation of Black death. It was a polarizing gesture that immediately problematized spectatorship, literally coming between (*inter* + *venire*) the visitor and the work of art. There was no neutral position available: your race predetermined how you would be perceived

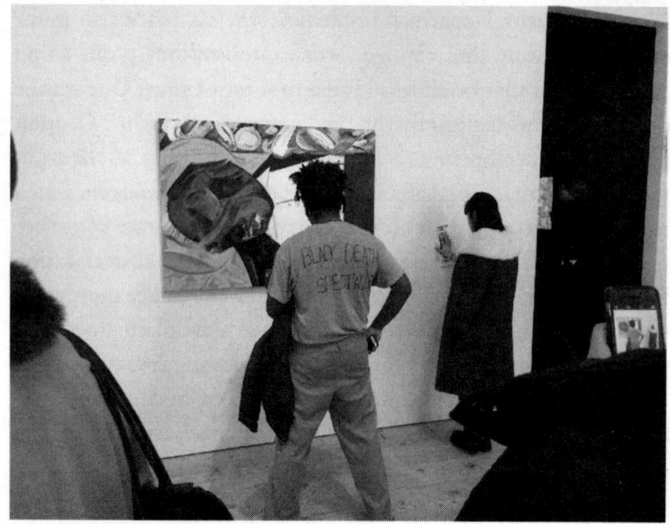

Parker Bright protests in front of Dana Schutz's *Open Casket* at the Whitney Biennial, 2017. Screengrab from gofundme.com/parkerbrightprotest.

in that space, regardless of what you thought of Schutz's painting. It was a thorn, and acutely uncomfortable.[87] Bright's gesture led to a flurry of confused debate whose target was unclear: was Dana Schutz the enemy, or the Whitney Museum, or white supremacy?

Meanwhile, Bright's image circulated on social media, where he predictably encountered both support and criticism. It even led to his gesture being appropriated by an artist in Paris, in an uncanny repetition of the co-option he was protesting in the work of Dana Schutz.[88] Yet Bright's intervention at the Biennial served as a form of conjunctural analysis, pointing to the limitations of museum representation. Although the two curators of the 2017 Biennial were Asian-American, and a substantial percentage of the works were by artists of colour and/or referred to Black history, the inclusion of Schutz's painting ignited a fierce dispute over cultural appropriation: which groups in society have access to the pain and trauma of other groups. The museum had no curators of colour on its permanent staff, and it had never even occurred to the institution that some viewers might find Schutz's painting troubling or offensive – particularly in the wake of extrajudicial killings by the police and Trump's recent ascent to power.

Bright's protest in 2017 was an isolated gesture, and confined to the art world. By the time of George Floyd's murder by police on 25 May 2020, collective indignation and frustration could no longer be contained. Mobilized by frustration and indignation, thousands of people poured onto the streets to denounce white supremacy and systemic racism, calling to defund the police, abolish prisons, and to reallocate resources to public education and welfare. One aesthetic consequence of this exhilarating wave of protests was a reckoning with the legacy of settler colonialism and New World slavery in monumental statuary across the US. The most popular gesture was iconoclastic, toppling statues to the ground in time-honoured fashion, or where this wasn't possible, simply beheading them.

In a number of cases, however, the monuments were left in place, but altered: red paint daubed like blood on the hands of Christopher Columbus; graffiti added; or images of victims projected onto the plinths. These actions directly inverted and re-semiotized the monuments' function – transforming glorifications of Southern generals who fought for slavery into memorials for those killed by a racist police force that murders with impunity. The visually striking tableaux that result are interventionist rather than iconoclastic. The activists know that the icon has power and that sometimes it is more potent to repurpose it than to drag it into the river. They seize a window of opportunity to reclaim public space, mobilize the media, and ignite debate through a strategic refocusing of attention. Such interventions push against the limitations of the intervention as a genre: its masculinism, its militarism, its whiteness, and its tendency to construct the artist (or artist collective) as hero-outsider.

The most striking of these interventions took place at the monument to General Robert E. Lee in Richmond, Virginia. An equestrian bronze statue atop an imposing white marble plinth in the middle of a prominent traffic island, the monument to General Lee had already been subject to numerous calls for removal, like many Confederate monuments over the past decade. Yet rather than toppling the statue outright, protestors festooned the marble base with candles and layers of brightly coloured graffiti, civil rights slogans, affirmations of Black love, and large-scale projected portraits of George Floyd and Breonna Taylor alongside civil rights heroes like Angela Davis, Harriet Tubman, and Malcolm X. A sign on the island read 'Welcome to Beautiful Marcus-David Peters Circle, Liberated by the People MMXX'.[89] That summer, the photographer Mel Cole captured a cross-section of activity on the traffic island. His images show a place abuzz with music, basketball, cookouts, dancing, games, a radical library, community. A monument endorsing slavery had been completely re-semiotized as a place to acknowledge collective grief but also to find joy in the present and to incubate a future. Unlike

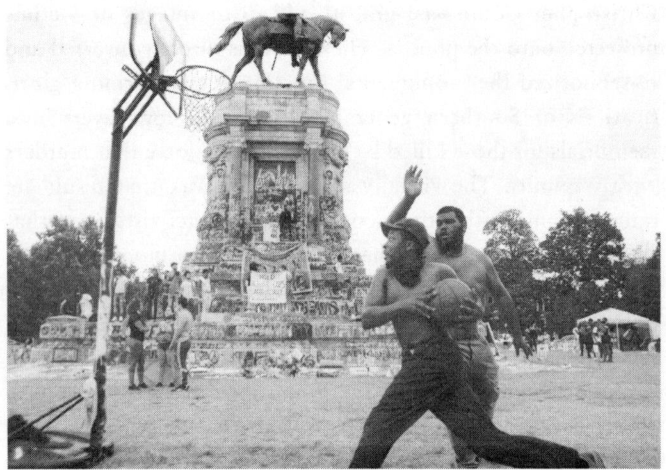

Mel D. Cole, *Richmond, VA, 6.20.2020*, 2020. Digital photograph.

Ensacamento, which recast authority in the negative (bagging the heads of national figures), protestors in Richmond overlaid a positive 'new skin' over a despised monument to assert a new civic constituency.[90] An empty grey traffic island with a pompous equestrian overseer was turned into a thriving locus of solidarity by changing the site's appearance, texture, function, and context. Its messaging was accordingly less ambiguous because it responded to an emergency present; rather than seizing the right moment, it claimed a moment that was long overdue.

Moral Relativism

Because aesthetic forms are fluid in their associations, the intervention – like all artistic strategies – is malleable in its politics. The meaning of any form depends on the conventions and connotations that circulate more broadly in culture and society. Over the last decade, the rise of the alt-right has problematized the left's monopoly on disruption; it has produced disturbing websites, protests, and even performances that seek to shock and transgress.[91] Cultural theorist Angela Nagle has persuasively shown how the legacy of the 1920s avant-garde and the 1960s counterculture, as well as Gramsci's theory of hegemony and counter-hegemony, have now been hijacked by the alt-right and ethno-nationalists.[92] Yet as the example of Italian Futurism demonstrates, that tradition was never so clearly leftist in the first place. On 6 January 2021, pro-Trump fanatics stormed the Capitol on the day of President Biden's certification by the Electoral College. One photograph from that day shows a man standing on a plinth alongside a bronze statue of Gerald Ford, having put a flag in the former president's hand and a red MAGA hat on his head. On a formal level, this intervention is the far-right mirror of the previous summer's attacks on Confederate-era monuments by Black Lives Matter protestors. Both groups transgress and make a claim on public space; both re-semiotize monumental statuary; both disrupt an existing social order, catalyse debate, and divide the public.

The uncomfortable conclusion is that disruption and transgression can no longer be automatically aligned with left or right, good or bad, however we construe them. Nagle rightly observes that transgression and subversion are 'ideologically flexible, politically fungible, morally neutral . . . and can characterize misogyny as easily as [they] can sexual liberation . . . anti-moral transgression has always been a bargain with the devil, because the case for equality is essentially a moral one'.[93] This tension can be seen in some of the interventions I have discussed. They tend to speak more to issues of freedom – freedom of speech, or the freedom to protest – than to issues of equality, redistribution, and justice. The exception is Parker Bright's intervention, which subjects artistic freedom to a moral test – and it is no coincidence that his gesture took place in a museum, rather than on the streets.

The next step, then, is to discuss ends as well as means. A nihilist, libertarian politics of transgression is substantially different from a politics of equality, justice, and futurity (as opposed to 'futurism'). This perhaps marks the limits of interventions: their speed, urgency, and radical subjectivity forecloses – perhaps inevitably – a consideration of strategic consequences. Their planning and horizon are short-term – but this is why they are effective in their moment. Attention to an intervention that goes viral is only ever brief and intense. Yet this is also the source of their strength as a catalyst for public debate and a focus for dissent. If one intervention spirals headlong into violence and hatred, then another can be prefigurative – a way to generate glimpses of the *not yet*, channelling rebellious energies of desire for a life that could be.

Despite the problems of social media circulation, and the shortcomings of short-term thinking, the intervention opens up a dynamic role for artists today: articulating the contradictions of our conjuncture in new ways, and generating a new set of terms. In the final chapter, I turn to a more conventional type of art that is far less controversial. In its lack of provocation, however, it allows us to understand another approach to the operating system of contemporary art.

4

Déjà Vu: Invoking Modernist Architecture and Design

At any point in the past thirty years, you could open an art magazine or go to a commercial gallery and find work by artists who are fascinated by 'modernist movements and collectives', who are drawn to 'forgotten modernist constructions that have crumbled over time', and whose work is 'based on' or 'inspired by' a modernist precursor – 'evoking the modernist architecture of Mies van der Rohe' or 'immersing themselves in Lina Bo Bardi's world'. Every year there seems to be yet another exhibition 'dedicated to the reanimation of aspects of Western European modernism' and 'the fragmentary evocation of the icons of modernist architecture'. One constant refrain describes the 'failure' of modernist utopias: photographs 'critiquing modernism's doomed utopias'; paintings offering 'a critical meditation on social utopianism'; and sculptures showing 'the absurd failure of large-scale, ambitious projects, such as Modernist Utopias'.[1]

Rather like research-based art (discussed in Chapter 1), contemporary art that references modernism has secured a place as a serious, historically minded alternative to the flashy presentism of the art market's big players. The artists who produce this work tend to be articulate, intellectually curious, and engaged with cultural history and politics. Perhaps for this reason, their work has never received sustained critical analysis. Despite its orientation toward the past, there seems to be a reluctance to subject this trend in contemporary art to a diachronic evaluation. None of the curators that have assembled exhibitions of this work have, to my knowledge, ever attempted to describe its emergence and development. One side effect of contemporary art that addresses history, as we have already seen with research-based art, is that it tends to occlude its own art-historical interrogation. Critics repeat information about the artist's topic, rather than situating the work in relation to a longer lineage of contemporary art now decades old and spanning at least two continents.

The sheer number of artists since the early 1990s who have quoted modernist architecture and design underlines the collective nature of attention in the most obvious sense: a multi-generational attraction to the modernist past that only seems to increase as more and more artists discover its austerely appealing aesthetic. But it also points to the problems with collective attention in the context of artistic production. A trend can gradually harden into conformism, overriding earlier artistic values such as originality and unconventionality.

A conscious engagement with history has arguably become one of the hallmarks of art since the 1990s – in research-based installations, video essays, documentaries, image archives, pseudo-museums, re-enactments, lecture-performances, and artists' books.[2] Focusing on the citation of modernist architecture and design has the advantage of thrusting certain problems to the fore that are obscured in these other modes of artistic engagement with the past – questions of depoliticization versus reactivation, nostalgia versus reimagination, and historicity versus presentism. This is because modernist architecture, urban planning, and design all carry a concrete relationship to the world, and by extension to the future: they contain a blueprint for a way of living. They mediate between the individual and the social, and this utilitarian impetus (often perceived as utopianism) is one of the main reasons they hold such appeal for contemporary visual artists. As such, this chapter will not make a distinction between modernist architecture and design, since both are cited widely and interchangeably by contemporary artists.

Modernism, in this art, is understood primarily as *style*, albeit one shot through with different degrees of ideological content. I will be focusing on the three modernisms that appear most regularly in this work: the International Style and its aftermath in Western Europe and North America from the 1910s to the 1970s, also exported to Europe's colonies; Socialist Modernism from the Bolshevik Revolution of 1917 to the collapse of the Soviet Bloc in 1989–91, encompassing both the interwar avant-garde and postwar Socmodernism in Russia and Eastern Europe; and Tropical Modernism in Latin America, especially architecture and design associated with postwar developmentalism in the 1950s and 1960s, but occasionally stretching back earlier to the 1920s and 1930s. Modernism thus shifts its meaning and periodization according to geographical location; so too does the idea of *modernity* more broadly – a huge topic with which the iconography of modernist architecture and design is inevitably entangled. The blurring between modernism (as a style) and modernization (as a social and historical process) occurs most frequently in discussions of Latin American art, where critics and curators regularly follow Néstor García Canclini in framing Latin American modernity as 'unrealized'.[3] I have tried to contain this potential spillover by restricting observations about modernity in general to the footnotes.

Despite its quiet ubiquity, this art throws up many questions that have not been addressed by critics and curators. What kind of citational practice is taking place, and does it offer a new or distinct approach? Why does contemporary art refer incessantly back to the more 'useful' arts of architecture and design, and equate both of these with 'utopianism'? And what does the artistic obsession with modernism tell us about historicity in a digital era? For the art historian, this work also throws up problems central to the theme of this book. What kind of attention should we bring to such a large body of work, especially when so much of it circulates online? Choosing to elevate a few examples would miss the opportunity to confront the sheer quantity and sameness of this practice. What models should we turn to when the usual method – case study exceptionalism – feels inappropriate?

I first started to track this work about fifteen years ago, in the context of research into post–Cold War Europe. As time passed, and more and more examples kept appearing, my eyes began to glaze over. Breuer chair, check. Niemeyer curves, check. Slim pilotis, check. Deserted buildings, check. Certain structures were depicted over and again: the Bauhaus Dessau, the Barcelona Pavilion, the Villa Savoye, Brasília, the Farnsworth House, the Seagram Building. When I first presented this material in public, I had amassed so many examples across so many media – photography, painting, 16mm and 35mm film, video, drawing, sculpture, various types of prints – that I wanted to give my audience a sense of what I was navigating. I loaded all my pictures into a PowerPoint presentation, which I arranged in various sequences (chronological, geographical, architectural) and timed them to play alongside my talk. The results were somewhat overwhelming, but conveyed the desired impression of quantity and repetition.

A slideshow rolling automatically in the background was appropriate, because the attentional mode I find myself giving this work is like a camera panning across a scene without focusing on any one element. The digital equivalent of this is *scrolling*. As a way of looking, scrolling implies a flatness of affect: the boredom of repetition (next, next, next) that is only occasionally punctuated by a 'like' or a 'share', and even more rarely by a jolt of excitement and curiosity. Sometimes a work leaps out, but for the most part our attention moves on – we clock the reference and advance to the next image. Unlike pagination, scrolling produces an amorphous relationship to time and space. When scrolling through a webpage, it's often hard to locate how far we are through the material and we have no idea how much more there is to come. On Instagram or TikTok, the situation is worse: the feed is bottomless, because the algorithm endlessly generates more content.

I have since uploaded hundreds of images onto a WordPress site that links to information about each work, and am continually adding examples. I encourage the reader to scroll through this for illustrations.[4] More than any of the preceding chapters, then, this one is unthinkable without the internet.[5] Most of the works I have only seen as images online. Rather than disqualifying me from commentary, this reflects how many of us see art today: we look at JPEGs more than we stand in galleries. Often we look at JPEGs to decide whether we should go and stand in a gallery, especially after the pandemic forced us online to an unprecedented degree. Although this is undoubtedly not what the artists intend, it underscores the hybridity of contemporary spectatorship.

While this chapter considers a large number of images, my method exists in tension with 'distant reading', formulated in 2000 by literary scholar Franco Moretti. For Moretti, the digitalization of nineteenth-century literature enabled a different set of research questions to come to the fore – questions that did not concern individual works but large international categories and literary genres (such as the gothic novel).[6] The translation of distant reading to art history has been strained – perhaps unsurprisingly, given that images cannot be subject to written search terms without tagging and categorization. The early issues of *The International Journal for Digital Art History* (founded in 2015) apply quantitative methods to objects as varied as seven centuries of portraiture, Aby Warburg's *Mnemosyne Atlas*, and everything on 'WikiArt paintings'. The results are unsatisfying: a new language of art history in which the datasets precede the research questions, rather than research questions emerging from (and engaging with) observations or current debates about the work.

Artist and digital theorist Lev Manovich, a regular contributor to this journal, developed a complementary method he calls 'cultural analytics' to study a contemporary visual culture of big data.[7] His datasets have grown steadily bigger – from thousands, to hundreds of thousands, to millions – with images drawn from Google street view, selfies on Instagram, and geotagged images shared on Twitter. Cultural analytics, like distant reading, pressures the traditional humanities attachment to elite objects. Manovich's resulting visualizations are striking, yet the research questions are weak or non-existent: *One Million Manga Pages* (2009–), for example, is all visualization, a morass of data awaiting a researcher to offer an interpretation.[8] In other projects, key analytic terms like 'cultural event' or 'emotional response' are taken for granted rather than problematized. At worst, the translation of visual research into the language of data can seem pointless – as when Manovich and his team analyse 776 paintings by Van Gogh to assess whether the artist's use of colour changed after his move from Paris to Arles in 1888, as claimed on the Van Gogh Museum website.[9]

Although the research for this chapter is underpinned by hundreds of works, I've tried to navigate the difference between distant reading and close-focus analysis by using examples to extrapolate conclusions that remain qualitative rather than computational, driven by questions of tone and attitude. My goal is to provide a historical overview of a genre of contemporary art while also retaining the specificity of individual works of art. At the same time, I want to underscore the extent to which this genre is culturally symptomatic. It has a complicated and ambivalent relationship to digital technology – evidenced in the model of historicity that we find therein and its remarkably consistent aesthetic over the last thirty years.

Tracking Tatlin

To date, no critics or curators have tracked the development of this work. One way to begin this is by turning to one of the most widely cited referents, Vladimir Tatlin's visionary *Monument to the Third International* (1919–20).[10] While most of the examples date from after 1990, the earliest examples can be found in the 1960s and 1970s. The best-known is Dan Flavin's series of thirty-nine *Monuments to V. Tatlin*, begun in 1964 and wrapped up in time for the 'end of history' in 1990. Flavin turned to Tatlin's work for a model of abstract, technological rigour, almost entirely unrelated to the social goals of the Revolution; his first neon light sculpture, *the diagonal of May 25, 1963* (1963), is dedicated to the Romanian modernist sculptor Constantin Brancusi. By calling his own prefabricated fluorescent tube sculptures 'monuments', Flavin was clearly making a wry joke – albeit one harder to appreciate now that his works are themselves iconic, found in every major collection, and extremely citable. (Portuguese artist Ângela Ferreira's recursive one-liner *Monument to D. Flavin* (2008), for example, combines Flavin's series and Tatlin's *Monument* into a single sculpture.)

In the 1980s, this art entered an ironic register associated with cultural postmodernism. Despite its problems, the term *postmodernism* provides a useful tool (and foil) for tracking the changing relationship to modernist design circa 1990. In Eastern Europe, the 'retroavantgarde' activities of the multi-disciplinary Yugoslav collective Neue Slowenische Kunst (NSK) provides a model of such postmodern remixing.[11] The Sisters of Scipion Nasice, the performance wing of NSK, performed underneath a reconstruction of Tatlin's *Monument* in the Cankarjev dom in Ljubljana (*Baptism under Triglav*, 1986). The set was designed by Miran Mohar, a founding member of NSK's visual art collective IRWIN. The latter's icon paintings, produced continuously since the group's founding in 1983, remix the dominant visual imageries that traversed modern Slovenia. IRWIN deliberately conflate the progressive and regressive – Italian Futurism, Soviet Constructivism, Fascist and Socialist Realism, and the tropes of nineteenth-century nationalism (deer, eagle, sower) – suggesting that all forms of state symbolism are undesirably ideological.[12] At the same time, these imageries are rescued and partially redeemed as part of a new collective iconography for the post-Tito era.

A handful of Russian artists associated with 'Sots art' reference Tatlin's *Monument* in the 1980s and 1990s, including Leonid Sokov and Aleksandr Kosolapov. Here the iconography is summoned and evacuated in a single move: Tatlin is one more empty signifier, along with Stalin, Marilyn Monroe, and Coca-Cola. Or a vodka brand – as in Sokov's painting *Tatlin's Tower with Stolichnaya* (1996), in which the monument snugly wraps around a bottle, and both point towards a glowing sun. Slavic scholar Svetlana Boym observes that for this generation of Russian artists, Tatlin's tower is less a symbol or model than simply 'part of the ludic cultural archaeology of the twentieth century'.[13] For a younger generation of artists experiencing *glasnost*, however, Tatlin's *Monument* was acquiring different connotations. Yuri Avvakumov's sculpture *Perestroika Tower* (1990) transforms the *Monument* into scaffolding, into which is embedded a copy of Vera Mukhina's monumental sculpture *Industrial Worker and Collective Farm Girl* from 1937. Here it is no longer Soviet communism and Western consumerism that are set at odds, but Constructivism and Socialist Realism, mashed up into one new national supersignifier as the country was disintegrating.

After the collapse of communism, a flourishing of references to Constructivism takes place outside Russia. Zaha Hadid's series of drawings and paintings *The Great Utopia* (1992) builds upon her longstanding interest in Suprematist and Constructivist architecture. Executed as exhibition designs for a Guggenheim exhibition of the same name, the series creates an analogy between two spirals, Tatlin's and Frank Lloyd Wright's.[14] More typical of this decade, however, is for Tatlin's *Monument* to be semiotically charged as a symbol of the Soviet social project, but in a plaintive register – each time signifying utopian longing and its failure, often through the use of poor materials. A sculpture by Cuban artist Kcho, *To the Eyes of History* (1995), reconstructs

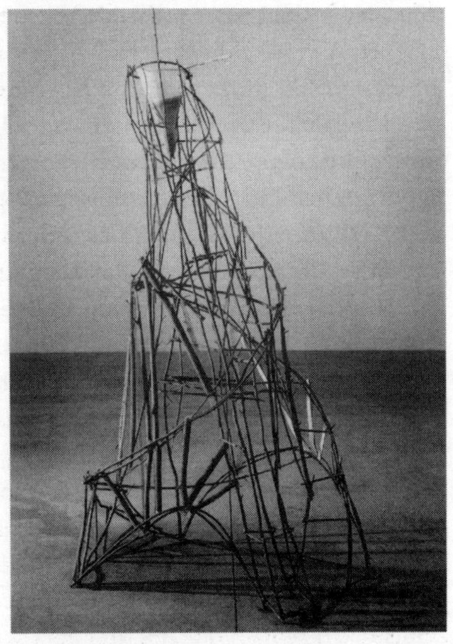
Kcho (Alexis Leyva Machado), *To the Eyes of History*, 1992–95. Twigs, plant fibres, and fabric coffee filter.

Tatlin's *Monument* in driftwood and twine to become a drip coffee-maker. Produced during the Cuban Special Period following the dissolution of the Soviet Union, the sculpture is an indictment of utopian political aspirations: when faced with the reality of life in Cuba, Tatlin's structure embodies a grand idea gone wrong.[15]

Post-2000, Tatlin's *Monument* starts to be inflected with different associations: less a vehicle for lamenting the 'failure of modernism' than a potential seed for reactivation. Polish artist Grzegorz Klaman used the *Monument* to subversive ends when he was commissioned to create a public sculpture as a monument to the Solidarity movement. *Gates II* (2000) slyly replaces the group's conservative Christian iconography with Tatlin's unmistakeable spiral, asserting the ongoing importance of the Third International. In this instance, Tatlin serves as a leftist correction to the historical record. Elsewhere, reactivation is suggested through an ongoing attachment to poor materials, and on a more domestic scale. French artist Michel Aubry set to music a small maquette of the *Monument* built of wooden slats and reeds (*Mise en musique du Monument à la IIIe Internationale*, 2000), while Greek artist Kostis Velonis jerry-rigged an assemblage version from old furniture (*Reconstruction of Tatlin's Monument to the Third International as an Instrument of Research for Domesticity*, 2009). Working in collaboration with an Aboriginal community in Sydney, US artist Michael Rakowitz produced a version of the *Monument* from reclaimed wood, and turned it into a broadcasting device for a local radio station (*White Man Got No Dreaming*, 2008). Catalan artist Domenèc, meanwhile, reimagines Tatlin's *Monument* as a functional climbing frame for children (*Playground [Tatlin in Mexico]*, 2011).

A complementary approach since 2000 has been the addition of scale and bling, in a sardonic commentary on art's revolutionary ambitions turned status symbols for the oligarchy. Ai Weiwei's ironically opulent twenty-three-foot-tall chandelier, *Fountain of*

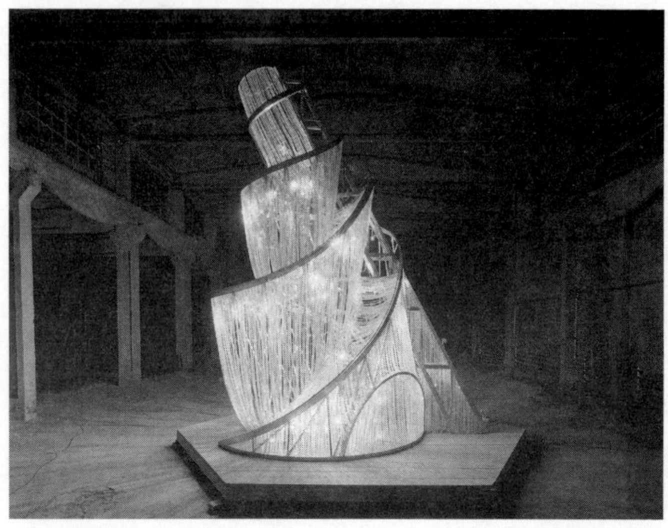

Ai Weiwei, *Fountain of Light*, 2007. Steel and glass crystals on a wooden base. Installation view, Ai Weiwei Studio, Beijing.

Light (2007), glitters with 32,400 crystals but is grounded on the floor, unable to rotate and devoid of functional usage. (A subsequent version, dated 2016, has been acquired by the Louvre Abu Dhabi.) Electroboutique's *3G International* (2010), an iPhone in the shape of Tatlin's *Monument*, attempts something similar but symptomatizes a more local problem: how the concepts of utopia and the historical avant-garde have been reduced to formalism and leveraged by Russian artists as national brands recognizable to the international art world.[16]

By the 2010s, the *Monument* has become a beacon standing for the impossible beauty of revolutionary ambition, but also the melancholy of its inability to be realized. In the work of neo-Marxist Russian collective Chto Delat, living under Vladimir Putin's corrupt regime of authoritarian neoliberalism, the pendulum swings back towards the plaintive. Tatlin's *Monument* appears numerous times in the group's work – for example, on the cover of the newspaper *Debates of the Avant-Garde* (2007), in the installation *Study, Study and Act Again* (2011–14), and in the sculpture *Untitled (Tatlin Tower)* (2013). In each instance, its diminished and precarious appearance conveys a sense of futures

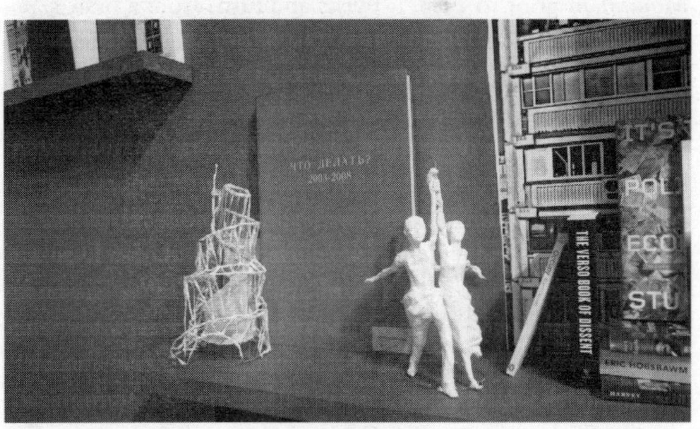

Chto Delat, *Untitled (Tatlin Tower)*, 2013. Installation view, *Art Turning Left: How Values Changed Making 1789–2013*, Tate Liverpool, 2013.

once dreamt but now lost. Together with the group's broader redeployment of early twentieth-century aesthetics (Constructivism, Socialist Realism, the Brechtian *songspiel*), the mood is one of melancholic yearning for past models of solidarity and resistance. Here, modernism appears as wholly a concern of the past, even when reactivation is ostensibly desired, and even depicted with contemporary actors. A similarly wistful mood informs the appearance of Tatlin's *Monument* in the performance *Works in Public Collections* (2014), by Romanian artists Alexandra Pirici and Manuel Pelmus. Three dancers assume a pose that momentarily takes the form of Tatlin's recognizable shape, but disappears before a minute has elapsed, to be replaced by another recognizable work of art.

A whole spectrum of approaches to twentieth-century socialism thus nestle within the spirals of Tatlin's model, which today reads as the symbol of artistic utopianism *tout court*. The locations of the artists are not insignificant: countries with a historical relationship to communism (Cuba, Russia, China, Poland, Romania), plus European countries experiencing the dismantling of the welfare state. The global proliferation of Tatlin citations is striking when compared to the number of works referencing the *Monument* prior to 1989. It twists and turns from a ludic signifier, to an ironic reference, to a plaintive object of desire, to potential yet perpetually unrealized reactivation. Of course, Tatlin's *Monument* could only assume such symbolic force once communism was no longer seen as an active threat: Tatlin can only be taken seriously as a referent when state socialism is defunct and no longer has political potency.

From Interrogation to Invocation

Outside of the narrow lens of Tatlin, the overall arc of contemporary artists' relationship to modernist architecture is strikingly similar. In the 1980s, a handful of artists express a scepticism towards modernism, regarding it as suspicious and totalitarian;

in short, as dystopian. In the early 1990s, after the breakup of the Soviet Union, art addressing modernist architecture and design begins to appear more frequently, if unevenly, in Eastern and Western Europe and North and South America, reflecting the regional rollout of neoliberalism and its relationship to the end of communism. What is meant by modernism begins to fragment, but the tone is consistent. After 2000, the modernist past is no longer to be mocked or critiqued; irony, cynicism, and pastiche are rare. Instead, modernism becomes an object of fascination, deserving close attention and research. Reverence and nostalgia ensue.

In the early 1990s, during the first, brief phase of this art, artists reflected critically on modernist architecture and planning more broadly. The work of Swiss artist Christian Philipp Müller exemplifies this kind of earnest interrogation. His research-based installation *Forgotten Futures* (1992) traces the connections between several late-modern utopias from the 1950s: the Philips Pavilion for the 1958 World Expo in Brussels (in which Le Corbusier collaborated with composers Iannis Xenakis and Edgard Varèse), Nicolas Schöffer's book *The Cybernetic City* (1969), and Veit Harlan's film *Different from You and Me* (1957), which explores the then-taboo subject of homosexuality and German laws against it. Müller's installation comprises a model of the pavilion, a reconstruction of the 'miniscule bureau' (or tiny office) from Le Corbusier's studio in Paris, a black box in which Varèse's eight-minute composition is played, a display of his scores alongside Le Corbusier's original Modular drawings, an information panel about Schöffer's vision for a cybernetic city, a vitrine with more original documents from Le Corbusier's archives, and a cinematic showcase of Harlan's film. As this description indicates, Müller's reference points are more central to the project than their spatial arrangement as an installation. *Forgotten Futures* augurs a type of research-based installation that was to flourish more fully after the millennium (discussed in Chapter 1) – a model less interested in making arguments than in creating open-ended informational displays, aggregating minor histories from outside the canon.[17] Müller's installation gestures to a queer critique of Le Corbusier's pristine spaces, which in the artist's view did not allow for any of life's contingencies: 'personal conflicts, sexuality, affects, the unforeseen, the irrational and alternative histories'.[18]

In the US, by contrast, a last gasp of critical irreverence can be seen in Sam Durant's *Abandoned Houses* (1994–95): six scale models of the Case Study Houses, constructed from cheap materials like foamcore and cardboard, which are burned, punctured with holes, and defaced with graffiti.[19] Like Müller's installation, the critique also concerns repression: Durant's accompanying collage series makes clear that his point is about the constitutive exclusion of class in California modernism (the Case Study Houses were intended to be affordable but have become collectors' items). In the photomontage *Modern Moon* (1994), a white party girl drops her shorts to bare her bottom in the mid-century

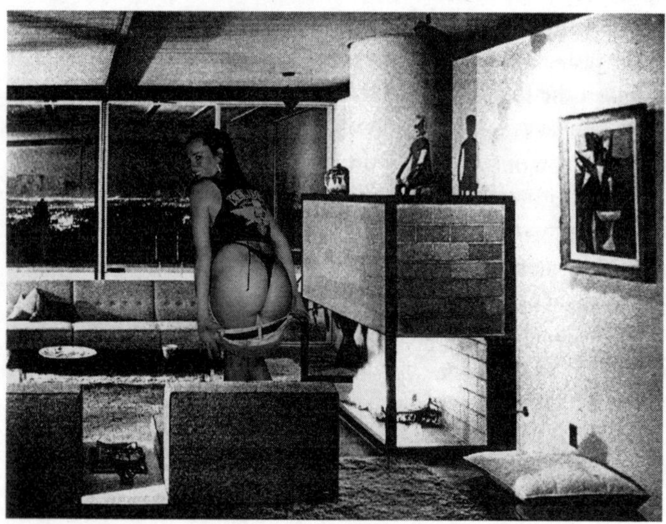

Sam Durant, *Modern Moon*, 1994. Collage on photocopy.

modern interior, bringing a trashy, raucous (full-colour) present into conflict with the controlled geometrical poise of the (black-and-white) living room.

Durant's acerbic takedown was soon out of sync with the general mood. Modernist design was about to be recuperated as a signifier of good taste, with the full imprimatur of art-world approval. *Wallpaper**, a glossy monthly magazine dedicated to interior design, architecture, and fashion, was launched in London in 1996 and consolidated the branding of 'mid-century modern' as lifestyle. *Wallpaper** indicated not only a changed relationship to modernism after its rejection by postmodernists, but the emergence of a young, affluent class who had graduated from thrift-store grunge to globe-trotting professionalism – signalled by the acquisition of Eames chairs, Saarinen tables, and Le Corbusier chaise longues. A 1998 article in the *New York Times* identified a 'Wallpaper Generation', arguing that the magazine did not so much pioneer as consolidate a trend already visible in furniture stores, pop videos, advertising, and celebrities buying up houses by John Lautner and Richard Neutra in Los Angeles. Mid-century modern became synonymous with grown-up good taste, especially if you could score a vintage original. A similar taste led artists to modernist architecture in their work, and collectors to acquire it.

By the end of the decade, it was not just modernist architecture that had been rehabilitated. Rebranded and depoliticized, the idea of utopia came to acquire a magnetic status for artists and curators. Formerly applied only to exhibitions of the Soviet avant-garde, the word became artistic shorthand for any kind of better world – propelled by Nicolas Bourriaud's advocacy of 'microtopias' in *Relational Aesthetics* (1998) and the itinerant exhibition 'Utopia Station' in 2003.[20] Around the turn of the millennium, modernism and utopianism became interchangeable terms; *utopia* became a descriptor exportable to any and every context, unburdened by political affiliation or ideology. Delinked from its negative associations with communism, it could now refer to any artistic proposition, even a small-scale convivial event. More often, however, it served as wishful thinking rather than as a catalyst for a new political imaginary. 'Utopian' became a catch-all descriptor for modernist design, regardless of whether or not it possessed a social vision or was ever realized.[21] Ironically, the works most cited by artists are examples from the postwar period, when the International Style fell into the hands of private individuals and corporate clients. Ubiquitous icons like the Seagram Building (1958) and private homes like Le Corbusier's Villa Savoye (1928–31), Mies van der Rohe's Farnsworth House (1945–51), and Philip Johnson's Glass House (1949) are all elite set pieces far removed from a socialist vision of a better life for all citizens. In order for the equation between modernist architecture and utopia to take place, both terms had to be de-ideologized and rendered generically applicable.

After 2000, modernist architecture's visions came to be seen as admirable, even enviable. From this point on, art quoting modernist architecture consistently offers a respectful tone of overall approval that can be described as *invocation*.[22] The contemporary work turns to older modernist referents and accrues authority from their reputation. Invocation is evidenced in artists' enthusiasm for the proper name: celebrated figures assume a disproportionate centrality – above all, Le Corbusier, Mies van der Rohe, and Oscar Niemeyer. Gradually, less canonical names began to be recovered, including those of women architects and designers (Eileen Gray, Charlotte Perriand, Lina Bo Bardi) and Eastern European modernists (Exat 51, Vjenceslav Richter, Zofia Stryjeńska, Oskar Hansen). While these works have produced a more inclusive picture of modernism, anticipating the 'multiple modernities' of museum collection displays, they exhibit the same attachment to nominalism. The cast might be new, but the plot remains the same.

A signal example of invocation in the global mode can be found in Florian Pumhösl's installation *Modernology (Triangular Atelier)* (2007), a work largely unintelligible without the list of proper names undergirding its abstract formalism. A series of black display screens allude to an exhibition organized in Japan in 1914 by the German Expressionist gallery Der Sturm, and to the triangular atelier of Japanese avant-garde designer Murayama Tomoyoshi; hanging on the screens are three textile works made in 1955 by Gutai artist Atsuko Tanaka, and eight abstract paintings on glass (by Pumhösl) that reference the Bauhaus painter and designer Walter Dexel; nearby are two Lucite display cases containing editions of the Japanese propaganda magazine *Front* from 1943. As in Müller's *Forgotten Futures*, proper names crowd the installation, but without a larger goal beyond tracing the transnational network. The references are as important as the layout (if not more so), positioning the artist not just as the creator of a spatial experience but as a respectful curator of citations.

Invocation marks a new phase of appropriation art. For much of the twentieth century, appropriation as an artistic strategy signalled a defiant, subversive approach to cultural objects: think of Dada photomontage, Surrealist found objects, and Situationist *détournement*. This began to shift with Pop Art in the 1960s, which – at least outside the US – was characterized by various degrees of ambivalence and uneasy pleasure. During the 1980s, appropriation artists competed to do the least possible with a pre-existing image repertoire (think Sherrie Levine or Richard Prince). In more recent usage, the term has acquired wholly negative connotations. When coupled with the word 'cultural', appropriation denotes white artists (or those from hegemonic centres) borrowing a signifier from a culture perceived as less powerful and/or with less cultural capital, and financially benefitting from this quotation.

Invocation, I would like to argue, represents a different approach: it is neither subversive (like *détournement*) nor replicative (like appropriation art) nor extractive (like cultural appropriation). Its hallmark, by contrast, is veneration. Contemporary artists rarely reference modernist architects and designers in an iconoclastic fashion. This work has no place in a lineage of avant-gardist vandalism that stretches from Duchamp's mischievous graffiti upon the Mona Lisa (*LHOOQ*, 1919), to Ai Weiwei destroying a 2000-year-old vase (*Dropping the Urn*, 1995), to Jake and Dinos Chapman defacing a set of Goya prints (*Insult to Injury*, 2004). Contemporary invocation art treats the proper name with respect. There are works that are playful (e.g., the Villa Savoye in pink felt or photoshopped with graffiti; a melting resin rendition of the Seagram Building), but the tone of these ludic efforts is affectionate; they keep the name (and form) intact to convey the desired one-liner.

What takes place across this art amounts to a secular version of what anthropologists describe as an appeal to ancestral spirits as a higher power. A name or artifact from the artist's own cultural milieu is invoked to lend significance to the contemporary object, consolidating the older object's importance while simultaneously legitimating the artist's place in that culture. The attitude is summed up by Portuguese artist Leonor Antunes, a prolific exponent of this genre: 'I feel that my role as an artist is also to talk about the relevance of other people's work. I want to make my work part of this trajectory of thought.'[23] Antunes frequently invokes female modernists, from well-known figures like Annie Albers, Lina Bo Bardi, Clara Porset, and Eileen Gray to lesser-known examples like Trude Guermonprez, Kay Sekimachi, Michiko Yamawaki, and Greta Grossman – sometimes within a single installation.

While such an approach has the advantage of bringing back to light overlooked cultural producers, it also risks blending different national histories and aesthetics into one ahistorical modernist soup. Goshka Macuga, born in Poland but based in London since 1989, not only cites a wide range of European modernist artists (and display strategies) but includes actual examples of their work inside her carefully staged installations and artist-curated exhibitions. Her installations have included references to or research into Eileen Agar, Paul Nash, El Lissitzky, Lily Reich,

Pablo Picasso, Aby Warburg, *The Cabinet of Dr Caligari* (1920), the Cabaret Voltaire, and the theosophist Madame Blavatsky, among others. The coexistence of these disparate references has led critic Martin Herbert to observe that Macuga 'appears devoted to a conception of the modern as sheer simultaneity: all its moments existing at once, quantum physics–style, in some accessible elsewhere, amenable to recombination'.[24] To clarify, my point is not that contemporary art tells a 'wrong' or misleading history of modernism. Rather, my argument is that invocation produces history in a register of simultaneity and aggregation rather than change or development: 'everything, everywhere, all at once'.

Invocation thus marks a key difference between art since the 1990s and previous artistic engagements with architecture. In the 1970s, for example, artists approached the architecture of their day with a distinct agenda, and without recourse to specific, named architects. For example, Dan Graham's architectural sculptures in two-way mirror glass from 1978 onwards engage with the history of pavilions but also the use of glass and steel in corporate atria and shopping malls. Gordon Matta-Clark's cutting and dismantling of abandoned buildings sought to explore what he called 'anarchitecture', while Martha Rosler's photo series *In the Place of the Public: The Airport Series* (1983–) documents airports as contemporary non-places. It is only since the arrival of the internet that historical research and remixing has become prevalent in contemporary art. Online resources facilitate research into the past, but also make possible the decontextualized download and ahistorical recombination of images, and the foregrounding of named individuals. Time and space get levelled into one geographically and historically homogeneous unit of 'the modern', all of which is up for grabs.

Why Modern?

As the transnational tracking of references to Tatlin's *Monument* indicates, 1989 is a key factor in the rise of this artistic genre: the fall of communism, the rise of a post-socialist condition, and disenchantment with the so-called triumph of neoliberalism.[25] But other factors, more central to the operation of contemporary art as a cultural industry, have provided material infrastructure for this engagement with the past.

One of these is residency programmes. As the Iron Curtain was lifted, artists from the West went exploring. The DAAD (Deutscher Akademischer Austauschdienst) studio residency programme in Berlin was an early incubator for this genre. Numerous artists elected to memorialize GDR-era buildings and monuments, or to depict their demolition: notable examples include Jane and Louise Wilson's *Stasi City* (1997) and Tacita Dean's films *Ferhnsehturm* (2001) and *Palast* (2004). The mood is less a yearning for a social project than a fascination with history's traces in architecture, the imprint of ideology upon design.[26] Eastern European artists, by contrast, tend to focus on the architecture and design of postwar socialism. A transition from cynicism to rehabilitation can be seen here too. In the early 1990s, the attitude towards the Soviet past began with moral ambivalence, tainted by the regime's associations with totalitarianism – as seen in the work of Dan Perjovschi (Romania), Deimantas Narkevičius (Lithuania), and Anri Sala (Albania).[27] By the mid-2000s, the mood is more nostalgic and appreciative – as seen in the work of Goshka Macuga, David Maljković (Croatia), Paulina Ołowska (Poland), and Tobias Putrih (Slovenia), all of whom trained in Western European art schools. Maljković takes as his starting point the experimental architecture of Yugoslav modernism. His low-tech video trilogy *Scenes for a New Heritage* (2004) assumes the form of homespun science fiction based on the monument to partisan resistance at Petrova Gora Memorial Park, designed by Vojin Bakić and completed in 1981. Maljković is less interested in critiquing or mourning Yugoslav modernism than in the 'attempt to create new platforms on the ruins of existing grounds': in other words, wiping the monument clean of ideology and validating it as a new form of sculptural heritage.[28]

The rise of biennials, often in tandem with residency programmes and facilitated by the arrival of low-budget airlines, further encouraged site-specific work alluding to the host city or country.[29] Brazilian modernism, particularly the iconic buildings of Oscar Niemeyer, became a point of reference for artists who went through the residency programme Capacete in Rio de Janeiro (founded 1998) or exhibited at the São Paulo Biennial, held inside Niemeyer's 1954 pavilion. The German artist Matthias Müller created the film *Vacancy* in 1998, using segments of amateur footage and feature films shot on location in Brasília in the early 1960s, while French artist Dominique Gonzalez-Foerster shortly afterwards produced her video *Brasília* (1998) and the exhibition 'Tropical Modernism' (1999), held in Mies van der Rohe's Barcelona Pavilion.[30] By 2009, curator Adriano Pedrosa could organize an entire edition of the annual survey exhibition 'Panorama de arte Brasiliera' out of work by non-Brazilian artists addressing Brazilian modernism. These artists tend to be captivated by the country's iconic modernist architecture, rather than addressing contested issues of race and *mestiçagem*.[31]

Education, however, remains a decisive factor – especially the rise of exchange programmes, international graduate programmes, and PhDs in Fine Art. In Latin America, many artists born in the late 1960s and early 1970s were trained as architects rather than as visual artists, among them Alexander Apóstol (Venezuela), Pedro Reyes (Mexico), and Tomás Saraceno (Argentina).[32] A significant number of these artists subsequently undertook graduate training in European art schools. Educational institutions in cities with a strong history of modernist architecture and design have provided especially important incubators for this genre of work. In Austria, artists graduating from the Universität für angewandte Kunst in Vienna have gravitated towards the city's émigré architects in Los Angeles (Rudolf Schindler, John Lautner, Pierre Koenig, the Case Study Houses) – as seen in the work of Dorit Margreiter, Mathias Poledna, and Florian Pumhösl. The Modern Institute, a commercial gallery founded in Glasgow in 1997, has long supported artists interested in re-evaluating Britain's modernist heritage (Martin Boyce, Toby Paterson, Eva Rothschild, Simon Starling), many of whom trained at the Charles Rennie Mackintosh–designed Glasgow School of Art. The Rijksakademie van beeldende kunsten and the Rietveld Academie in Amsterdam have both encouraged attention to the rich historical context of De Stijl and European modernism more generally, which are invariably referenced positively in the work of their alumni.[33]

It is conspicuous that artists from South Asia or North Africa who reference European modernist architecture have all studied in Western art schools. Consider the Pakistani Seher Shah, who has made collages based on Le Corbusier's *La Ville Radieuse*, or the Algerian Kader Attia, whose installation *Untitled (Ghardaïa)* (2009) is based on Le Corbusier's interest in M'zab architecture and innovatively moulds a model of the desert city in couscous. The publication *Chandigarh Is in India* (2016) presents the work of ten artists who have made work about Le Corbusier's complex in that city, and all but one were trained outside India.[34] The majority of artists invoking modernist architecture are white Europeans and Latin Americans who have trained in Europe. I have yet to find a Nigerian artist invoking Maxwell Fry and Jane Drew's library at Ibadan University; to spend one's time on colonial architecture would make no sense. When modernist architecture does appear in African art, it is more usually in the register of the futuristic (e.g., Angolan artist Kiluanji Kia Henda's photo series 'Icarus 13', 2006) or the fantastical (e.g., the sculptures of Congolese artist Bodys Isek Kingelez).

A collective attention to modernism can thus be tracked through residencies, biennials, and education, but it also parallels the simultaneous rise of initiatives to preserve the modernist heritage. In Western Europe and the Americas, specialist agencies dedicated to protecting modernist architecture began to flourish around the same time as this genre of work. In 1995, the international body Docomomo (Documentation and Conservation of the Modern Movement) was established to foster interest in, and protect, modernist architecture as heritage.[35] Modernist architecture's now canonical status is best signalled in the recognition of numerous buildings as UNESCO World Heritage Sites, established in 1972 to acknowledge 'the exceptional universal value of a cultural or natural site which deserves protection for the benefit of all humanity'.[36] All but one of the modernist buildings on UNESCO's list were added after 2000, and the line-up reads like a roll call of popular references in contemporary art.[37]

In socialist and former socialist countries, however, contemporary art citing modernist architecture often has a political valence that is lacking in the West. Modernism – both avant-garde and postwar – continues to be associated with the suffering and deprivation of the communist era. In neoliberalized East Germany and Poland, the norm is not preservation but erasure of the relatively recent past in favour of anodyne new corporate architecture. The 2008 demolition of the GDR-era Palast der Republik in Berlin (1976) became a cultural flashpoint, cited in many works of art.[38] In such contexts, contemporary art has the capacity to assume a public expression of dissent and resistance. Paulina Ołowska's attempt to restore socialist-era neon signage in Warsaw is one of the few artistic projects to have led to cultural reinscription in the urban fabric. Many of the neons that illuminated the Polish capital in the 1960s and 1970s were designed by artists for state monopolies and promoted generic activities (such as hairdressing, sports, museums, drinking milk, reading books), but they had been removed by the 2000s. Ołowska's refabrication of these neons led not only to their reinstallation (notably the *Volleyball Player* of 1961 on Marszałkowska Street) but to the acquisition of the neon fabricator's archive by the Museum of

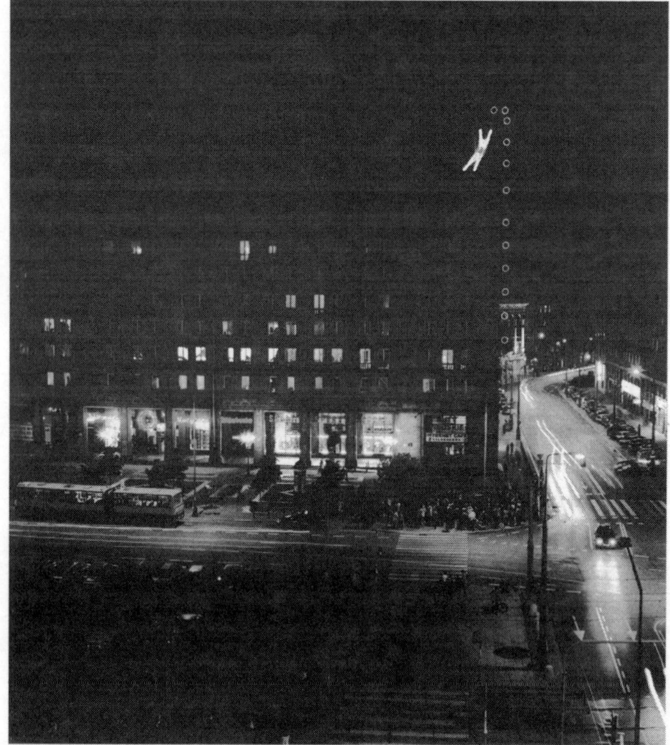

Paulina Ołowska, *Siatkarka (Volleyball Player)*, 2006. Refabricated neon sign, Warsaw.

Modern Art, Warsaw. Today the reinstalled neons function as a form of anonymous public art, discrete pockets of socialist visual culture that resist the gravitational pull of homogeneous global commerce.

In socialist Venezuela, which shares with Brazil and Cuba a strong tradition of modernist architecture, this iconography has taken a more bourgeois path. Modernist architecture first appeared in contemporary art in the wake of Hugo Chávez's rise to power in 1998; among the middle classes, there was a fear that Venezuela was about to lose its oil-rich modernity and go into reverse. Lacking residency programmes and the lure of a biennial,

Venezuela's architectural history has largely been a subject for local artists, most of whom participate in elite nostalgia for the heyday of mid-century modernism.[39] In the early 2000s, Alexander Apóstol began photographing anonymous modernist buildings in Caracas. His series *Residente Pulido* (2001–) documents abandoned residential buildings constructed in the 1940s and 1950s by immigrants from Europe, who were themselves nostalgic for middle-class suburban European architecture.[40] In 2006, Juan Araujo began a series of modestly scaled paintings focusing on modernist private houses built during the Venezuelan oil boom of the 1950s: Gio Ponti's Villa Planchart (1953–7) and Carlos Raúl Villanueva's Casa Caoma (1951–2), but also Oscar Niemeyer's house Canoas in Rio and Lina Bo Bardi's Casa de Vidro in São Paulo (both 1951). It's telling that these images focus on private dwellings rather than large-scale public projects, perhaps because many of the latter are associated with the dictatorship.[41] Invocation serves two functions here: both a wistful retrieval of the past and a point of national pride.

Across Europe and the Americas, we find a general pattern from postmodern irony to critique, and from rehabilitation to invocation. This shift is less easy to trace in other parts of the world, in part because the phenomenon of artists invoking modernist architecture is less widespread, and in part because what constitutes modernism (and its demise) is tied to political histories that manifest artistically through a different gamut of signifiers. The chronology I am focusing on is necessarily Eurocentric because the key themes evoked by this art – modernity, utopia, historicity – are explicitly grounded in a body of architecture and design that is both localized and deemed to have been superseded. The contemporaneity of Euro-American art is thus bound up with architecture as a mode of historical reckoning in a manner entirely different to the way in which it appears in, say, Chinese art of the 1990s.

A comprehensive survey of the ways in which modernist architecture resonates among contemporary artists outside the

Euro-American axis is not possible here, but a brief comparison to Asia is informative. Throughout the 1990s and 2000s, a dominant theme in group shows of Chinese contemporary art was rapid urban change. Artists like Zhang Dali, Weng Fen, Birdhead, and Wang Qingsong focused on the chaotic energy and accelerated growth of the country's emergent megacities.[42] Modernization, not modernist architecture, is the focus. In the new millennium, Cao Fei turned to the human cost of this modernization in poignant video works centring outsourced factory labour (*Whose Utopia?*, 2006) and the lived experience of alienation in the contemporary urban sprawl of Beijing (*Haze and Fog*, 2013). In both works, she indelibly centres human experience: collaborating with factory employees to realize a 'fairy tale' of alternative roles for themselves, or depicting the city's inhabitants as surreal protagonists of a zombie flick. Taiwanese artist Chen Chieh-Jen uses modern architecture to frame a more overtly Marxist critique: his oneiric video installations of former factories, soon-to-be-demolished housing blocks, and Cold War–era military bases are all shown populated by their former workers (e.g., *Factory*, 2003; *Happiness Building*, 2012), setting past and present empires into juxtaposition.[43]

By contrast, Japanese artists tend to focus on architecture of all eras in the aftermath of earthquakes (e.g., Ryuji Miyamoto, Keizo Kitajima, Meiro Koizumi), and a substantial body of work has arisen post-Fukushima, much of which takes the form of social practice (e.g., Koki Tanaka, Chim Pom). In the Asian context, architecture is more likely to be seen as a site of political trauma or natural catastrophe, rather than as a locus of historical reflection and cultural nostalgia. The social cost is foregrounded more than abstract formal geometry and the invocation of specific architects. As a result, the visual language is more varied and distinctive, more willing to engage with the present, and less bound up with historical yearning.

Déjà Vu

In catalogues and essays, two dominant ways of reading this genre of work emerge, both deploying recent philosophy. The first is the 'hauntological', loosely indebted to Jacques Derrida, which argues that art citing modernism is undead or ghostly because the modern has not been laid to rest.[44] The second, 'potentialization', takes its lead from Giorgio Agamben and maintains that contemporary works of art attempt to retrieve the unrealized potential of modernism.[45] Derrida and Agamben offer competing relationships to political temporality: either the melancholy of spirits nagging from the future (Derrida) or the wistful hope for potentialization (Agamben). What emerges from both these arguments is the centrality of *historicity* for contemporary art: an estranged relationship to the past, and a struggle to bridge the gap between then and now.[46] Yet neither are adequate for an art-historical account of this genre, which needs to juggle the artists' fascination with modernism, a conflicted relationship to ideology, and the repetition of these returns to modernism over thirty years. Every year another exhibition on the same theme; every year the rediscovery and promotion of another minor modernist; every year another painting/film/installation/photo series expanding the repertoire of historical figures.

Each time I encounter another contemporary example, I feel like I've seen it before. On the one hand, this is how collective attention operates to produce a trend, and eventually a convention. It leads to a tacit consensus about what makes good art and how it should look. For artists, a certain kind of affirmative critical attention is guaranteed – in part because the artists' own attitude towards the modernist past is affirmative. However, this genre has now become so persistent and enduring that it symptomatizes something more. One term to describe the effect of this repetition is *déjà vu*. As with any genre of work, there are better and worse examples, yet the prevailing tone is surprisingly uniform.

In 1996, Italian philosopher Paolo Virno theorized déjà vu as a post–Cold War political paralysis synonymous with the 'end of history': a loss of control, a distanciation from agency, the feeling of watching yourself live.[47] His book is fraught with the millenarian pessimism of its moment, but offers some useful pointers. An overabundance of memory paralyses action, he writes, and encourages melancholy; déjà vu is thus a 'public pathology' resulting from an excess of memory, a surfeit of history.[48] Virno never mentions the technological underpinnings of what he calls the 'blind mania to collect', yet hypermnesia has clearly been exacerbated by the tsunami of real-time documentation and archiving enabled by digital media. As Bernard Stiegler reminds us, memory has always been exteriorized – whether as writing, photographs, card indexes, or databases.[49] Today, the internet is the ultimate substrate and repository of memory, but arguably goes a step further in its colonization of all previous technologies. The appearance and texture of earlier exteriorizations are now levelled, unified, and uniformly experienced as digital.[50]

Media historian Peter Krapp argues that the term *déjà vu* emerged at the end of the nineteenth century in the wake of new media technologies like photography, telegraphy, and phonography. These inventions complicated our relationship to the familiar, allowing it to appear in decontextualized form, and to be repeated. The result was a foreboding sense of experiencing the present as if it were a memory, as captured in Sigmund Freud's landmark essay 'The Uncanny' (1919). Krapp argues that mass media technologies, by granting access to repetition in unprecedented ways, not only instigated the déjà vu effect, but harnessed that effect, and ended up transforming the experience of déjà vu itself – from an uncanny sense of unfamiliarity to 'a sense of the overly familiar, the tediously repetitive, the already known, the always present'.[51]

This contemporary, colloquial meaning of déjà vu, as the feeling of having experienced something before, is the one that I will mobilize to describe the effect of invocation. Déjà vu denotes not an aesthetic of derealization (e.g., the presentation of modernist architecture as alienated or uncanny, which anyway is rare) but the viewer's reaction to encountering, again and again, decade after decade, an iconography that seems stuck in a permanent loop of repetition. The déjà vu effect results from a common approach to the modernist heritage: an invocation that both cements the significance of that referent and legitimates the younger artist while simultaneously *emptying* the referent of ideological content. This shared approach is, in turn, compounded by the internet as a new intellectual technology for understanding the past.

The basic structural unit of reproductive technology – the print, the photograph, the film, the 35mm slide, and video – is the rectangle. In the 1910s and 1920s, the rectilinear geometry of

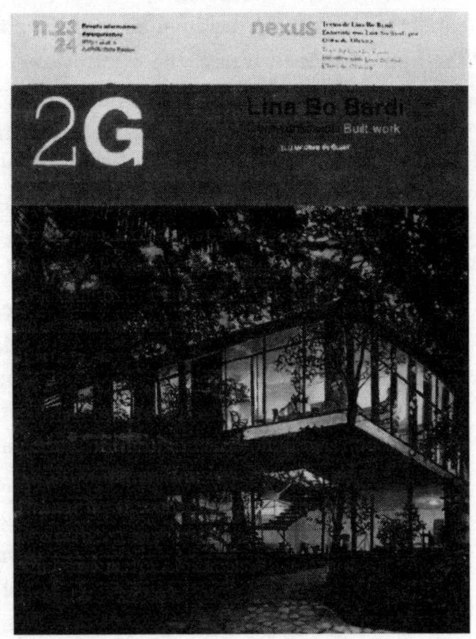

Juan Araujo, *Rivista 2G no.23 and 24*, 2006.
Oil on paper and wood.

the International Style circulated first and foremost *as* photography (in architectural photo-books and magazines) rather than as first-hand experiences. Indeed, the whole development of modernist architecture was indebted to North American industrial silos and factories that European architects only experienced through photography.[52] This photographic history is echoed in the paintings of Juan Araujo, mentioned above, which draw attention to the circulation of these buildings as reproduced images; one series, for example, is based on photographs that appear inside and on the cover of architecture magazines. Then as now, the geometrical occupation of the camera/canvas/frame is irresistible, resulting in a formal poise that diminishes the capacity for disjunction and contradiction.

The assertion of the rectilinear has been compounded by the rectangular screen interface that dominates our lives. Invocation's respect for the modern precedent so often ends up replicating the original's linear geometry, since it looks so beautiful and satisfying within the rectangularity of the photograph, the print, the film and video frame, the 35mm slide . . . to say nothing of Instagram and every single webpage. Even when buildings are represented in the form of a ruin or empty shell, the rectangularity of the frame (the canvas, the installation shot, the video projection, the gallery) serves to reproduce and maintain a sense of geometric, rational order.

In some artists' work, the consistency of this rectilinear aesthetic can erase the difference between benign and oppressive forms of modernism. The work of German painter Günther Förg offers an indicative example. Förg began photographing modernist architecture in the 1980s, including the Bauhaus Dessau, the Barcelona Pavilion, and notable examples of Italian modernism such as the Casa Malaparte in Capri and the Casa del Fascio in Como. Yet his images of the controversial IG-Farben Haus (built 1928–30, photographed 1999) are as neutral as his images of buildings by émigré Bauhaus architects in Tel Aviv and Jerusalem (built in the 1940s and '50s, photographed in 2001). Nothing in

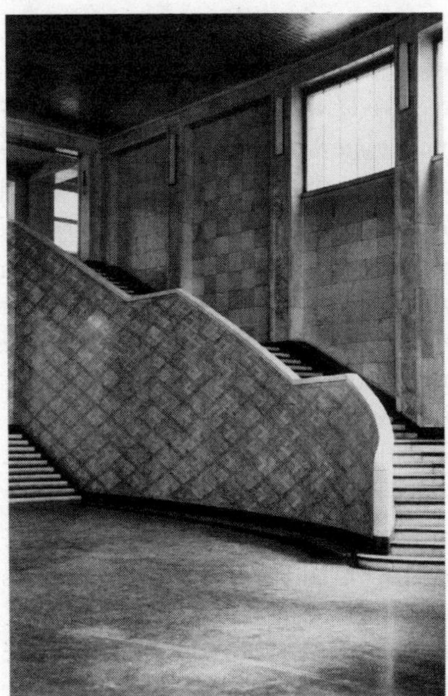

Günther Förg, *IG-Farben-Haus VII,* 1996. Colour photograph.

his image acknowledges the changing ideological function of the IG-Farben factory – from the headquarters of the chemical conglomerate that manufactured Zyklon B for the concentration camps to the location of the Allied European Forces, from which the Marshall Plan was implemented. His artistic presentation of modernist architecture as vacant mirrors his ideological emptying out of political history for the essence of pure form.[53]

Depopulation becomes a key strategy, because the presence of people grounds an image in a specific moment or era. It also distracts from the pleasure of rectilinear composition, and lessens the image's abstract power. By depicting buildings as empty structures, the artist can present modernist architecture as outside time: both historical (in this case, modern) and contemporary. It can be idealized as an empty palace for the viewer's eyes alone, unsullied by human presence. Despite the lure for artists of modernist design's social function, it is repeatedly displaced in this work from a site of action and social experimentation to a revered object. The past thus becomes a pristine image that evokes 'history' but as an abstracted style without context or users: a representation, a monument, a phantasmatic projection.

Nowhere is this effect more powerfully evinced than in one of the few works to analyse the economic status of modernist design in the global marketplace: Amie Siegel's forty-minute video *Provenance* (2013).[54] Focusing on Pierre Jeanneret's furniture designed and fabricated for Le Corbusier's complex in Chandigarh in the 1950s, the video shows this furniture exported and sold at high prices to the discerning 1 per cent. Siegel's twist is to tell the story backwards: the video opens with shots of penthouse apartments and luxury yachts where the furniture currently finds a home, then cuts to an auctioneer in Paris where the chairs sell for $30,000 each; from here we see the studio where they are photographed for the auction catalogue; the refurbishment workshop in Belgium, and finally Chandigarh itself, where the seats are stacked up, dusty and unused outside the university library. Siegel's video is rare in tracing the provenance of design objects from the homes of high-net-worth individuals (pristine and uninhabited, more like private museums than lived spaces) back to palaces of public learning (the university in Chandigarh, well-worn with use). *Provenance* could potentially offer a blistering critique of the elite co-option of communal luxury, but it tells this story in a visual language as luxurious and leisurely as the private dwellings wherein this furniture now resides.[55] The circularity of this aesthetic is acknowledged but also cynically reinforced by Siegel's decision to film the sale of *Provenance* at auction on 19 October 2013, at Christie's London. The resulting six-minute video *Lot 248* (2013) is shown alongside *Provenance* and a third work, *Proof (Christie's 19 October 2013)* (2013), the printer's proof of the auction catalogue paper for *Provenance*, embedded in Lucite. While Siegel's work honours and documents a past vision of design for the public good, it also panders for patronage to an elite that has expedited its privatization.

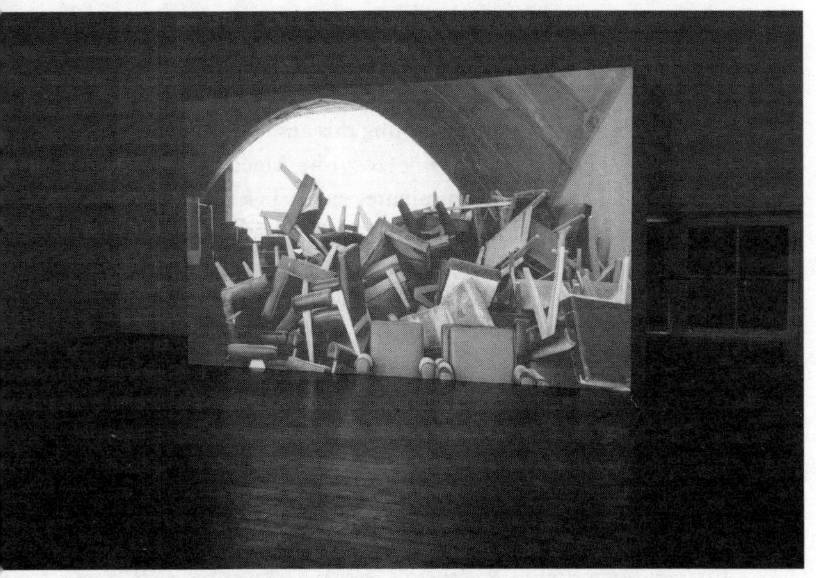

Amie Siegel, *Provenance*, 2013. Installation view at MAK, Vienna.

So it's not hard to see why contemporary art's fascination with modernism has been welcomed by collectors and enthusiastically accommodated within museums. It's tempting for acquisition boards to take the easy option when faced with a choice between a contemporary work that quotes an iconic object already in the collection (such as a Rietveld chair or a Mondrian painting), or having to entirely rethink an institution's acquisitions policy in the face of a long-term project or performance that not only resists commodification but seeks to establish new criteria for the work of art. It is telling that within a year of its production, Siegel's *Provenance* and its two related spinoffs were acquired by the Metropolitan Museum of Art in New York. Contemporary art that invokes a well-known artist, architect, or designer offers a sense of comfort and brand security, while also conferring status by association on the younger artist.[56]

It's also telling that very few of these artists have decided to address racial, class, or totalitarian discord – the 'dark side of modernism'. Among those who do, it's striking that reverence for the modernist referent still ends up dominating any attempt to produce a friction that might challenge or undermine the architecture. The difficulty of disrupting this aesthetic regime can be seen in *This Functional Family* (2007) by Argentine artist Judi Werthein. This seventeen-minute video inserts Surinamese inhabitants into Brinkman and Van der Vlugt's Sonneveld House in Rotterdam (1933), juxtaposing black-and-white archival images with her own colour footage. The soundtrack is the Sonneveld House's own acoustiguide, which explains the history of the building and (among other things) Albertus Sonneveld's source of wealth in the tobacco industry. Werthein juxtaposes this with candid footage of white tourists ambling around the house and staged vignettes of an immigrant family, dressed in 1930s costumes, at home in the house and waited on by young Caucasian women. Reversing the racial dynamic to create a *Verfremdungseffekt*, Werthein's work awkwardly oscillates between instructional video and thought experiment. The actors

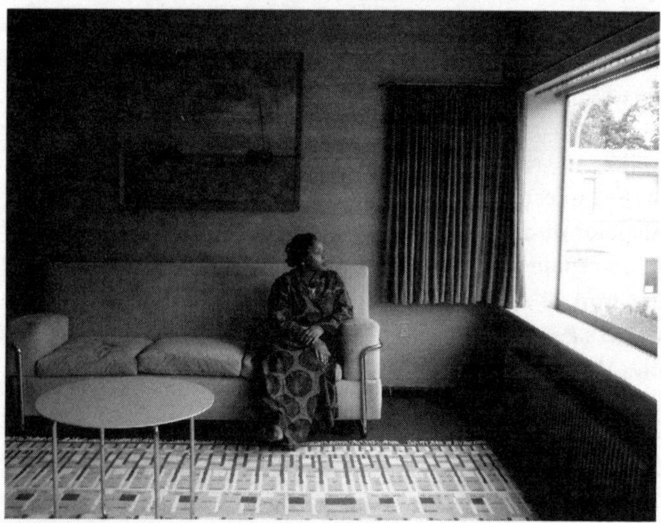

Judi Werthein, *This Functional Family*, 2007. Single channel video (still).

struggle to look at home in a pristinely empty set, whose geometric harmony nevertheless dominates the framing of each scene. Werthein's video is rare in presenting modernist architecture as inhabited. While it lacks the HD slickness and smooth camerawork of Siegel's *Provenance*, it still evidences a formal subordination to rectilinear geometry and the European tradition. Such attempts to include the spectre of everything that doesn't belong in the usual vision of modernist efficiency and hygiene – women, immigrants, people of colour, the working class (maids, cleaners, gardeners) – always seem to end in the same aesthetic register: the dissonant figures remain a secondary foil to the primary seduction of the architecture.

Through invocation, artists step into a speech act that is larger than their individual utterances: a broader discourse of citation and reference that is as much about fashion and advertising, heritage and preservation, and the tastes of a collecting class as it is about a former geopolitical *weltanschauung*. In this panorama, it seems paradoxical and striking that European modernism is being celebrated by artists and bought up by collectors at a time when European traditions are increasingly challenged not just by diasporas from the East and South, but also by new design values from China and the Far East – traditions disconnected from any genealogical root in the Bauhaus. It is tempting to see the motif of modernist architecture as an unconscious prophylactic against non-Western culture: a reaction formation to the marginalization of the West (or, at least, to the idea that such provincialization may be happening). Presenting familiar icons of the past arguably provides a sense of certainty, recognition, and comfort at a time when the future seems ever more uncertain.[57] Modernist architecture and design thus keep the idea of Europe alive, in however ruined a form – much like the 'postcolonial melancholia' identified by Paul Gilroy, with which he diagnoses Europe's inability to mourn the loss of its empire, leading to the repetition of an imperial impulse in the present.[58] This melancholy grips Europe and the Americas, even in those areas where it serves to express dissatisfaction with the new world order of neoliberalism and the erasure of socialist culture. In this vista, modernism is less a 'failed utopian project' than constitutive of a shared identity: an architecture that binds together Eastern and Western Europe, North and South America, in uneven and complicated shared histories.

The Project

The contemporary artistic meditations on modernist architecture and design that offer some friction with this model are more oblique, and have come from artists who engage with the social dimension of this legacy, rather than its selective evacuation. This work has a more distinctive and singular aesthetic – less indebted to the past and freer of burdensome reverence, while steadying its gaze on the present. I will conclude with two examples that show the possibilities of invoking modernist architecture and utopia to different ends. Both readings owe a debt to Black studies, which has sought to dismantle the foundational concepts of Enlightenment modernity and rethink them as an explicitly emancipatory call to the future. This conclusion therefore takes us far from the dyad of Eastern/Western Europe with which we began, leaving behind a Cold War logic to address a new set of coordinates more attuned to the needs of the twenty-first century.

The first artist is the US painter Kerry James Marshall. The presence of mass housing appears anonymously and regularly in the backgrounds of his paintings, where it serves to frame places of social gathering for his Black protagonists – from the five canvases of 'The Garden Project Series' (1993–94) to works like *7am Sunday Morning* and *Garden Party* (both 2003). Presented as unremarkable two-storey houses or mid-rise apartment blocks, the architecture is never the central subject in his paintings, but rather participates in the construction of a postwar urban normality. These unmodulated boxes for housing are

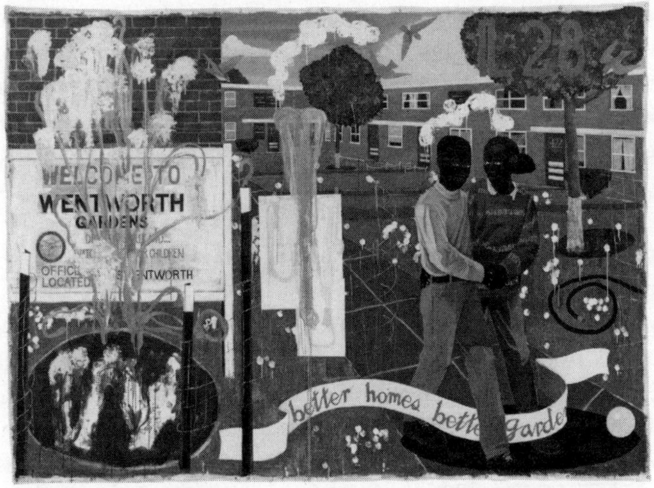

Kerry James Marshall, *Better Homes, Better Gardens*, 1994. Acrylic and collage on canvas.

unexpectedly framed as idyllic settings, pervaded by an atmosphere of measured calm, even optimism. In *Better Homes, Better Gardens* (1994), for example, a couple embraces next to a sign stating, 'Welcome to Wentworth Gardens'.

Marshall's series has been read as a critique of modernist architecture, because a number of Chicago projects are called 'Gardens' but there is nothing lush or appealing about these run-down inner-city estates.[59] Yet Marshall's paintings never depict deterioration; instead, they exude a tranquillity more associated with the pastoral. Although the top right of *Better Homes, Better Gardens* is stamped with the housing project code 'IL 2-8', the painting's title unfurls on a cheerful banner in the bottom right. Bluebirds and a glorious sunburst fill the sky. The flowers are out. A dribbly smear of pale blue paint – which initially invites misreading as graffiti or other sign of neglect – becomes legible as some kind of fountain erupting from the picture plane. The painting depicts not what exists (by the mid-1990s: acute poverty and dysfunction) but what *could* be – indeed, what *should* be. Through an exercise of visualization in the present, the generic geometries of public housing frame a new, harmonious relationship between the residents and their environment: not the contrived infinity of a perfectly empty glass box in nature, but the peacefulness of a community whose unthreatened self-sufficiency has its own utopian impetus.[60]

Art that foregrounds the social dimensions of architecture usually steps away from the various media discussed so far: photography, painting, prints, film, video. Instead, it adopts other aesthetics and formats, like performance, documentary, or social practice. Thomas Hirschhorn's *Gramsci Monument*, located at Forest Houses in the Bronx during the summer of 2013, is one of a series of participatory installations that the artist has made since 2001. Each 'monument' is dedicated to a modern thinker and located on a low-income housing project on the outskirts of a metropolitan centre.[61] Hirschhorn eschews brand-name modernist architecture in favour of anonymous social housing, which becomes the discreet but ever-present backdrop for a temporary intergenerational, interracial, interclass community who gather for lectures, poetry readings, radio broadcasts, exhibitions, and performances.[62] As with all of Hirschhorn's monuments, the economic and racial differences between residents and visitors to Forest Houses were often acutely visible and awkward, but neither were they swept aside. Instead, they existed as a group challenge: could this temporary gathering somehow work? The collision of demographics and activities created a social montage that was as disjunctive as it was beautiful. A schedule of activities on a makeshift plywood stage included a white German philosopher rattling off some impenetrably abstruse musings on Gramsci; ignoring him nearby, a group of Black and brown teenagers were more interested in practising their dance routines. Later the same day, poet and theorist Fred Moten rhapsodized to a small group of listeners on 'the projects as a project':

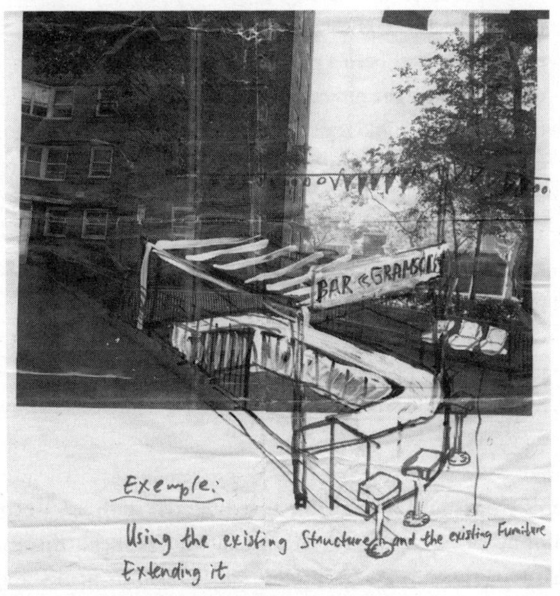

Thomas Hirschhorn, preparatory sketch for *Gramsci Monument*, 2013. Ink on paper.

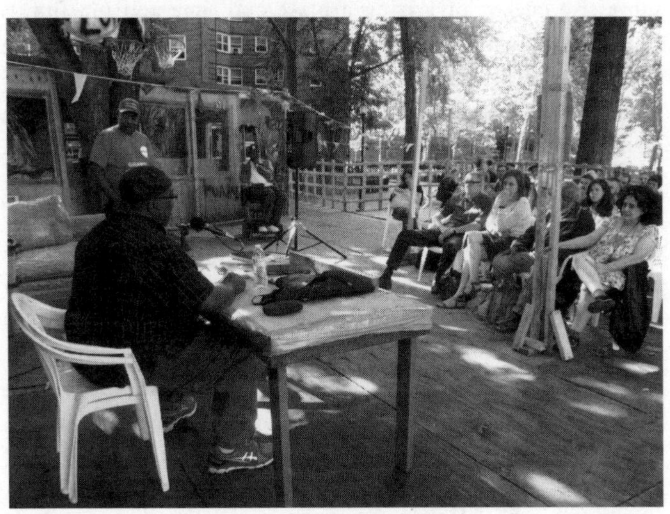

Thomas Hirschhorn, *Gramsci Monument*, 2013. Forest Houses, Bronx, New York. Poetry session with Fred Moten, 14 August 2013.

if the projects become a project from outside
then the projects been a project forever. held in
the projects we the project they stole. we steal
the project back and try to give it back to them.
come on, come get some of this project. we protect
the project with our open hands. the architect is in mining
and we dispossess him. we protect the project by handing.
let's bust the project up. let's love the project. can the
projects be loved? we love the projects. let's move
the projects. we project the projects. I'm just
projecting the project's mine to give away. I'm not
mine when I dispossess me I'm just
a projection . . .[63]

Moten's words and intonation have lingered with me since that afternoon, since they refute the déjà vu I've been discussing. For Moten, there is no architectural determinism: no 'failure' or 'modern ruin', no architect to revere, only the resistant and subversive energy of seizing a place and time and making it your own. Moten's recursive wordplay points to a richer lived experience of place than the pristine isolation of a penthouse with Pierre Jeanneret chairs. It points – like Hirschhorn's *Monuments* as a whole – to the urgency of reinhabiting, repopulating, reoccupying, and re-(dis)-possessing such spaces for a provisional community right here, for a future that's happening right now. Marshall, Moten, and Hirschhorn break with déjà vu in favour of the *not yet*: they mark a shift from depopulation to inhabitation, from formalism to social experiment, from nostalgia to imagination, from historicity to futurity. But they are outliers. For the most part, the trope of modernist architecture and design in contemporary art serves only to re-present canonical design history as style for the apolitical tastes of the collecting class. The art that results is more symptomatic than singular: armchair admiration for the past, and an inability to act in the present.

The historical transitions of the past decade mark the invocation of modernist architecture and design as decisively passé, belonging to a now-gone historical conjuncture. Right-wing populism, surveillance capitalism, a global pandemic, and the urgencies of climate change have changed our priorities in unimaginable ways. This is not to claim that modernism has nothing to teach us; far from it. Nor is it to deny the value of art's mnemonic function, which remains a source of profound cultural identification and solace. My call is for uses of the past that go beyond the security blanket of invocation. Much like utopian architecture, visual art has the capacity to envisage new ways of being together, to prefigure the future in the present, to propose visions of the world that are both representations and aspirations. Rather than gazing spellbound in the rear-view mirror, artists are ideally situated to dream up potent new images. These don't need to be grand schemes, just experiments in thinking and seeing the world more imaginatively.

Epilogue

For the last twenty years, if not longer, there have been anxieties about the impact of the internet and social media on our attention. This book has tried to grasp this period through a discussion of four artistic strategies in contemporary art and performance – research-based installation art, performance exhibitions, interventions, and invocations of modernist architecture. Each of these strategies owes their current manifestation to the internet and social media, whose platforms have become entangled with what we understand by knowledge, social relationships, publicness, and memory.

The non-linear thinking enabled by hypertext and the internet led to amateur and participatory but also information-heavy ways of undertaking research and presenting this in installation form (Chapter 1). It also created a context in which visual literacy was subject to new challenges and levels of saturation. The instantaneity of digital communication provided a foil for the return of duration in performance, while at the same time borrowing social media's 24/7 approach to sociality, generating a hybrid spectatorship that is simultaneously on- and offline (Chapter 2). The attention economy has not always been rejected by artists; on some occasions it is mobilized to reach globally dispersed new audiences, while also showing how art can be a mode of expressive dissent in illiberal contexts (Chapter 3). The virtualization of history and the ubiquity of the rectangular interface have consolidated an appreciation of modernist architecture and design – even if this has led to a certain flattening of historical distance, and a repetition of aesthetic forms (Chapter 4). Most strikingly, perhaps, against earlier fears of postmodern presentism, the widespread availability of online digital archives and image repositories has encouraged contemporary artists to look backwards and recover non-hegemonic, marginal histories. Spectatorship, meanwhile, has settled into a continual flow of actual and virtual, both equally intertwined and valued as modes of seeing and thinking. None of these developments could have been predicted in the early 1990s.

In 2023, however, a new set of technological anxieties emerged, centred on artificial intelligence and its threat to our humanity. Generative pretrained transformers (GPTs) use algorithms to analyse data patterns, and on the basis of pre-existing examples produce outputs that resemble human creations. These offer new challenges to authorship and to culture more broadly. An initial burst of public fascination and amazement has already given way to suspicion at the predictability and sterility of computer-generated text and images. Critics lament the coldness, emptiness, and repetitiveness of AI music, pictures, and writing, largely because they are ungrounded in the pain and pleasure of lived human experience. My instinct is to agree. But we should also learn from the past: AI will inevitably leave its mark upon contemporary art and performance, but how artists will metabolize this new technology is yet to be established. An obvious speculation is that a greater premium will be placed on live performance and social processes – in other words, art that requires irreplaceable human skill sets. After all, you can't use DALL-E and Midjourney to execute social experiments in public space.

But artists never respond in straightforward ways. AI will likely become one more form of ready-made, generating unintended and unexpected (and yes, probably also undesirable) effects, once artists and performers have figured out how to manipulate this new prosthetic – just as artists over the past two centuries internalized, rejected, and ambivalently reorganized their work around photography, cinema, television, video, and the internet. This degree of fear and delirious excitement has been seen before. AI is just one more knowledge instrument; at best, it will drive us to new forms of creativity and collaboration, generating further hybrid outcomes. But the optimism should probably end here. Scientists estimate that AI will use more energy than the entire human workforce; culturally, it risks doubling down on the dullest consequences of a technologically uniform, automated world. More than this is hard to say. For better or worse, our destinies are entwined with digital technology, and in ways that go far beyond matters of attention.

Acknowledgements

To say this book has felt absolutely interminable says perhaps less about my skills as a writer (I'm relatively fast) than it does about the condition of long-form writing about contemporary art. It's straightforward enough to rattle out your thoughts for a magazine: you make a few arguments, capture a slice of time, and the turnaround is relatively fast. When you sit longer with a subject and dig in, the conjuncture inevitably shifts; practices mutate, values change, and suddenly everything needs rewriting. Nothing sits tidily in the past. Every week there's a new show, another performance, another article. Historicizing contemporary art is like trying to analyse the view from a speeding car.

The grants that assisted research for this project to come into being go back a decade. The first was a Clark Art Institute Fellowship in spring 2013 that gave me the luxury of space and time to read. An Andy Warhol/Creative Capital Grant in 2017 provided generous support at a crucial moment. A Graham Foundation Grant in 2019 didn't quite come to fruition in the way I was hoping, but was a useful exercise nonetheless. Throughout this research the New York Public Library at 42nd Street has been a godsend; many thanks to all the members of staff there who let me roost in the Shoichi Noma Reading Room and later the Wertheim Study.

Many audiences at many institutions around the world listened to early versions of these chapters. I thank everyone who asked questions and made suggestions; it was invaluable to hear what landed and what didn't. I will briefly mention those audiences who had to put up with the first iteration of each chapter: at the Onassis Foundation, Athens (Chapter 1), at Skulptur Projekte Münster (Chapter 2), at Manchester University (Chapter 3), and at the Migros Museum of Art, Zurich (Chapter 4).

CUNY Graduate Center students in my seminars *Black Box/White Cube* (spring 2016), *Art, Attention, Technology* (spring 2019), *Interventions* (spring 2021), and *Attention/Internet* (spring 2022) were formative for this project in so many ways. I have been lucky enough to learn from them, some of whom also became research assistants in various capacities: Joseph Henry, Tie Jojima, and Rachel Valinsky. Emeline Boehringer helped to secure the image permissions. Extra thanks to Flora Brandl who read an entire draft and made helpful comments. Former doctoral students have also remained inspiring interlocutors, especially Lindsay Caplan, Arnaud Gerspacher, Gemma Sharpe, and Jonah Westerman.

Many artists, curators, editors, and friends contributed thoughts and feedback at key moments. Tania Bruguera takes precedence as an ongoing interlocutor, friend, and the unconscious of Chapter 3. Thanks to all the artists, curators, scholars, and dancers who fielded questions, visited my classes, or otherwise helped to bounce ideas around: Kader Attia, Anna Boghiguian, Boris Charmatz, Luis Camnitzer, Ekaterina Degot, Ricardo Dominguez, Annie Dorsen, Alex Farqharson, Mark Franko, Andrea Geyer, Jessie Gold, Kenny Goldsmith, Julieta González, Maria Gough, Boris Groys, Nicolás Guagnini, Hristoula Harakas, Trajal Harrell, Maria Hassabi, Michael Helland, Maggie Iversen, Ana Janevski, David Joselit, Carrie Lambert-Beatty, Xavier Le Roy, Pablo León de la Barra, David Levine, Jill Magid, Mickey Mahar, David Maljković, Paige Martin, Rabih Mroué, Paulina Ołowska, Vincenzo Pernice, Ben Piekut, Alexandra Pirici, Walid Raad, David Riff, Julia Robinson, Jay Sanders, Elizabeth Schambelain, Richard Schechner, Shelley Senter, Jacques Servin,

Simon Starling, David Thompson, David Velasco, Christophe Wavelet, and Catherine Wood. Thomas Elsaesser and Okwui Enwezor sadly passed away before the book was finished, but both asked me incisive and memorable questions. So too did Marion von Osten, who generously shared her perspectives on artistic research in the 1990s.

At the CUNY Graduate Center I am blessed with terrific colleagues and generous interlocutors with inspiring politics. Thanks to Jennifer Ball, Peter Eckersall, David Grubbs, Anna Indych-Lopez, Rachel Kousser, Siona Wilson, and especially Romy Golan. The members of the Committee for Globalization and Social Change have been invaluable intellectual companions – especially Anthony Alessandrini, Herman Bennett, Susan Buck-Morss, Duncan Faherty, Uday Mehta, Joan Scott, Jesse Schwartz, Julie Skurski, and Gary Wilder. Thanks also to Katherine Carl and the Center for Humanities, who provided a platform to collaboratively brainstorm artistic research and digital technology in 2011 and 2012 respectively.

Linda Norden helped me through the pandemic more than words can say by lending me apartment 10d. Large chunks were also revised on Raabestrasse; thank you Florian Malzacher and Joanna Warsza.

It's not customary to acknowledge illegal file-sharing sites, but two years of research would have been lost without them. Thank you to all the anonymous organizers and participants who take risks to share these materials, and thereby to set ideas free. Please distribute this book in a similar spirit. Which leads me to Verso: thank you, Leo Hollis and Mark Martin, for your ongoing support!

The biggest thanks is to Nikki Columbus for listening to me work things out during so many lectures, making the post-talk dinners fun afterwards, pushing back on my ideas, and editing the crap out of my rambling drafts.

This book is dedicated to radiant Helio, who has disordered my attention in the most beautiful way imaginable.

Notes

Introduction: OS XXI, Disordering Attention

1. *Sun and Sea (Marina)*, a collaboration between director Rugilė Barzdžiukaitė, writer Vaiva Grainytė, and composer Lina Lapelytė, won Lithuania a Golden Lion for best national pavilion at the Venice Biennale in 2019. It was first staged in Vilnius in 2017 as a one-hour theatre piece. For Venice, it was looped to fill eight hours. It continues to tour internationally, usually in theatres, with variable duration.
2. *The Sound of Morning* was a ninety-minute performance presented at the intersection of Orchard and Rivington Streets as part of the Performa Biennial, 14–16 October 2021. It has not been reperformed.
3. Performance studies and queer studies, by contrast, have been particularly diligent at bestowing attention on practices considered minor and fleeting by art historians.
4. Close looking has even entered a conservative phase in the 'slow' movement, which has emerged as a direct reaction to digital image saturation. See Arden Reed, *Slow Art: The Experience of Looking, Sacred Images to James Turrell*, Berkeley: University of California Press, 2019. For a sociological critique of the 'slow' lifestyle movement (e.g., slow food, staycations, and slow living), see Sarah Sharma, *In the Meantime: Temporality and Cultural Politics*, Durham, NC: Duke University Press, 2014.
5. Dominic Pettman, *Infinite Distraction: Paying Attention to Social Media*, Cambridge: Polity, 2016, p. x.

6. See for example Sherry Turkle's *Reclaiming Conversation: The Power of Talk in a Digital Age*, New York: Penguin Press, 2015, and the Time Well Spent movement, founded in 2016 by former Google executive Tristan Harris and Oxford ethicist William James, and the latter's *Stand Out of Our Light: Freedom and Resistance in the Attention Economy*, Cambridge, UK: Cambridge University Press, 2018. The exception is Jenny Odell's *How to Do Nothing: Resisting the Attention Economy*, Brooklyn, New York: Melville House, 2019. Odell is an artist and mentions several examples of artistic refusal, including Tehching Hsieh in the 1980s and Pilvi Takala in the 2000s. She sees these artists in the tradition of Diogenes, Bartleby, and Thoreau, creating a 'third space' of noncompliance.
7. Crary maps this shift not just through the history of scientific experiments but in the transition from the seventeenth-century camera obscura (in which perception emerges spatially from a shared social field, because the image fills a room in which one stands with others) to the early nineteenth-century stereoscope (in which perception is exclusively optical, binocular, and immobilizing, because the two images synthesize in the viewer's retina). Jonathan Crary, *Techniques of the Observer: On Vision and Modernity in the Nineteenth Century*, Cambridge, MA: MIT Press, 1990.
8. William James, *The Principles of Psychology* (1890), Vol. 1, Cambridge, MA: Harvard University Press, 1983, chapter XI, pp. 381–2. We tend to use *attention* and *focus* interchangeably, but they are not quite the same thing: attention can be scattered, dispersed, or distracted, while focus conveys a sense of laser-beam directionality. Focus, in other words, is one type of attention.
9. James, *The Principles of Psychology*, p. 381, my emphasis.
10. Geniuses, James writes, are 'commonly believed to excel other men in their power of sustained attention' (*The Principles of Psychology*, p. 400).
11. The colonial underpinnings of observation and rationality are critiqued by Aníbal Quijano in 'Coloniality and Modernity/Rationality', *Cultural Studies* 21:2–3 (2007), pp. 168–78.
12. Jonathan Crary, *Suspensions of Perception: Attention, Spectacle, and Modern Culture*, Cambridge, MA: MIT Press, 1999, chapter 1. For an earlier, incisive discussion of time and labour, see E. P. Thompson, 'Time, Work-Discipline, and Industrial Capitalism', *Past & Present* 38 (1967), pp. 56–97.

13. In Frederick Taylor's 'Lecture on Management' (1907), the speed, movement, and capacity of each worker is carefully calculated in order for the company's productivity to double or even treble in output. See 'Report of a Lecture By and Questions Put to Mr F. W. Taylor: A Transcript', *Journal of Management History* 14:3 (2008), pp. 214–36.
14. The department store, by contrast, was designed to set the gaze in motion. See Anne Friedberg, *Window Shopping: Cinema and the Postmodern*, Berkeley: University of California Press, 1993.
15. See Tony Bennett's Foucauldian account in *The Birth of the Museum: History, Theory, Politics*, London: Routledge, 1995, especially chapters 2 and 3. Sir Henry Cole, art educator and first director of the South Kensington Museum (1857–73), argued that opening museums on Sundays would lead to the moral improvement of the working-class man. A museum visit after church, for example, would supply 'his refreshment there in company with his wife and children, rather than leave him to booze away from them in the Public house and Gin Palace'. As for young children, Cole assures the reader, museums can teach them not just to 'behave gently' but to 'respect property'. Henry Cole, *Fifty Years of Public Work of Sir Henry Cole, K.C.B., Accounted for in his Deeds, Speeches and Writings*, 2 vols, London: George Bell & Sons, 1884, p. 368, p. 356.
16. See Martha Ward, 'Impressionist Installations and Private Exhibitions', *The Art Bulletin* 73:4 (1991), pp. 599–622.
17. For a history of exhibition display centred on MoMA, see Mary Ann Staniszewski, *The Power of Display: A History of Exhibition Installations at the Museum of Modern Art*, Cambridge, MA: MIT Press, 1998; for a German history, see Walter Grasskamp, 'The White Wall: On the Prehistory of the "White Cube"', in Marianne Eigenheer, Dorothee Richter, and Barnaby Drabble (eds.), *Curating Critique*, Frankfurt: Revolver, 2007, pp. 316–39.
18. Russell Burdekin notes that Wagner did not likely achieve full darkness until the end of the century, due to the difficulty of extinguishing gas lamps. The practice of dimming lights had been used in British theatres in the 1850s; Wagner simply represents a consistency of application, and with the aim of intensifying audience attention to the entire work rather than creating ambiance for a single scene. Burdekin, 'Darkening the Auditorium in the Nineteenth Century British Theatre', *Theatre Notebook* 72:1 (2018), pp. 47–8.

19. Richard Sennett, *The Fall of Public Man*, New York: Vintage Books, 1976, p. 206.
20. Katy Sedgman, *The Reasonable Audience: Theatre Etiquette, Behaviour Policing, and the Live Performance Experience*, Basingstoke: Palgrave Macmillan, 2018, chapter 5.
21. See for example the UK's Theatre Charter (2014), at theatre-charter.co.uk.
22. Mariah Tyler, 'Fifteen Museum Etiquette Errors and How to Avoid Making Them', *Travel and Leisure*, 17 May 2016, at travelandleisure.com.
23. See for example Laura Mulvey, 'Visual Pleasure and Narrative Cinema' (1976), in *Visual and Other Pleasures*, Basingstoke: Palgrave Macmillan, 1989, pp. 14–26; Simone Browne, *Dark Matters: On the Surveillance of Blackness*, Durham, NC: Duke University Press, 2015; Fred Moten's poetics of 'fugitivity' are explored in numerous publications, including his *Consent Not To Be A Single Being: Black and Blur*, Durham, NC: Duke University Press, 2017; Marlon Bailey, *Butch Queens Up in Pumps*, Ann Arbor: University of Michigan Press, 2013; Jane Garland-Thomson, *Staring: How We Look*, Oxford: Oxford University Press, 2009.
24. James, *Principles of Psychology*, p. 382.
25. These high-capacity cinemas (which seated between 1,000 and 5,000 viewers) offered mixed programmes of vaudeville acts, musical numbers, and films. Among the best known were the Wintergarden and UFA-Palast am Zoo (in Berlin) and the Roxy Theater (in New York).
26. Siegfried Kracauer, 'The Little Shopgirls Go to the Movies' (1927), in *The Mass Ornament: Weimar Essays*, Cambridge, MA: Harvard University Press, 1995, pp. 291–304.
27. Kracauer, 'Cult of Distraction' (1926), in *The Mass Ornament*, p. 326.
28. See Theodor Adorno and Max Horkheimer, 'The Culture Industry: Enlightenment as Mass Deception' (1944), in *Dialectic of Enlightenment*, London: Verso/NLB, 1997; Jacques Ellul, *The Technological Society*, New York: Vintage Books, 1964; Marshall McLuhan, 'The Agenbite of Outwit' (1963), in *Media Research: Technology, Art and Communication*, ed. Michel Moos, London: Routledge, 1997, pp. 121–5.
29. See for example Neil Postman, *Amusing Ourselves to Death: Public Discourse in the Age of Show Business*, New York: Penguin Books, 1986.

30. Tania Modloski, 'The Rhythms of Reception: Daytime Television and Women's Work', in E. Ann Kaplan (ed.), *Regarding Television: Critical Approaches. An Anthology*, Frederick, MD: University Publications of America, 1983, p. 71.
31. Raymond Williams, *Television: Technology and Cultural Form* (1974), London: Routledge Classics, 2003, pp. 86–7.
32. See for example Maggie Jackson, *Distracted: The Erosion of Attention and the Coming Dark Age*, New York: Prometheus Books, 2008; Nicholas Carr, *The Shallows: What the Internet is Doing to Our Brains*, New York: Norton, 2010; Pettman, *Infinite Distraction*.
33. Sherry Turkle, *Alone Together: Why We Expect More from Technology and Less from Each Other*, New York: Basic Books, 2011, chapter 10.
34. Bernard Stiegler, *Taking Care of Youth and the Generations*, Stanford, CA: Stanford University Press, 2010, p. 72. See also Bernard Stiegler, *Nanjing Lectures 2016–2019*, London: Open Humanities Press, 2020, p. 13.
35. The notable exception is Walter Benjamin, who attempts to redeem distraction as a receptive state for the formation of new habits. Somewhat enigmatically, he describes architecture as the art best received in a state of distraction – haptically, rather than optically – in 'The Work of Art in the Age of Mechanical Reproduction' (1936), in *Illuminations: Essays and Reflections*, New York: Fontana, 1973, p. 233.
36. Paul North, *The Problem of Distraction*, Stanford, CA: Stanford University Press, 2012, prologue.
37. Curiously, the 'hyper' in hyperattention seems to connote only greater spread (i.e., numerical quantity) rather than greater intensity. N. Katherine Hayles, 'Hyper and Deep Attention: The Generational Divide in Cognitive Modes', *Profession* (2007), p. 187.
38. Cathy Davidson, *Now You See It: How the Brain Science of Attention Will Transform the Way We Live, Work, and Learn*, New York: Viking, 2011, p. 287.
39. As a graduate student in the 1990s I spent many hours engaged in 'hyper' research with print publications. As a result of the pandemic, it is my idea of a library that has changed – no longer a physical space, but an archive of pdfs.
40. Stiegler, *Taking Care of Youth and the Generations*, pp. 77–8. Stiegler devotes many pages to agreeing and disagreeing with Hayles's concept of hyperattention.

41. In later writing, Stiegler argues for digital technology as a pharmakon, that is, as both poison and a remedy. Bernard Stiegler, 'The Digital, Education, and Cosmopolitanism', *Representations* 34:1 (2016), p. 158.
42. Jonathan Crary, *24/7: Late Capitalism and the Ends of Sleep*, London: Verso, 2013, and *Scorched Earth: Beyond the Digital Age to a Post-Capitalist World*, London: Verso, 2022.
43. Crary, *Scorched Earth*, p. 2.
44. Crary, *Scorched Earth*, pp. 39–40.
45. For a history of ADHD from inside the psychiatric profession, see Russell Barkley, 'History of ADHD', in Barkley (ed.), *Attention-Deficit Hyperactivity Disorder*, New York: Guilford Press, 2015, pp. 3–50. For a critical counter-history of ADHD diagnoses and medication, see Kenneth Rogers, *The Attention Complex: Media, Archaeology, Method*, New York: Palgrave Macmillan, 2014, chapter 4.
46. Alan Schwarz and Sarah Cohen, 'ADHD Seen in 11% of US Children as Diagnoses Rise', *New York Times*, 31 March 2013.
47. See Sami Timimi and Eric Taylor, 'ADHD Is Best Understood as a Cultural Construct', *British Journal of Psychiatry* 184 (2004), pp. 8–9. Critical ADHD Studies has recently begun to be formulated in the UK, calling for a critical and intersectional revision of the field. See 'Critical ADHD Studies: Call for Abstracts', 23 May 2022, at ddhuijg.com.
48. Dr Michael Anderson on prescribing Adderall to middle-school parents, cited in Alan Schwarz, 'Attention Disorder or Not, Pills to Help in School', *New York Times*, 9 October 2012.
49. Hayles, 'Hyper and Deep Attention', pp. 190–1.
50. Rogers, *The Attention Complex,* pp. 159–60.
51. The first usage of 'attention economy' is frequently credited to Nobel Prize–winning economist Herbert Simon in a lecture from 1971, but the phrase only appears in the Q&A session, when another economist sums up Simon's contribution. The bulk of Simon's lecture focuses on efficient organization and administration; in passing he alludes to the problem of 'information overload', a term recently made fashionable by Alvin Toffler's bestseller *Future Shock* (1970). Herbert Simon, 'Designing Organizations for an Information-Rich World', in Martin Greenberger (ed.), *Computers, Communications, and the Public Interest*, Baltimore: Johns Hopkins University Press, 1971, pp. 40–1.
52. Georg Franck, 'Ökonomie der Aufmerksamkeit', *Merkur*, September 1993, pp. 748–61. See also Franck, *Mentaler Kapitalismus: Eine*

politische Ökonomie des Geistes, Munich/Vienna: Carl Hanser Verlag, 2005.

53. Michael Goldhaber, 'The Attention Economy and the Net', *First Monday* 2:4 (1997).
54. Thomas H. Davenport and John C. Beck, *The Attention Economy*, Cambridge, MA: Harvard Business School Press, 2001.
55. Here I take my lead from Jules Gill-Peterson's neurofeminist critique of attention, 'Neurofeminism: An Eco-Pharmacology of Childhood ADHD', in Victoria Pitts-Taylor (ed.), *Mattering: Feminism, Science, and Materialism*, New York: New York University Press, 2016, pp. 188–203. Gill-Peterson suggests a longer, alternate history of attention that de-prioritizes cognitive modes (like reading and writing) and instead turns to embodied forms of entrainment and expression (like dance) that don't play into the binary of deep vs hyper attention. She describes a neurofeminist approach as one that disavows the nature/culture divide and regards the brain as *biocultural*: biology, culture, the body, and the social are inextricable.
56. Yves Citton, *The Ecology of Attention*, Cambridge: Polity Press, 2017 (first published in French, 2014), p. 31, italics in original. By way of example, Citton mentions the Islamophobia of the French mediasphere, which leads him to notice if a woman is wearing a hijab. Italian theorist Tiziana Terranova makes a similar point when she concludes that attention is not a scarcity or a commodity but inseparable from 'the invention and diffusion of common desires, beliefs, and affects', thus opening up to an economy of social cooperation – although she doesn't provide examples. Terranova, 'Attention, Economy and the Brain', *Culture Machine* 13 (2012), p. 13.
57. Citton, *The Ecology of Attention*, p. 198.
58. Stiegler and Crary allude to care as a salutary defence against the programming industries and exploitation respectively.
59. See for example the work of Carol Gilligan, Nel Noddings, and Joan Tronto.
60. Christina Sharpe, *In the Wake: On Blackness and Being*, Durham, NC: Duke University Press, 2016. Jennifer C. Nash draws a useful lineage of Black feminist care in 'Practicing Love: Black Feminism, Love-Politics, and Post-Intersectionality', *Meridians: Feminism, Race, Transnationalism* 11:2 (2013), pp. 1–24.
61. At the same time, care has limitations, as disability activists have long argued: it is associated with dependency, coercion, and

paternalistic intervention, rather than positive associations of reciprocity and interdependence. See Jonathan Herring, 'The Disability Critique of Care', *Elder Law Review* 8 (2014), pp. 1–14. For an aesthetic critique of care, see Maggie Nelson, *On Freedom: Four Songs of Care and Constraint*, New York: Graywolf Press, 2021, p. 23, p. 69.

62. Tina Campt, *A Black Gaze: Artists Changing How We See*, Cambridge, MA: MIT Press, 2021. Campt offers the most succinct definition of a 'black gaze' in 'Adjacency: Luke Willis Thompson's Poethics of Care', *Flash Art* 327 (2019), pp. 42–9.
63. Alois Riegl explored the difference between haptic visuality and optical visuality in *The Group Portraiture of Holland* (1902), which was taken up by Walter Benjamin in 'The Work of Art in the Age of Mechanical Reproduction' (1936). Campt makes no reference to Riegl or Benjamin; her points of reference are to articulations of critical Black spectatorship by bell hooks in 'The Oppositional Gaze: Black Female Spectators', in *Black Looks: Race and Representation*, Boston, MA: South End Press, 1992, pp. 115–131, and Manthia Diawara in 'Black Spectatorship: Problems of Identification and Resistance', *Screen* 29, 1993, pp. 66–75.
64. Michael Fried, 'Art and Objecthood', *Artforum*, September 1967, and *Absorption and Theatricality: Painting and the Beholder in the Age of Diderot*, Chicago: University of Chicago Press, 1980. Throughout his career, Fried has denounced 'theatrical' modes of spectatorship (which directly address the viewer) and argued for 'absorption' as a mode of beholding that makes the viewer less self-conscious of spectating.
65. See for example Hal Foster's introduction to 'Questionnaire on "The Contemporary"', *October* 130 (2009), p. 3. Since then, a slew of publications under the category of the 'global modern' have appeared, demonstrating many alternative ways to being a 'modernist' or 'contemporary' art historian. Many of these have been regionally focused studies on mid-twentieth-century modernism. Few have attempted a global purview on the scale of David Joselit's *Heritage and Debt: Art in Globalization*, Cambridge, MA: MIT Press, 2020.
66. The sigmoid curve, or s-curve, describes the peak-and-decay model of viral attention: a slow start, followed by huge acceleration, then the tipping point, after which there is inertia. See Karine Nahon and Jeff Hemsley, *Going Viral*, Cambridge: Polity Press, 2013, chapter 2.

67. See clairebishop.commons.gc.cuny.edu.
68. For McLuhan, 'Art as radar acts as an "early alarm system," as it were, enabling us to discover social and psychic targets in lots of time to prepare to cope with them.' Marshall McLuhan, *Understanding Media: The Extensions of Man* (1964), Berkeley, CA: Gingko Press, 2011, Preface to the second edition, p. 16.
69. In this, *Disordered Attention* differs from Janet Kraynak's approach to artists in *Contemporary Art and the Digitalization of Everyday Life*, Berkeley: University of California Press, 2020.
70. Franco Moretti, 'Conjectures on World Literature', *New Left Review*, January–February 2000, p. 57. He continues: 'if, between the very small and the very large, the text itself disappears, well, it is one of those cases when one can justifiably say, Less is more. We always pay a price for theoretical knowledge.'
71. Stephen Best and Sharon Marcus, 'Surface Reading: An Introduction', *Representations* 108 (2009), pp. 1–21.
72. Here I follow Stiegler's approach to technology as prosthesis but more closely Donna Haraway's claim that 'machines can be prosthetic devices, intimate components, friendly selves . . . The machine is us, our processes, an aspect of our embodiment.' Haraway, 'A Cyborg Manifesto', in *Manifestly Haraway*, Minneapolis: University of Minnesota Press, 2016, p. 61, p. 65.
73. Brian Massumi, *Parables for the Virtual: Movement, Affect, Sensation*, Durham, NC: Duke University Press, 2002, p. 85. See also footnote 5, p. 269: Massumi pushes back against the idea of television as a discrete unit having an 'effect' on the public (as another discrete unit) by rethinking transmission as a change in potentiality.
74. This sentence is an attempt to update Raymond Williams's argument that a technology like television is not an 'effect' but the emergence of a new social complex that also includes ways of communicating, financial institutions, and cultural expectations. Williams, *Television*, p. 25.

1 Information Overload: Research-Based Art

1. Artist-curators assemble works by other artists, often displaying them alongside non-art objects, and in ways that reflect the artist-curator's own aesthetic and method of thinking. In the 'archival turn', artists aggregate materials to combine the personal and the historical, often aiming to generate a counter-archive or counter-memory. See Hal Foster, 'An Archival Impulse', *October* 110 (2004), pp. 3–22.

2. James Elkins, 'Artists with PhDs', at jameselkins.com. Tokyo National University of Fine Art and Music (now the Tokyo University of the Arts) established a PhD programme in 1977, but it did not result in research-based art of the kind I am describing in this chapter. Because the US has so few doctoral programmes in Fine Art, New York's Whitney Independent Study Program, founded in 1968, can be considered both a precursor to the rise of the studio art PhD programme and an outlier, as a one-year programme that awards no degrees.
3. For an overview of the literature, I refer the reader to Tom Holert's list in *Knowledge Beside Itself: Contemporary Art's Epistemic Politics*, Berlin: Sternberg Press, 2020, pp. 82–4. Note also the inaugural issues of *Art & Research* (Glasgow, 2008) and the *Journal for Artistic Research* (Amsterdam, 2011), the special issue of *transversal* on 'Art/Knowledge: Overlaps and Neighbouring Zones' (March 2011) and the special issue of *Texte zur Kunst* on 'Artistic Research' (June 2011).
4. In Europe, PhDs tend to be self-funded, unlike doctoral education in the US. In the UK, PhDs are explicitly money-making entities: funding for departments is higher for those with a doctoral programme, which incentivizes the recruitment of fee-paying students, especially from outside the EU.
5. Hito Steyerl, 'Aesthetic of Resistance?', in Florian Dombois, Ute Meta Bauer et al. (eds.), *Intellectual Birdhouse: Artistic Practice as Research*, London: Koenig Books, 2012, p. 55.
6. For an early critique of the neoliberal university, see Bill Readings, *The University in Ruins*, Cambridge, MA: Harvard University Press, 1997.
7. Howard Singerman, *Art Subjects*, Berkeley: University of California Press, 1999.
8. One significant incubator for research-based art has been New Institutionalism; see Alex Farquharson, 'Bureaux de Change', *Frieze*, 2 September 2006. Another is the biennial, as argued by Holert in *Knowledge Beside Itself*, p. 70.
9. The best of these is Holert's *Knowledge Beside Itself*, which focuses on the 'epistemization' of contemporary art, and Steyerl's 'Aesthetic of Resistance?'
10. This is true also for reviews of research-based art. Critics invariably reiterate details of the artist's chosen research topic, providing yet more informational context, and rarely pay

attention to form. An exception is Susanne von Falkenhausen's 'Rules of Research', *Frieze d/e*, Autumn 2012, pp. 117–20.

11. Lange referred to herself as a 'Researcher-Photographer', pursuing social science research and advancing a leftist point of view with her art. FSA captions were sometimes added by Roy Stryker who hired and managed the FSA photographers.
12. Goldblatt was influenced by the work of FSA photographers, which he first saw around 1960. See Okwui Enwezor, 'Matter and Consciousness: An Insistent Gaze from a Not Disinterested Photographer' (1998), in *Fifty-One Years: David Goldblatt*, Barcelona: MACBA, 2001, pp. 39–40.
13. In 1935, Walter Benjamin noted that captions had become 'obligatory' in magazines, governing our reading of a photograph, because they 'have a character altogether different from the title of paintings' in their precision and prescriptiveness. Benjamin, 'The Work of Art in the Age of Mechanical Reproduction' (1936), *Illuminations: Essays and Reflections*, New York: Schocken Books, 2007 (1968), p. 226.
14. See Michel Chion, *The Voice in Cinema*, New York: Columbia University Press, 1999; David Oscar Harvey, 'The Limits of Vococentrism: Chris Marker, Hans Richter and the Essay Film', *SubStance* 41:2 (2012), p. 7.
15. Nora Alter and Timothy Corrigan cite as early examples D. W. Griffiths's *A Corner in Wheat* (1909), films about cities in the 1920s (Cavalcanti, Ruttman, Vertov, Vigo), and Sergei Eisenstein's unrealized version of Marx's *Capital*. See Alter and Corrigan (eds.), *Essays on the Essay Film*, New York: Columbia University Press, 2017, p. 2.
16. Hans Richter, 'The Film Essay: A New Type of Documentary Film', in Alter and Corrigan (eds.), *Essays on the Essay Film*, pp. 89–92.
17. Hans Haacke, in Jeanne Siegel, 'An Interview with Hans Haacke', *Arts* 45:7 (1971), p. 21. He goes on to add, 'Of course, I don't believe that artists really wield any significant power. At best, one can focus attention.'
18. Vilém Flusser, 'Crisis of Linearity', trans. Adelheid Mers, *Bootprint* 1:1 (2007), pp. 19–21.
19. Vilém Flusser, *Into the Universe of Technical Images*, Minneapolis: University of Minnesota Press, 2011 (1985), pp. 57–8.
20. *A Thousand Plateaus* helped to legitimize non-linear forms of argumentation and the production of an ambiguous, open-ended

aesthetic that stood in reaction to the Marxist didacticism of 1970s art. Deleuze and Guattari's writing was particularly appealing to artists because of its visual metaphors – the herd, the pack, the line of flight – and a vitalism that flatteringly reinforces the idea that artistic gestures are endlessly creative, resistant, and open-ended.

21. Green's *Import/Export* invites comparison with two signal exhibitions at the Dia Center: 'Democracy' by Group Material (1988) and 'If You Lived Here . . .' by Martha Rosler (1989). Both projects assembled works of art, posters, slogans, photography, and research materials in themed installations addressing democracy, education, the AIDS crisis, and homelessness. Yet they were activist and polemical: although a great diversity of information was displayed, the textual components positioned the viewer as the recipient of an already synthesized position.
22. Two grey cubicles at either end of the installation contain black boxes labelled 'Data' and 'Funk', whose materials can be browsed and handled if the viewer wears white gloves.
23. George Landow, *Hypertext: The Convergence of Contemporary Critical Theory and Technology*, Baltimore: Johns Hopkins University Press, 1992, pp. 4–5. See also Jay David Bolter, *Writing Space: The Computer, Hypertext, and the History of Writing*, Mahwah: Lawrence Erlbaum Associates, 1990. In hindsight, the claims around hypertext were wildly overstated: hypertext only allows the reader to chart their own path through pre-given material, not to add to, edit, or question this material.
24. George Landow, *Hyper/Text/Theory*, Baltimore: John Hopkins University Press, 1994, p. 35, cited in Renée Green, 'The Digital Import/Export Funk Office' (1995), in Gloria Sutton (ed.), *Other Planes of There: Selected Writings, Renée Green*, Durham, NC: Duke University Press, 2014.
25. Landow, *Hypertext*, p. 184.
26. Nizan Shaked, *The Synthetic Proposition: Conceptualism and the Political Referent in Contemporary Art*, Manchester: Manchester University Press, 2017, p. 51; see also footnote 64 on pp. 58–9 for a list of some of the publications included in the installation.
27. Renée Green, in Russell Ferguson, 'Various Identities: A Conversation with Renée Green', *World Tour: Renée Green*, Los Angeles: LA Museum of Contemporary Art, 1993, p. E58.
28. Leo Steinberg discusses the work of Robert Rauschenberg, Jasper Johns, and Andy Warhol (among others) as exhibiting a perceptual

shift from horizontality to verticality (in *Other Criteria: Confrontations with Twentieth-Century Art*, Oxford: Oxford University Press, 1972, p. 84). Since Steinberg's essay, horizontality is no longer a 'symbolic allusion to hard surfaces such as tabletops, studio floors, charts, bulletin boards', but an internalization of data management display (tabletops, shelves, vitrines).

29. See François Cusset, *French Theory: How Foucault, Derrida, Deleuze, & Co. Transformed the Intellectual Life of the United States*, Minneapolis: University of Minnesota Press, 2008. Another important point of reference was Fredric Jameson's influential call for an 'aesthetic of cognitive mapping'.
30. French and British art schools preferred to centre Deleuze and Guattari. In German-speaking countries, artists arrived at theory either through education in the US (especially the Whitney ISP) or via self-taught feminist collectives, since local art schools were largely anti-theoretical, geared towards painting and sculpture, and dominated by male professors. Photocopies of recently translated texts by Judith Butler, Deleuze, Donna Haraway, and Michel Foucault were circulated and shared in an activist spirit that owed much to punk and DIY, such as the *Copyshop* publications by the Düsseldorf collective BüroBert. These were distributed in collaborative 'project exhibitions' that aimed to contribute to a counter-public sphere.
31. 'No authorial voice, nor any other narrative device, is used to tie the carefully chosen scenes together; the full structure of the network comes together solely in the mind of the viewer . . . It certainly doesn't follow a particular line of argument that would assume a proposition, conclusion, or deduction. It is not conceived as a sequence in time but as constructed coexistence in space.' Ursula Biemann, 'Counter-Geographies in the Sahara', in Susanna Witzgell and Gerlinde Vogl (eds.), *New Mobilities Regimes in Art and Social Sciences*, London: Routledge, 2016, p. 164, p. 173.
32. Biemann's implicit critique of mainstream media differs from what Alfredo Cramerotti calls 'aesthetic journalism': practices that do not develop their own mechanisms of narration, but instead rely on photo-reportage and the model of television journalism. See Cramerotti, *Aesthetic Journalism*, Bristol and Chicago: Intellect, 2009, p. 40.
33. For an excellent representative selection of this work, see Okwui Enwezor's exhibition 'Archive Fever: Uses of the Document in Contemporary Art', International Center of Photography, New York, 2008.

34. The approach can be seen in García Torres's artist talk at Dia: Chelsea, New York, 27 February 2012, at diaart.org.
35. It should be clear that I am sceptical about the success of these artists' attempts to fuse the individual and the historical. More successful, in my view, is John Akomfrah's use of archival footage to reconstruct the life of cultural theorist Stuart Hall, interweaving his life with world historical events, and music, in his poignant three-screen video *The Unfinished Conversation* (2012).
36. Foster, 'An Archival Impulse', p. 21.
37. Mario García Torres, in Montse Badia, 'The Structures of Art: An Interview with Mario García-Torres', *A*Desk* 104, 20 October 2012, at a-desk.org.
38. Nicolas Bourriaud, *Postproduction. Culture as Screenplay: How Art Reprograms the World*, Berlin: Sternberg Press, 2006, p. 18. Bourriaud is not describing artistic research but cultural assemblage more generally (sampling, hacking, DJ-ing); nevertheless, his term is a useful one to capture a sense of digital drift.
39. Similar pantheons can be found in the work of Sam Durant (in pieces referencing Robert Smithson and the Case Study Houses), Jonathan Monk (Sol LeWitt, Ed Ruscha, Bruce Nauman, Lawrence Weiner, Jeff Koons), and Rirkrit Tiravanija (John Cage, Marcel Broodthaers, Felix Gonzalez-Torres).
40. This could be seen as another form of 'invocation', as discussed in Chapter 4: the younger artist successfully invokes his hero and benefits from this adjacency.
41. Saidiya Hartman, 'Venus in Two Acts', *Small Axe* 12:2 (2008), pp. 1–14.
42. David Joselit, 'On Aggregators', *October* 146 (2013), pp. 12–14.
43. David Joselit, in 'The Epistemology of Search: An Interview with David Joselit', *ARPA Journal* 2 (2014), at arpajournal.net.
44. Tillmans has long been attentive to non-hierarchical modes of installation. Exhibitions of his photographs freely mix personal images with commercial commissions, and incorporate many different genres (portraits, landscapes, still lives) and milieus (nightclubs, political protests, domestic scenes).
45. Wolfgang Tillmans, interview with Lorena Muñoz-Alonso, *Latitudes* blog, 10 November 2010, at lttds.blogspot.com.
46. 'Studying Truth with Wolfgang Tillmans' is archived at tate-tillmans.s3-website.eu-west-2.amazonaws.com.

47. Appropriately, Tillmans designed a pink canvas tote bag printed with a world cloud as merchandise for his MoMA retrospective, 'To Look Without Fear'.
48. Peter Schjeldahl, 'The Polymorphous Genius of Wolfgang Tillmans', *New Yorker*, 10 October 2022.
49. The leading news sources were not traditional newspapers (*New York Times*, *Wall Street Journal*, etc.) but Yahoo, Google News, and CNN.
50. I still recall the visceral jolt of finding sponsored posts in my Instagram feed in 2013, and once more, in 2018, when ads began appearing in my *New York Times* app that directly related to my phone conversations.
51. A recent article identifies two new types of pedestrian whose visual attention is divided between the virtual and the physical: 'smartphone zombies', who walk slowly while absorbed in their phone screens, and 'post-flâneurs', whose wandering gaze shuttles between virtual and physical space. Gorsev Argin et al., 'Between Post-Flâneur and Smartphone Zombie: Smartphone Users' Altering Visual Attention and Walking Behavior in Public Space', *International Journal of Geo-Information* 9:12 (2020), pp. 1–26.
52. Jakob Nielsen, 'How Little Do Users Read?', Nielsen Norman Group, 5 May 2008, at nngroup.com.
53. N. Katherine Hayles, 'How We Read: Close, Hyper, Machine', in *How We Think: Digital Media and Contemporary Technogenesis*, Chicago: University of Chicago Press, 2012, p. 61. Hayles is citing Jakob Nielsen, 'F-Shaped Pattern for Reading Web Content', Nielsen Norman Group, 16 April 2006, at nngroup.com.
54. I recall a friend reporting with dismay an experience of visiting an archive with the then-director of Documenta, who pulled out a box at random and immediately declared the contents sufficiently interesting to include in her exhibition – a classic instance of time-expedient sampling.
55. Susanna Newbury, 'Things We Think With', *X-tra Contemporary Art Quarterly* 18:1 (2015), at x-traonline.org.
56. Geert Lovink, *Sad by Design*, London: Pluto Press, 2019, p. 150.
57. An excerpt of the video in Forensic Architecture's installation *The Long Duration of a Split Second* is available on YouTube.
58. Eyal Weizman, 'Introduction: Forensis', in Weizman (ed.), *Forensis: The Architecture of Public Truth*, Berlin: Sternberg, 2014, p. 13.

59. Forensis denotes both the production of evidence (by trawling open-source images and information in the public domain) and questioning the practice of evidence-making. Weizman, 'Introduction: Forensis', p. 12.
60. Working under the name of an invented collective, The Atlas Group, Raad amassed a fictional archive of the Lebanese Wars of 1975 to 1990: photographs, notebooks, and films that indirectly and obliquely revealed the war's deleterious effect on individuals, places, and the social psyche. See theatlasgroup1989.org.
61. Walid Raad, 'Walkthrough, Part I', *e-flux* 48, October 2013, at e-flux.com.
62. Walid Raad, in conversation with Seth Cameron, *Brooklyn Rail*, 9 December 2015, at brooklynrail.org.
63. Raad has long engaged with Jalal Toufic's ideas about the 'withdrawal' of cultural objects following trauma. See Toufic, *The Withdrawal of Tradition Past a Surpassing Disaster*, Forthcoming Books, 2009, at jalaltoufic.com.
64. Mark Leckey in conversation with Mark Fisher, 'Art Stigmergy', *Kaleidoscope Almanac of Contemporary Aesthetics* 11 (2011), at kaleidoscope.media.

2 Black Box, White Cube, Grey Zone: Performance Exhibitions and Hybrid Spectatorship

1. See Michael Paulson and Michael Cooper, 'Filming the Show: Pardon the Intrusion? Or Punish It?', *New York Times*, 6 October 2019.
2. The Theatre Charter campaign (2014) and Cumberphone Campaign (2015) both originated in the UK and sought to improve audience behaviour by restricting phone usage during performances. See cumberphonecampaign.wordpress.com. The Theatre Charter website seems to have been taken down but the group still tweets @TheatreCharter.
3. See Amy Qin, 'A New Weapon for Battling Cellphones in Theatres: Laser Beams', *New York Times*, 14 March 2016. For an overview of popular literature that targets mobile phones for disapproval, see Katy Sedgman, *The Reasonable Audience: Theatre Etiquette, Behaviour Policing, and the Live Performance Experience*, Basingstoke: Palgrave Macmillan, 2018, chapter 4.
4. Yondr pouches were first introduced in 2014 in a school context. For their use in theatres, see Chris Jones, 'Cellphones Are Disrupting Theatres Everywhere', *Chicago Tribune*, 1 October 2019.

5. In this essay I use 'live art' to denote the full spectrum of live performance in the museum: music, theatre, dance, and performance art.
6. Jerry Saltz, 'This Renovation Plan Will Ruin MoMA, and the Only People Who Can Stop It Aren't Trying', *New York Magazine*, 25 March 2014, at vulture.com.
7. Sven Lütticken, 'Dance Factory', *Mousse* 50, October 2015, p. 91, p. 96.
8. Allison Hugill, 'The Instagrammable Angst of Anne Imhof', *Momus*, 5 October 2016.
9. André Lepecki, *Singularities: Dance in the Age of Performance*, New York: Routledge, 2016, pp. 172–5.
10. Lepecki, *Singularities*, p. 173.
11. Hal Foster, *Bad New Days: Art, Criticism, Emergency*, London: Verso Books, 2017, pp. 128–9.
12. Siobhan Burke, 'Maria Hassabi's "Plastic" Sends Dancers Crawling Through MoMA', *New York Times*, 23 February 2016.
13. Performance is also increasingly present in commercial art galleries and art fairs, but the focus of this chapter is the museum due to its commitment to public access and historical record.
14. The first example of a group show is 'A Choreographed Exhibition' at the Kunsthalle Sankt Gallen, 2008. See Erin Brannigan, 'Dance in the Gallery: Curation as Revision', *Dance Research Journal* 47:1 (2015), pp. 3–25.
15. See Claire Bishop, 'The Perils and Possibilities of Dance in the Museum: MoMA, Whitney and Tate', *Dance Research Journal* 46:3, pp. 62–76. In 1948, MoMA presented 'An Evening on American Dance' in its auditorium, which included performances by Maria Tallchief, Pearl Primus, José Limon, Charles Weidman, and others.
16. Jasper Johns, Robert Morris, Robert Rauschenberg, Frank Stella, Stan VanDerBeek, and Andy Warhol (among many others) designed sets for the Merce Cunningham Dance Company. Visual artists who performed at Judson include Robert Morris, Robert Rauschenberg, and Carolee Schneemann, while the Judson Church gallery hosted exhibitions and happenings by Jim Dine, Allan Kaprow, and Claes Oldenburg, among others.
17. Deborah Hay, letter to John Baur, 14 November 1968, Whitney Museum Archive, Container 1, Folder 23.
18. Robert Wilson's twelve-hour opera *The Life and Times of Joseph Stalin* (1973) at the Brooklyn Academy of Music, for example,

provided a separate space to which the audience could retreat for food and drink.

19. See Claire Bishop, *Artificial Hells: Participatory Art and the Politics of Spectatorship*, London: Verso, 2012, chapter 8.
20. See Claire Bishop, 'Ruled Out', *Artforum*, October 2013, pp. 127–8. Prior to the pandemic, performance was a staple presence in art fairs, albeit as ornamental adornment rather than integral to sales. In 2014, Frieze Art Fair in London introduced a section called 'Live', while in 2016 the Foire internationale d'art contemporain (FIAC) in Paris launched 'Parades', a performance festival produced in collaboration with the Louvre.
21. In the UK, artists Pollard and Forsyth re-enacted legendary rock gigs from 1996 onwards (The Smiths, David Bowie) while Rod Dickinson re-enacted the Jonestown mass suicide (2000) and the Milgram Experiment (2002); the best example remains Jeremy Deller's *The Battle of Orgreave* (2001). In Cuba, Tania Bruguera re-enacted the work of Ana Mendieta, beginning in 1986, shortly after the artist's death, until 1996. Performance re-enactments for video are a separate category but began around the same time (e.g., Mike Kelley's *Fresh Acconci*, 1995).
22. See for example Klaus Biesenbach and Hans-Ulrich Obrist's performance exhibition '11 Rooms', held at Manchester International Festival in 2011: each artist was given a small white box (akin to an art fair booth) to present one work for the duration of the exhibition.
23. Christophe Wavelet, in Bojana Cvejić, 'Interpreting Works Without Works: Interview with Christophe Wavelet on some aspects of Quatuor Albrecht Knust', *Maska* 94–5 (2005), p. 70.
24. Bojana Cvejič, *Choreographing Problems: Expressive Concepts in Contemporary Dance and Performance*, Basingstoke: Palgrave Macmillan, 2015, p. 172.
25. See the comments by Jérôme Bel and Xavier Le Roy in 'A Conversation between Christophe Wavelet, Jérôme Bel, and Xavier Le Roy', in *Peripheral Vision and Collective Body*, Bolzano: Museion, 2008, p. 89, p. 97. In some cases, the connection to visual art was personal (Jérôme Bel was married to French visual artist Dominique Gonzalez-Foerster); in other instances, the choreographer trained at an art school (Maria Hassabi at California Institute of the Arts).
26. From 2009 to 2018, Boris Charmatz took over the Centre National Choréographique de Rennes and renamed it 'Musée de la Danse',

where he made works specifically for museums and galleries (e.g., *expo-zéro*, 2009; *20 Dancers for the XX Century*, 2012). Bel showed in the 2007 Lyon Biennial and adapted work for MoMA in 2012 and 2016. Le Roy has adapted his solo works into a self-standing gallery exhibition (*'Retrospective'*, 2012, discussed below) and was included in Skulptur Projekte Münster in 2017. Maria Hassabi began making 'live installations' for exhibition spaces in 2013 (discussed below) and was included in Documenta 14, 2017.

27. Sehgal, quoted in Elizabeth Carpenter, 'Be the Work: Intersubjectivity in Tino Sehgal's *This Objective of that Object*', Walker Art Center blog, 2014, at walkerart.org.
28. Biesenbach, in 'Performance vs. Acting', instructional video by the Museum of Modern Art, at moma.org. A distaste for performance is particularly prevalent among an older generation of art historians – not just Foster but Benjamin H. D. Buchloh in 'The Entropic Encyclopedia', *Artforum*, September 2013, p. 313.
29. Rebecca Schneider, *Performing Remains: Art and War in Times of Theatrical Re-enactment*, London: Routledge, 2011, p. 130.
30. See for example the articles on curating performance in *Performing Arts Journal* 34:1 (2012) and in *Theater* 44:2 (2014); the special issue of *Dance Research Journal* 46:3 (2014); and articles in *Mousse* 50, October 2015.
31. Mark Franko and André Lepecki, 'Editorial: Dance in the Museum', *DRJ* 46:3 (2014), p. 1, my emphasis.
32. See Trajal Harrell's comments in D. Everitt Howe, 'Dance in the Ruins', *Mousse* 50, October 2015, p. 78; Hassabi's comments in Harry Thorne, 'Maria Hassabi: Stillness is the Move', *Frieze*, 16 April 2018; and Sarah Michelson's in Hilarie M. Sheets, 'When the Art isn't on the Walls', *New York Times*, 22 January 2015.
33. Richard Schechner defines 'event time' as a measurement found primarily in sports games and only occasionally used in theatre; his example is the first scene of Jean Genet's *The Maids* (1947), which has to be completed before an alarm clock rings. By contrast, I use event time in opposition to performances that run continuously throughout the day and have no apparent beginning or end. Schechner, 'Approaches to Theory/Criticism', *Tulane Drama Review* 10:4 (1996), p. 28.
34. Within visual art, the term *black box* began to be used in the 1990s to refer to the darkening of galleries to show video installations and other projected media. In this essay, I am using it exclusively to refer to the spaces of experimental theatre from the 1960s onwards.

35. The classic expression of this position is Brian O'Doherty, *Inside the White Cube: The Ideology of the Gallery Space*, Berkeley: University of California Press, 1986, p. 14.
36. Mary Anne Staniszewski, *The Power of Display: A History of Exhibition Installations at the Museum of Modern Art*, Cambridge, MA: MIT Press, 1998, p. 70.
37. For a history of black box theatre, see David Wiles, *A Short History of Western Performance Space*, Cambridge: Cambridge University Press, 2003, chapter 8.
38. Jerzy Grotowski, 'Towards a Poor Theatre' (1968), in Grotowski, *Towards a Poor Theatre*, New York: Routledge, 2002; Peter Brook, *The Empty Space*, New York: Atheneum, 1968.
39. Grotowski, 'Towards a Poor Theatre', pp. 41–2. See also p. 19: 'By gradually eliminating whatever proved superfluous, we found that theatre can exist without make-up, without autonomic costume and scenography, without a separate performance area (stage), without lighting and sound effects, etc. It cannot exist without the actor–spectator relationship of perceptual, direct, "live" communion.'
40. Giorgio Agamben, 'What is an Apparatus?', in '*What is an Apparatus?' and Other Essays*, Stanford: Stanford University Press, 2009, p. 14. Because the apparatus (in Agamben's account) constructs a behaviour, I prefer it to classic film theory's account of the cinematic apparatus as the ideological production of a spectating subject who identifies with the (gendered) point of view onscreen.
41. The main disruptions in both theatre and cinema are auditory: phones ringing, people whispering, coughing, and unwrapping sweets. See George Home-Cook, *Theatre and Aural Attention: Stretching Ourselves*, New York: Palgrave Macmillan, 2015, p. 3.
42. Tate curator Catherine Wood describes this institutional struggle in Wookey, *Who Cares? Dance in the Gallery and Museum*, London: Siobhan Davies Dance, 2015, p. 34.
43. See choreographer Jennifer Lacey in conversation with Mathieu Copeland, *Choreographing Exhibitions*, Dijon: les presses du réel, 2013, p. 123.
44. Michael Sanchez, '2011: Art and Transmission', *Artforum*, Summer 2013, pp. 294–301. He continues: 'Such fluorescent-lighting systems became ubiquitous in galleries in the mid- to late 2000s, at the same time that galleries began systematically posting images of their exhibitions on their websites.'

45. See for example artist Simon Denny, in Brigitte Oetker and Nicolaus Schaufhausen (eds.), *Attention Economy*, Berlin: Sternberg Press, 2013, p. 64.
46. *PLASTIC* was a co-production between the Hammer Museum (in Los Angeles), the Stedelijk Museum (Amsterdam), and MoMA (New York).
47. The dancers recall how visitors to *PLASTIC* referred to the dancers as 'it'. Noelle Bodick, 'Body Art: Maria Hassabi's Dancers Discuss *PLASTIC*', *Blouin Art Info*, 15 March 2016.
48. See the comments by dancer Michael Helland in Bodick, 'Body Art', and Hassabi in Thorne, 'Maria Hassabi'.
49. There was, however, a discreet ambient soundtrack by composer Marina Rosenfeld, which provided a means of signalling time to the dancers.
50. The precedent for looping is in exhibitions of film, the first of which was 'Projected Art' at Finch College in New York in 1966. The exhibition's central innovation was that 'you could walk in, watch, leave, come back, watch, leave again, without feeling conspicuous and without that terrible solemn holy-ritual quality of sitting fixed in an auditorium seat'. Judith Shantnoff, 'Report from New York', *Film Quarterly* 20:4 (1967), p. 75.
51. Maria Hassabi, e-mail to the author, 7 November 2015. Video footage of *Plastic*, can be found on YouTube.
52. See Thomas J. Lax, 'Maria Hassabi: Glances', Museum of Modern Art brochure, 2016, p. 8.
53. Dancer Mickey Mahar, interview with the author, 23 May 2017. For the dance conference *Inventur* (Dusseldorf, 2017), and in collaboration with Hassabi, I interviewed several of her dancers (including Mahar) about their experience of the audience while performing *PLASTIC*, and superimposed this over a range of Instagram posts about the work: vimeo.com/261864861.
54. See for example Claudia La Rocco, 'Present Tense', *Artforum*, 29 February 2016.
55. Xavier Le Roy, quoted in 'Xavier Le Roy', *Artforum*, 29 October 2014.
56. Xavier Le Roy in conversation with the author, New York, 13 September 2011. Marcella Lista refers to the 'sculpture' display mode as a '"freeze frame" inspired by the photographic capturing of a performance'. Lista, 'Play Dead: Dance, Museums, and the "Time-Based Arts"', *Dance Research Journal* 46:3 (2014), pp. 6–23.

57. When the dancers weren't performing in one of these three modes, they occupied a separate space for rehearsal and research that was also visible to the public.
58. For video footage of *'Retrospective'*, see vimeo.com/127403961.
59. This reset, and even the accompanying buzzing sound, was used by Tino Sehgal to signal the arrival of new visitors in *This Objective of That Object*, 2004.
60. Bojana Cvejič, 'Xavier Le Roy's *'Retrospective'*: Choreographing a Problem, and a Mode of Production', in Cvejič (ed.), *'Retrospective' by Xavier Le Roy*, Dijon: Les presses du réel, 2014, p. 10.
61. See Scarlet Yu, in Marisa Hayes, 'Exposer la danse au musée: Entretien avec Scarlet Yu', *Repères: Cahier de danse* 38/39 (2017), p. 6. Le Roy shared with me his folder of images showing audiences taking photographs of *'Retrospective'*.
62. Unauthored exhibition booklet for Anne Imhof's *Angst*, Kunsthalle Basel, 2016, p. 1, p. 3, at kunsthallebasel.ch.
63. Imhof's centring of performer Eliza Douglas, who also models for Balenciaga, cements this association. For video footage of *Faust*, see YouTube.
64. Lepecki, *Singularities*, p. 172.
65. Lepecki, *Singularities*, p. 175.
66. Drury Lane Theatre could seat 2,300 prior to 1791; after its rebuilding in 1794, capacity increased to 3,600 and the noise was considerable. A German visitor to London noted the chaos with amazement; see Felicity Nussbaum, *Rival Queens: Actresses, Audiences, and Eighteenth-Century British Theater*, University Park: University of Pennsylvania Press, 2010, p. 134.
67. Jeffrey Ravel, *The Contested Parterre: Public Theater and French Political Culture, 1680–1791*, Ithaca: Cornell University Press, 1999, p. 19.
68. Condillac noted how 'the spectators mutually prompt each other, through the examples they give each other, to fix their gaze on the stage'. Abbé de Condillac, *Essai sur l'origine des connaissances humaines* (1746), cited in Ravel, *The Contested Parterre*, p. 55.
69. Denis Diderot, 'Réponse à la lettre de Madame Riccoboni' (1758), cited by Ravel in *The Contested Parterre*, p. 55.
70. Mårten Spångberg, in Nikki Columbus, 'Attention Must Be Paid For', *Parkett* 94 (2014), p. 32. One critic described *La Substance* as 'a little like watching a sunset. It changed just enough to hold your gaze'. Gia Kourlas, 'Kicking Back: Nature of Choreography Revised, with Beer Cans', *New York Times*, 13 January 2014.

71. Mårten Spångberg, email to the author, 19 September 2016. Tellingly, Spångberg describes the dancers' behaviour and speech in *La Substance* as 'like three women/people going to a museum'. Imhof also made adjustments to *Faust* by sending text messages to the performers, whose phones were visible and charging beneath the glass floor.
72. Spångberg, quoted in Anas Sareen, 'Mårten Spångberg's Slouching Disco', *Zürich Moves! Festivalblog* 2016, at zuerichmoves2016.tumblr.com.
73. Richard Schechner, 'Selective Inattention: A Traditional Way of Spectating Now Part of the Avant-Garde', *Performing Arts Journal* 1:1 (1976), pp. 8–19.
74. Schechner, 'Selective Inattention', pp. 15–16. For a critique of Schechner, see Rustom Bharucha, 'A Collision of Cultures: Some Western Interpretations of the Indian Theatre', *Asian Theatre Journal* 1:1 (1984), pp. 1–20.
75. Subsequent presentations have been shorter, due to the expense of housing the company internationally: three days at Tate Modern; five days at MoMA; two days at Mudam, Luxembourg; ten days at the Centre Pompidou; four days at the Volksbühne, Berlin. My description is based on presentations at Wiels and MoMA. De Keersmaeker has since gone on to make other works for museums and galleries, including *Forêt* at the Musée du Louvre (2022).
76. 'Relaxed performance' (RP) is a term introduced to the UK theatre in 2009, to North American theatre in 2011, and to Asian theatre in 2014. RP denotes a loosening of rules around audience behaviour in order to accommodate neurodiverse patrons' needs. Audience members are allowed to move around, make noise, leave, and return to the theatre as needed. The house lights are partially dimmed rather than fully turned off. Although RP was originally designed for customers with autism, it now caters to all neurodiverse audiences. Thanks to Hui Peng for this research.
77. David Sillito, 'Philip Glass: Have a Sleep During Einstein on the Beach', BBC News, 4 May 2012.
78. On occasion, dance has served as a critical intervention into the museum. In Boris Charmatz's performance-exhibition 'Moments: A History of Performance in Ten Acts' at ZKM (2012), dancers improvised with and around historical works of art. Ralph Lemon's series of 'Value Talks' at MoMA, 2013–14, interrogated the museum's value system, albeit for a small, non-public audience.

79. Liberate Tate (2010–) pressured the museum to divest itself of BP sponsorship via numerous 'oil spill' actions at Tate Modern and Tate Britain, while Gulf Labor intervened at the Guggenheim on 1 May 2015, showering the rotunda with On Kawara flyers to protest the museum's labour practices in the United Arab Emirates. A similar strategy was deployed in 2019, at the same museum, by P.A.I.N. (Nan Goldin's campaign to remove Sackler sponsorship from the arts).
80. Annelies Van Assche and Kareth Schaffer respectively refer to these as autodramaturgy, hyperreferentiality and hyperindividualism. Van Assche and Schaffer, 'Flexible Performativity: What Contemporary Dancers Do When They Do What They Do', *TDR* 67:1 (2023), pp. 203–22. Their arguments are corroborated by Mickey Mahar: 'I haven't taken a dance class in three years, but I rehearse my eyes all the time. Because with this museum work, your eyes have to be super well-trained. I think that's what separates a lot of dancers that are successful from those that aren't – the intentionality of the gaze, working out the subject position from which to perform.' Mahar, interview with the author, 23 May 2017.
81. Thomas DeFrantz, 'Dancing the Museum Black: Activist Animations of the Social', in Susanne Franco and Gabriella Giannachi (eds.), *Moving Spaces: Enacting Dance, Performance, and the Digital in the Museum*, Venice: Edizioni Ca'Foscari, 2021, p. 108.

3 Seizing the Moment: Interventions

1. Mario Ramiro, 'Grupo 3Nós3: The Outside Expands', *Parachute* 116 (2004), p. 47.
2. Mario Ramiro, 'Between Form and Force: Connecting Architectonic, Telematic and Thermal Spaces', *Leonardo* 31:4 (1998), p. 248.
3. See Nahon and Hemsley, *Going Viral*, chapter 2.
4. Filippo Tommaso Marinetti, 'The Futurists, The First Interventionists. Manifesto of Italian Pride', in Gunter Berghaus (ed.), *F. T. Marinetti, Critical Writings*, New York: Farrar, Straus and Giroux, 2006, p. 227. The text was first published in 1929 but is based on a letter Marinetti sent to Francesco Cangiullo in 1914.
5. The black-and-yellow flag is that of the Hapsburg monarchy. It's important to note that Marinetti refers to their actions as 'demonstrations' rather than interventions, for example in F. T. Marinetti,

Guerra, sole igiene del mondo, Milan: Edizioni futuriste di poesia, 1915, p. 157. By spring 1915, the Interventionist position won out and Italy declared war on Austria–Hungary.

6. Joan Neuberger, 'Culture Besieged: Hooliganism and Futurism', in Stephen P. Frank and Mark D. Steinberg (eds.), *Cultures in Flux: Lower-Class Values, Practices, and Resistance in Late Imperial Russia*, Princeton: Princeton University Press, 1994, chapter 10.
7. Vladimir Markov, *Russian Futurism: A History*, Berkeley: University of California Press, 1968, p. 138.
8. See André Breton, 'Artificial Hells. Inauguration of the 1921 Dada Season', *October* 105 (2003), pp. 3–10.
9. See Inti Guerrero, 'Flávio de Carvalho: From an Anthropophagic Master Plan to a Tropical Modern Design', *Afterall* 24 (2010), p. 115. There is no documentation of *Experiência no. 2* (1931), only the artist's written account of walking against the flow of a religious procession, leering at the women participants; later, when arrested, he claimed he was simply analysing crowd psychology.
10. Jonah Westerman has traced the emergence of 'performance art' as a hegemonic category in North Ameria to circa 1979, with new dedicated journals (e.g., *High Performance*, 1978), the first history (RoseLee Goldberg's *Performance: Live Art 1910–1970*, New York: Harry N. Abrams, 1979) and the first Performance Studies department (at New York University, 1980). Westerman, 'Performance circa 1979: The Invention of a Medium and Some Consequences', seminar at CUNY Graduate Center, 29 October 2019.
11. In Asia, the terminology is different. In Hong Kong, performance art is translated as *xingdong yishu* (action art), but on mainland China the phrase used from the 1980s onwards is *xingwei yishu* (behaviour art). In Japan, the Anglicism *hapuningu* was used from the mid-1960s onwards, with the Anglicism *pafomansu* entering in the 1980s. Indigenous Japanese terms include *gishiki* (ritual or ceremony), *jiken* (event or incident), and *hokusetsu kōdō* (direct action). In Korea, performance before the 1980s was referred to as 'happenings', 'events', 'gesture art' or 'incidents'. Thanks to Flora Brandl for this research.
12. *Intervención*, in Spanish, has long been used in the sense of military imposition, but always in reference to historical conflict (e.g., French Intervention in Mexico).
13. John Coatsworth, 'United States Interventions', *ReVista: Harvard Review of Latin America*, Spring/Summer 2005, at revista.drclas.harvard.edu. Unsurprisingly, in the vast literature on government

interventions, the US is a prominent subject, particularly in relation to Latin America. See Alan L. McPherson (ed.), *Encyclopedia of US Military Interventions in Latin America*, Vol. 1, Santa Barbara, CA: ABC-CLIO, 2013.

14. United Nations General Assembly, 36th session, 1981–82, 'Declaration on the Inadmissibility of Intervention and Interference in the Internal Affairs of States', at digitallibrary.un.org/record/27066.
15. See Ernesto 'Che' Guevara, *Guerrilla Warfare*, New York: Monthly Review Press, 1961, section 3.
16. Décio Pignatari, 'Teoria da Guerrilha Artística' (1967), in Pignatari, *Contracomunicação*, São Paulo: Perspectiva, 1971, pp. 157–66; Julio le Parc, '¿Cultural Guerrilla?', *Robho*, 1968, at julioleparc.org. See also Germano Celant, 'Arte Povera: Appunti per una guerriglia', *Flash Art* 5 (1967), p. 3; for Celant, the Arte Povera artist as *guerrigliero* uses mobility, location, and the surprise of new materials to commit aesthetic violence.
17. Frederico Morais, 'Contra a Arte Afluente: O Corpo é o Motor da Obra', *Revista de Cultura Vozes* 1:64 (1970), p. 59.
18. Morais, 'Contra a Arte Afluente', p. 49, translation by Tie Jojima. The Brazilian artists mentioned by Morais were nevertheless using their own terminologies, including *propisição* (proposition; Oiticica), *interção* (insertion; Meireles), *situação* (situation; Barrio), and of course *acción* (action). Brazilian artists intervened in print media throughout the 1970s, inserting classified ads into newspapers (e.g., Meireles, Daniel Santiago) or altering their front pages (e.g., Antonio Manuel's *Clandestinas*, 1975). See *Arte-Veículo: Intervençoes na mídia de massa Brasiliera*, São Paulo: Sesc Pompeia, 2018.
19. Viajou sem Passaporte referred to their actions as *intervenções humanas* (human interventions), reflecting their training in theatre. Members of Viajou met those of 3Nós3 through classes at the Escola de Artes e Comunicações at the University of São Paulo. See Patricia Morales Bertucci, *Intervenção Urbana, São Paulo (1978–1982): o espaço da cidade e os coletivos de arte independente Viajou Sem Passaporte e 3Nós3*, PhD dissertation, Universidade de São Paulo, 2015, p. 83.
20. This began to change during the relaxation of authoritarian rule under President Geisel (1974–79). Prior to this moment, US support for the 1964 coup was not widely known, and not referred to as an 'intervention' until 1976. In Neale Ronning's anthology *Intervention in Latin America* (New York: Knopf, 1970), he notes that

intervention is an 'emotionally packed word in Latin America' because of the long history of European and US challenges to that region's sovereignty.

21. Mira Schor, 'Girls Will Be Girls', *Artforum*, September 1990, p. 125.
22. For a critical history of public art in the 1960s, see Miwon Kwon, *One Place After Another: Site-Specific Art and Locational Identity*, Cambridge, MA: MIT Press, 2002. In Brazil, the biennial public art exhibition 'Arte/Cidade', held in São Paulo, took *intervenções urbanas* as its focus from 1992 onwards. It drew on the intervention's associations of marginality and risk from the 1970s but functioned, for the most part, like most other large-scale public art biennials of the 1990s. In 2002, a significant number of works were sited in Zona l'Este, a district considered dangerous and off-limits to a white middle-class public. Visitors' unease was exacerbated by an exhibition guide based on a nineteenth-century map that didn't correspond to the present-day urban plan. Even in the company of the curators we could not visit a handful of projects, which had been taken over by the homeless (*Highway House-&-Garden* by Acconci Studio) and a local drug dealer (a kiosk by Atelier van Lieshout).
23. Osvaldo Sánchez, 'Curatorial Framework' (2005), InSITE, at insiteart.org.
24. These debates were largely set in motion by MoMA's controversial exhibition '"Primitivism" in Twentieth-Century Art: Affinity of the Tribal and the Modern' (1984). Paradigmatic artist-curated exhibitions in its wake include Jimmie Durham's 'We the People' (1987) and Fred Wilson's 'Rooms with a View' (1989). Joseph Kosuth's 'The Play of the Unmentionable' (1990), by contrast, was made in reaction to right-wing attacks on National Endowment for the Arts funding.
25. *Mining the Museum* stimulated so much enthusiasm that 'children's museums, natural history museums, science centers, and art museums suddenly wanted "Fred Wilsons" of their own'. Lisa Corrin, '*Mining the Museum:* An Installation Confronting History', *Curator* 36:4 (1993), p. 312.
26. See David Gibbs, *First Do No Harm: Humanitarian Intervention and the Destruction of Yugoslavia*, Nashville: Vanderbilt University Press, 2009.
27. William Pope.L, cited on the Museum of Modern Art website, 2019, at moma.org/calendar/exhibitions/5059.

28. For a discussion of this comment, see Joanna Fiduccia, 'Lacks Worth Having: William Pope L and Land Art', *Shift* 8 (2015), pp. 7–22.
29. See 'Yeguas del Apocalipsis', at english.yeguasdelapocalipsis.cl, and Juliana Sandoval Alvarez, '"I Speak for My Difference": Las Yeguas del Apocalipsis, Memory, and Performance in Chile's Transition to Democracy', *The Public Historian* 41 (2019), pp. 116–43.
30. 'We came together to provoke . . . Before the advent of democracy, it was in part us *maricas* [queers] who enunciated what others couldn't or wouldn't say.' Las Yeguas, cited in Victor Hugo Robles, 'History in the Making', *NACLA Report on the Americas* 31:4 (1998), n.p.
31. Hammons arranged for his gesture to be photographed by Dawoud Bey but did not exhibit the images for almost a decade.
32. In early 1990s Russia, the newspaper critics were themselves artists and curators, so the primary audience for these actions also had the capacity to report on them. Ekaterina Degot, conversation with the author, 10 March 2021.
33. Artist Anatoly Osmolovsky observed that such radical acts were not concerned with symbolism but with 'suddenness and a special atmosphere', using gestures that have 'simplicity, reaching to elementary, accuracy, archetypical themes or precise absurdity'. See osmopolis.com/tihiy_parad.
34. *Art activism* and *dissidence* are often complementary terms: we tend to use the former for group opposition in liberal democracies, and the latter for individual resistance under repressive regimes. Interventions can blur this distinction.
35. See Ondine Chavoya, 'Internal Exiles: The Interventionist Public and Performance Art of Asco', in Erika Suderberg (ed.), *Space, Site, Intervention: Situating Installation Art*, Minneapolis: University of Minnesota Press, 2000, p. 202.
36. David García and Geert Lovink, 'The ABC of Tactical Media' (1997), at nettime.org.
37. Critical Art Ensemble, *Electronic Civil Disobedience and Other Unpopular Ideas*, New York: Autonomedia, 1996.
38. See Ricardo Dominguez, 'The Zapatistas FloodNet: From Automation to Autonomy and Back', *ASAP/Journal* 4:2 (2019), pp. 292–4. EDT's *FloodNet* made the Mexican government's website automatically reload with error messages such as 'Error 404_Democracy not found' and 'Error 404_Justice not found'. It is archived at anthology.rhizome.org.

39. For archived footage of the BBC interview, see 'Bhopal Disaster – BBC – The Yes Men' on YouTube.
40. Aldo Damian Menendez, 'Art Attack: The work of ARTECALLE', in Coco Fusco (ed.), *Corpus Delecti: Performance Art of the Americas*, London: Routledge, 2000, p. 255.
41. Rachel Weiss, 'Performing Revolution: Arte Calle, Grupo Provisional, and the Response to the Cuban National Crisis, 1986–1989', in Greg Sholette and Blake Stimson (eds.), *Collectivism after Modernism: The Art of Social Imagination after 1945*, Berkeley: University of California Press, 2005, p. 122.
42. Weiss cites the response of *Juventud Rebelde*, the official newspaper of the Young Communist League, for whom the group's use of public space was less worrying than widespread knowledge of their actions. Weiss, 'Performing Revolution', p. 129.
43. Tania Bruguera, in *Claire Bishop in Conversation with/en conversación con Tania Bruguera*, New York: Cisneros, 2020, chapter 2. All subsequent quotes by Bruguera are taken from this publication.
44. Bruguera: 'When you make an artwork in which the meaning of the work is defined by a political situation that is unfolding, and when it involves as its material some of the elements generating the political situation . . . when control and consequences of the work are not in the hands of the artist but decided by a government or by those in power; when the work unleashes a chain of political responses or the creation of new policies . . . when people can see in the artwork a space to participate that they can't find in the political situation – then these are factors that render an artwork political timing specific.'
45. The Cuban government, like many other repressive regimes, micromanages culture and perceives all expressions of dissent as a threat. This should be borne in mind when we read Bruguera's ambitious list of prerequisites for political-timing-specific art (see footnote above).
46. Raymond Williams, *Marxism and Literature*, Oxford: Oxford University Press, 1977, pp. 128–35.
47. Menendez, 'Art Attack', p. 254.
48. Ernesto Leal quoted in Weiss, 'Performing Revolution', p. 124.
49. CUNY Graduate Center student Flora Brandl memorably critiqued the masculinism of interventions as 'metaphorically tied to acts of penetration: a brief insertion, discharge, and subsequent evacuation, heedless of the lingering consequences'.
50. Donald Egbert, 'The Idea of "Avant-garde" in Art and Politics', *The American Historical Review* 73:2 (1967), pp. 339–66.

51. See for example Geert Lovink, 'Information Warfare: From Propaganda Critique to Culture Jamming', in Lovink, *Dark Fiber: Tracking Internet Culture*, Cambridge, MA: MIT Press, 2002, p. 313.
52. Critical Art Ensemble, *Electronic Civil Disobedience*, p. 29.
53. Andrew Boyd (ed.), *Beautiful Trouble*, London: OR Books, 2012.
54. R. B. Onians, *The Origins of European Thought about the Body, the Mind, the Soul, the World, Time and Fate*, Cambridge: Cambridge University Press, 1988, pp. 343–8.
55. Joanne Paul, 'The Uses of Kairos in Renaissance Political Philosophy', *Renaissance Quarterly* 67 (2014), p. 46.
56. See Paul, 'The Uses of Kairos', p. 65. During the Renaissance, Greek and Roman deities were made to conform with Christian didacticism: this resulted in the iconography of Occasio being conflated with Fortuna, whose turning wheel dramatizes the downfall of those who seek worldly possessions and glory.
57. I will return to this idea of moral relativism; for now, it suffices to note the political undecidability of interventions whose politics might be far from clear, and even ambivalent.
58. Vladimir Lenin, cited in Georg Lukács, *Lenin: A Study on the Unity of His Thought* (1924), London: Verso, 2009, p. 29.
59. Régis Debray, *Revolution in the Revolution: Armed Struggle and Political Struggle in Latin America*, New York: Grove Press, 1967 (first published in French 1967). Nicolas Guagnini notes that artists throughout Latin America in the 1970s were familiar with Foquismo, in Guagnini, *The Counter-Public Sphere in the Condor Years*, New York: ISLAA, 2020, pp. 1–13.
60. As the 45th president of the United States knew well, a well-timed tweet in the early hours could distract and derail the media for days.
61. Voina member Alexei Plutser-Sarno reports that his post about the intervention had 3,000 comments and half a million views before being removed by moderators, at which point the YouTube video had been viewed 300,000 times. See 'The VOINA Art-Group (<<War>>). Actions 2006–2013', at plucer.livejournal.com.
62. Oliver Johnson, 'War on the Ru-net: Voina's *Dick Captured by the FSB* as a Networked Performance', *Third Text* 27:5 (2013), p. 599.
63. This phrase was used by one of the Innovation Award jury members, art historian and curator Ekaterina Degot, in 'Why I Voted for Voina', *Openspace*, 13 April 2011, at openspace.ru. Voina won the 2011 Innovation Award but declined to attend the award

ceremony, donating the money to political prisoners – just as criminal proceedings were being instigated against two of its members.

64. Masha Gessen, *Words Will Break Cement: The Passion of Pussy Riot*, New York: Riverhead Books, 2014, p. 35.
65. Voina, 'Dick captured by KGB / Voina's 65-metres-high Cock', *Livejournal*, 14 June 2010, plucer.livejournal.com/266853.html.
66. Alexei Plutser-Sarno, 'The VOINA Art-Group (<<War>>). Actions 2006–2013', at plucer.livejournal.com/266853.html and the original post at https://plucer.livejournal.com/265584.html. Johnson takes up this line of thinking, variously referring to the intervention as a 'blog-post artefact', 'a deliberately low-fi work of Internet art', a 'spontaneous guerrilla performance', and a 'networked performance' ('War on the Ru-net', p. 592).
67. Johnson, 'War on the Ru-net', pp. 602–3.
68. In Voina's own words, they aspire to be 'an artist-intellectual, in a manner of Russian libertarian decemberism . . . artist as romantic hero, who prevail[s] over the evil'. See en.free-voina.org/about.
69. Nadezhda Tolokonnikova and Yekaterina Samutsevich were members of Voina before co-founding Pussy Riot.
70. Gessen, *Words Will Break Cement*, chapters 6 and 7.
71. Elena Gapova, 'Becoming Visible in the Digital Age: The Class and Media Dimensions of the Pussy Riot Affair', *Feminist Media Studies* 15:1 (2015), p. 29. The video was first posted at pussy-riot.livejournal.com/12442.html.
72. Interventions by women tended to be limited to interior spaces, such as Lyudmila Gorlova's *A Happy Childhood* (1994), an event for a limited audience in a maternity ward.
73. Gapova, 'Becoming Visible in the Digital Age', p. 23, citing a report by the Levada Center, levada.ru/31-07-2012/rossiyane-o-dele-pussy-riot (in Russian).
74. Gapova, 'Becoming Visible in the Digital Age', p. 24.
75. *Tatlin's Whisper #6* (2009) was first performed at the Centro Wilfredo Lam as part of the tenth Havana Biennial.
76. See for example '#YoTeInvito a Nuestra Plaza el 30 a las 3' (Bruguera) and 'Yo también exijo – NormiQueen (Video Oficial)' (Normi Queen), both on YouTube. Bruguera issued two more open letters, one to Pope Francis (asking him to protect the freedom of Cubans), and another to the national newspaper *Granma*, which unsurprisingly was not published.
77. The ensuing nine-month drama was played out between the artist and the Cuban government, who duly adopted their respective roles

of dissident and oppressor. Each staged their own PR battle. For Bruguera, it was a question of mobilizing social media (given the limitations of internet access in Cuba, this was done largely by her sister in Italy with the support of the international art world) and in person during the Havana Biennial, to which she unofficially contributed by performing a durational reading of Hannah Arendt's *The Origins of Totalitarianism* (1951). The Cuban government, by contrast, deployed more traditional means of smearing Bruguera's reputation: sending a video to Cuban art schools denouncing her as a traitor, and removing her name from the list of official artists issued to visiting international curators and cultural organizations.

78. The consequences of the intervention were so disruptive for Bruguera that she eventually handed in her passport in 2021 and relocated to the US, in exchange for the Cuban government freeing twenty-five political prisoners.

79. Admittedly, this inflection was not helped by Bruguera's retelling of the events, in which *#YoTambienExijo* understandably becomes a narrative of interrogations, actions, and counter-actions between her and the government. Such a retelling, while gripping, focused on her own drama rather than the collective plight of cultural producers in Cuba.

80. T. J. Clark, 'On the Social History of Art' (1973), in Francis Frascina and Charles Harrison (eds.), *Modern Art and Modernism*, Abingdon: Routledge, 1982, pp. 255. My discussion of conjunctural analysis (see below) differs from Clark's since he is only invested in 'art at its greatest' (p. 252). That said, I adhere to his positioning of the work of art as a 'moment of historical coalescence' – the encounter between an individual artist, aesthetic traditions, and ideologies, all of which accrue meaning and in turn act on history.

81. Louis Althusser, 'Glossary', in *For Marx* (1965), London: Verso, 2005, p. 250. Althusser refers to Machiavelli as 'the first theorist of the conjuncture or the first thinker . . . to think *in* the conjuncture: that is to say, in its concept of an aleatory, singular case' (*Machiavelli and Us*, London: Verso, 1999, p. 18). See Juha Koivisto and Mikko Lahtinen, 'Historical-Critical Dictionary of Marxism: Conjuncture, Politico-Historical', *Historical Materialism* 20:1 (2012), pp. 267–77.

82. Hall's primary points of reference are Gramsci (who in turn was indebted to Machiavelli), and to a lesser extent Raymond Williams,

who coined the term 'structure of feeling' to problematize Gramsci's concept of hegemony.

83. A conjunctural analysis 'forces you to look at many different aspects, in order to see what the balance of social forces is and how you might intervene, or have a better idea of how to intervene effectively'. Hall, in Stuart Hall and Doreen Massey, 'Interpreting the Crisis', *Soundings* 44 (2010), p. 58.
84. Igor Ponosov argues that Voina's conflation of art and activism initiated a new era of civic disobedience and protest in Russia. Ponosov, 'Urban Art in Russia, Part 3: Rebirth of the Russian Street Art as Politically and Socially Engaged Art (2011–2012)', at eng.partizaning.org/?p=6462.
85. Ben Anderson, 'Emergency Futures: Exception, Urgency, Interval, Hope', *Sociological Review* 65:3 (2017), pp. 463–77.
86. At the same time, Anderson is doing what Hall would call a conjunctural analysis: he exposes the structural contradiction whereby 'emergency' is construed as a short-term measure by and for white power, both exacerbating and ignoring the long-term, endemic 'emergency' of antiblack racism in the US.
87. Bright's vigil echoes Kevin Quashie's work on 'Black Quiet'. Quashie's paradigmatic example is the raised fists of Tommie Smith and John Carlos at the Mexico Olympics in 1968, but the concept applies equally to more recent gestures of public interiority as resistance, such as American footballer Colin Kaepernick taking a knee during the national anthem (2016 onwards). See Kevin Quashie, 'The Trouble with Publicness: Toward a Theory of Black Quiet', *African American Review* 43:2–3 (2009), pp. 329–43.
88. Bright set up a Go Fund Me account to raise money to go to Paris and protest in front of the appropriation of his work at the Palais de Tokyo by the French-Algerian Neïl Beloufa. He explains his rationale and experience of online harassment in 'Help Parker Reclaim His Image' at gofundme.com.
89. Marcus-David Peters was a resident of Richmond murdered by the police in 2018. The General Lee monument was removed from its plinth by the city of Richmond on 8 September 2021.
90. Michael Shaw intriguingly refers to the monument receiving a 'new skin'. Shaw, 'Refacing the Robert E. Lee Monument in Richmond', *Reading the Pictures*, 25 June 2020, at readingthepictures.org.
91. See Christopher Grobe, 'The Artist is President: *Performance Art* and Other Keywords in the Age of Donald Trump', *Critical Inquiry* 46:4 (2020), pp. 764–805, particularly his description of a performance by

alt-right provocateur Milo Yiannapolis. Further examples can be found in the exhibition 'Political Art' at Ujazdowski Castle Centre for Contemporary Art, Warsaw, 2021.

92. Angela Nagle, *Kill All Normies*, London: Zero Books, 2017, chapter 2. For a more European perspective, see Sofía Bempaza, 'Aesthetic Practices of the New Right: Fake and Post-Truth as a Challenge for Transgressive Art and Cultural Practices', *medienimpulse* 58:2 (2020), pp. 1–34.
93. Nagle, *Kill All Normies*, p. 30.

4 Déjà Vu: Invoking Modernist Architecture and Design

1. All quotes in this paragraph are pulled from *Frieze*, *Artforum*, and press releases in New York galleries during 2013–14, when I first began presenting this material. Exhibitions devoted to contemporary art about modernist architecture seem to begin with 'I Moderni /The Moderns' at Castello di Rivoli (2003); see my website for subsequent examples: clairebishop.commons.gc.cuny.edu.
2. See for example curator Mark Godfrey, 'The Artist as Historian', *October* 120 (2007), pp. 142–3. I differ from Godfrey in wanting to parse the artist's relationship to the past – in other words, not just noting that an artistic interest in history exists but asking what this relationship to history comprises.
3. The phrase 'modernity without modernization' appears in Nestor García Canclini, *Hybrid Cultures: Strategies for Entering and Leaving Modernity*, Minneapolis: University of Minnesota Press, 1995, chapter 4.
4. clairebishop.commons.gc.cuny.edu.
5. Two blogs have been particularly useful for this research: Framing Ark (framingark.blogspot.com) by the curator and architect Fabrizio Gallanti, and Center for the Aesthetic Revolution by Pablo León de la Barra (centrefortheaestheticrevolution.blogspot.com), a valued interlocutor for my research.
6. In a series of essays from 2000, Moretti asks how forms and genres develop worldwide, not just in a handful of European countries that play an outsize role in literary history. See Franco Moretti, 'Conjectures on World Literature', *New Left Review*, January–February 2000. Moretti's approach is influenced by world-systems theory and Italian Marxism, but his default is to think cultural production in terms of colonial centres at the

vanguard. Peripheral regions can only follow suit, hybridizing genres in their wake.

7. Manovich positions cultural analytics in opposition to the digital humanities, which assess historical databases rather than living digital culture, and tend to sideline the visual. Lev Manovich, *Cultural Analytics*, Cambridge, MA: MIT Press, 2020, chapter 1.
8. See Cultural Analytics Lab, 'Exploring One Million Manga Pages with Supercomputers and HIPerSpace', at lab.culturalanalytics.info.
9. Manovich, *Cultural Analytics*, p. 172.
10. Tatlin's *Monument to the Third International* (1919–20) was a sculptural model for a building too technically ambitious to be realized: a 400m high spiralling tower whose levels rotated at different speeds. This section takes its lead from a prompt by art historian Maria Gough, who generously shared images with me.
11. Neue Slowenische Kunst was founded in Slovenia in 1983 with branches in theatre (The Sisters of Scipion Nasice), visual art (IRWIN), graphic design (New Collectivism), and music (Laibach). In 1994, IRWIN adopted the term 'retroavantgarde' to construct and propagate its own lineage of Eastern European modernism.
12. This conscious collection of references stands in contrast to Jameson's claim that postmodern artists engage in 'random cannibalization of all the styles of the past, the play of random stylistic allusion', thereby effacing history. Fredric Jameson, *Postmodernism, or, The Cultural Logic of Late Capitalism*, London: Verso, 1991, p. 18.
13. Svetlana Boym, *Architecture of the Off-Modern*, Princeton: Princeton University Press, 2008, p. 33. Tatlin's *Monument*, like Malevich's *Black Square* (1915), sporadically makes an appearance in Sots art and Moscow Conceptualism of the 1970s and 1980s.
14. During the 1980s, Hadid rejected the postmodern trend to return to historical styles and asserted the ongoing importance of modernism as an incomplete project. See Detlef Mertins, 'The Modernity of Zaha Hadid', in *Zaha Hadid*, New York: Solomon R. Guggenheim Foundation, 2006, pp. 33–8.
15. 'In Cuba if you have a refrigerator and it breaks, you have to find a way to make it work again, because you're never going to get another one. And if you can't make it work as a refrigerator, you have to find a way to make it useful doing something else. As far as Tatlin's tower goes, it was architecture that never worked, a bad idea from the beginning. So I had to find a way to make it useful

doing something else.' Kcho, cited in Alma Ruiz, 'Todo Cambia', *Kcho: Todo Cambia*, exhibition catalogue, Los Angeles: Museum of Contemporary Art, 1997, n.p.

16. See Keti Chrukhov, 'Art after Primitive Accumulation: Or, on the Putin-Medvedev Cultural Politics', *Afterall* 26 (2011), pp. 135–6. More recently, Soviet art of the 1920s has been co-opted by the Russian government: posters for the 2014 Sochi Winter Olympics based on Malevich, team outfits for the 2020 Rio Olympics based on Varvara Stepanova designs, and the interiors of the new terminal of Sheremetyevo airport based on numerous Constructivist works of art (2020). Thanks to Masha Chlenova for this reference.
17. Müller's project was a response to his own training in Switzerland: 'I was spoon-fed with modernism in my upbringing from day one. It was the foundation of my education and my later training as a graphic designer and artist.' By the early 1990s, Müller wanted to reassess this by turning back to the late 1950s, years that he understood to be the end of modernism, but also the moment when he was born (1957). Müller, in Sabine Breitwieser (ed.), *Modernologies: Contemporary Artists Researching Modernity and Modernism*, Barcelona: MACBA, 2009, p. 156.
18. Müller, in Breitwieser (ed.), *Modernologies*, p. 156.
19. The Case Study Houses are a series of thirty-six experimental residential homes designed by Richard Neutra, Charles and Ray Eames, Pierre König and others between the mid-1940s and mid-1960s. Not all the designs were built.
20. Nicolas Bourriaud, *Relational Aesthetics*, Dijon: les presses du réel, 2002. 'Utopia Station' at the Venice Biennale (2003) was co-curated by Hans-Ulrich Obrist, artist Rirkrit Tiravanija, and art historian Molly Nesbit, and toured widely after Venice.
21. Modernism was arguably stripped of a social project by the end of the 1930s, when the United States dismantled the principles of the International Style and replaced universalism with a regionalist modernism inflected by populist nationalism. See Keith Eggener, 'Nationalism, Internationalism, and the "Naturalization" of Modern Architecture in the United States, 1925–1940', *National Identities* 8:3 (2006), pp. 243–58.
22. My reading of invocation differs from that of Jan Verwoert, who uses Jacques Derrida's *Specters of Marx* to argue that contemporary art invokes 'the ghosts of unclosed histories'. Verwoert, 'Living with Ghosts: From Appropriation to Invocation in Contemporary

Art', *The Journal of Artistic Research* 1:2 (2007), p. 7. The recent trend for 'neo-ancestralism' – the use of invocation by artists exploring Black, indigenous, and pre-modern cultural forms – requires a study of its own.

23. Leonor Antunes, in Robert Preece, 'The Measure of Modernism: A Conversation with Leonor Antunes', *Sculpture* 41:2 (2022), p. 32.
24. Martin Herbert, 'Sifting Defunct Modernism in Search of Something Useful', *TATE Etc.* 15 (2009), p. 68.
25. Post-socialism in Eastern Europe denotes a double condition of radical change and persistent legacies: the collapse of the state, the privatization of public assets, the end of welfare, the introduction of the market, rising crime and unemployment, nostalgia for the past, and the continuation of political corruption and authoritarianism. In Western Europe, post-socialism is signalled by the gravitation of left-wing parties towards the centre, distancing themselves from unions and the old left to become pro-business and privatization.
26. Later works made during DAAD residencies that allude to the built environment of the GDR include Allora & Calzadilla's *How to Appear Invisible* (2009), and Phil Collins's *marxism today (prologue)* and *Use! Value! Exchange!* (both 2010). Tellingly, none of these videos reference a proper name but focus on a now-defunct aesthetic and political regime.
27. While the 1990s works of these artists do not depict architecture, they exude disapproval of the recently crumbled political order. The pre-eminent examples are Sala's *Intervista* (1998) and Narkevicius's *His-Story* (1998).
28. David Maljković, cited in Breitwieser (ed.), *Modernologies*, p. 18.
29. See for example British artist Simon Starling: 'The buildings of International Modernism became a focus for my travels, my mapping – my activity as an artist. I started to behave a bit like an architectural tourist; it gave some form to the practice.' Starling, in *Simon Starling: Cuttings*, Basel: Kunstmuseum Basel, Museum für Gegenwartskunst/Hatje Cantz, 1995, p. C2.
30. Gonzalez-Foerster's *Brasília* is part of a compilation of eleven videos distributed as *Parc Central* (1998–2003). It is not to be confused with her better-known installation *Brasília Hall* (1998).
31. See Julieta González's 'Extranjeros en todas partes', *Mamõyguara opá mamõ pupé, 31st Panorama da Arte Brasiliera*, São Paulo: Museu de Arte Moderna, 2009, p. 47. It is worth recalling that Oscar Niemeyer only died in 2012, at the age of 104; Brazilian

modernism is therefore an anomaly, having existed without interruption since the 1930s.

32. See Ana María Durán Calisto, 'Modernism and Contemporary Art in Latin America', in Antonio Sergio Bessa (ed.), *Beyond the Supersquare: Art and Architecture in Latin America after Modernism*, NY: Bronx Museum of the Arts/Fordham University Press, 2014, p. 19.
33. See for example the work of Rijksakademie graduates David Claerbout, Ryan Gander, Dora García, Jill Magid, David Maljković, Paulina Ołowska, Bojan Šarcevic, and Monika Sosnowska.
34. The exception is the artist-duo Thukral & Tagra, but their work is so abstract that the reference to Le Corbusier's complex would be difficult to detect without the extended caption. See Shanay Jhaveri (ed.), *Chandigarh Is in India*, Mumbai: The Shoestring Press, 2016.
35. See docomomo.com. Precedents include the Los Angeles Conservancy Modern Committee (or ModCom) in 1984 and London's Twentieth Century Society in 1992. The first modern Mexican buildings to be declared 'national patrimony' and receive legal protection were the Casa Barragán (in 1988) and Juan O'Gorman's house-studios for Diego Rivera and Frida Kahlo (in 1994); the Fomento Universal para la Difusión Arquitectónica de México was only founded in 2012. By contrast, Brazil's Serviço do Patrimônio Histórico e Artístico Nacional (SPHAN) was set up in 1937; leading modernist architects like Lúcio Costa were put in charge of cataloguing, legislating, and preserving what they saw as an 'authentic' Brazilian culture.
36. See whc.unesco.org/en/list.
37. Modernist examples on the UNESCO list include Brasília, the Ciudad Universitaria de Caracas, the Rietveld-Schröder House, the Luis Barragán house and studio, the central campus of the Universidad Nacional Autónoma de México, seventeen buildings by Le Corbusier, and the six Berlin housing estates designed by Taut, Wagner, Gropius, and others. A handful of architectural icons have been protected since the 1960s through private trusts – most notably Frank Lloyd Wright's Fallingwater (since 1963) and Le Corbusier's Villa Savoye (since 1965). The former was added to the UNESCO list in 2019; the latter in 2016.
38. The Palast was ideologically recoded as a negative building, both morally and historically, that needed to be erased in favour of a reconstruction of the imperial baroque Stadtschloss that had been destroyed during the Second World War. Works about the Palast

include the above-mentioned pieces by Tacita Dean (*Palast*, 2004) and Allora & Calzadilla (*How to Appear Invisible*, 2009), but also in Nina Fischer and Maroan el Sani's film *Palast der Republik – Weissbereich* (2001), Søren Lose's installation *Palast* (2008), and Reynold Reynolds's video *Last Day of the Republik* (2010).

39. The utopian promise of Latin American modernism was not that of Tatlin's technofuturist socialism, but bound up with postwar developmentalism during the 1950s and 1960s, and in the case of Venezuela, the discovery of oil. On the one hand, Latin American modernism-as-developmentalism signalled a rupture with chaotic backwardness, an expression of solidarity with the global south, and a cosmopolitan idea of identity and freedom; on the other, it was national rather than international in character, and many architects were happy to work with the dictatorships.
40. In *Residente Pulido*, Apóstol digitally 'seals' the windows and doors of these buildings using Photoshop so they come to resemble ceramics, referenced in subtitles that allude to European porcelain (Meissen, Limoges, Lladró, Capodimonte, Sèvres, etc.).
41. During Venezuela's military dictatorship of 1948–58, notable buildings like the Centro Simón Bolívar Towers (1954) and Ciudad Universitaria (1954) were inaugurated, as well as the eventually abandoned shopping centre (now prison) El Helicoide (1955).
42. 'Cities on the Move', a touring exhibition curated by Hou Hanru and Hans-Ulrich Obrist between 1997 and 1999, was one of the first major shows of contemporary Chinese art in Europe and foregrounded the unprecedented growth of Chinese megacities. See also Maurizio Marinelli, 'Urban Revolution and Chinese Contemporary Art: A Total Revolution of the Senses', *China Information* 29:2 (2015), pp. 154–75.
43. Retrospective approaches are much rarer. The photo series 'Assembly Hall' (2002–4) by Shao Yinong and Mu Chen documents former meeting places during the Cultural Revolution, but the approach is studiedly neutral, in keeping with the artists' aversion to propaganda.
44. Jacques Derrida, *Specters of Marx: The State of the Debt, the Work of Mourning, and The New International*, New York: Routledge, 1994. See for example Verwoert, 'Living with Ghosts'; Roger Buergel's statement 'Is Modernity Our Antiquity?' for Documenta 12, 2007; Boris Groys, 'Spectres of Communism: Contemporary Russian Art', New York: The James Gallery at CUNY Graduate Center, 2015.

45. Giorgio Agamben, *Potentialities: Collected Essays in Philosophy*, Stanford: Stanford University Press, 1999, chapter 11. The potentiality approach can be found in Herbert, 'Sifting Defunct Modernism'; Svetlana Boym, *The Future of Nostalgia*, New York: Basic Books, 2001, p. xi; Christine Ross, *The Past is the Present; It's the Future, Too: The Temporal Turn in Contemporary Art*, New York: Continuum, 2012; Uros Cvoro, *Transitional Aesthetics: Contemporary Art at the Edge of Europe*, London: Bloomsbury, 2018. Mieke Bal offers a semiotic model focusing on the use of the baroque by contemporary artists, whose wilful anachronism she describes as 'preposterous history'. See Bal, *Quoting Caravaggio: Contemporary Art, Preposterous History*, Chicago: University of Chicago Press, 1999.
46. By historicity I mean 'this primary experience of *estrangement*, of distance between self and self, to which the categories of past, present, and future give order and meaning, enabling it to be grasped and expressed'. François Hartog, *Regimes of Historicity* (2003), New York: Columbia University Press, 2015, pp. xv–xvi. Hartog's reading of historicity is richer than Jameson's use of the term in *Postmodernism, or, The Cultural Logic of Late Capitalism*, p. 284.
47. Paolo Virno, *Déjà Vu and The End of History* (1996), London: Verso, 2015.
48. Virno, *Déjà Vu*, p. 41, p. 47.
49. 'The digital is an intellectual technology, a technology of the mind. The mind always has a technical foundation: the mind is founded on the becoming-technical of the psyche.' Stiegler, 'The Digital, Education, and Cosmopolitanism', p. 158.
50. Consider how retro filters impersonate the look and feel of past technologies – sepia, vignette, silvertone, Polaroid, lens flare, light leaks – but are completely unmoored from any indexical relationship to the image.
51. Peter Krapp, *Déjà Vu: Aberrations of Cultural Memory*, Minneapolis: University of Minnesota Press, 2004, pp. ix–x.
52. Reyner Banham, *A Concrete Atlantis: US Industrial Building and European Modern Architecture 1900–1925*, Cambridge, MA: MIT Press, 1986. Walter Gropius's 1913 article on modern industrial architecture preceded his first visit to the United States by fifteen years; Le Corbusier published images of US industrial architecture in 1923 but did not visit the country until 1935.
53. Förg would be the first to agree with this assessment. See his comments in Dorothea Dietrich, 'Gunther Förg in His Own Words', *Print Collector's Newsletter* XX:3 (1989), pp. 82–3.

54. Siegel's video *Provenance* forms the first chapter of a three-part work of the same title, which also comprises the video *Lot 248* (2013) and the print *Proof (Christie's 19 October 2013)* (2013).
55. Kristen Ross, *Communal Luxury: The Political Imaginary of the Paris Commune*, London: Verso, 2016.
56. Ironically, turbocharging a contemporary work with the blue-chip reputation of a modernist precedent renders the former less distinctive and less available to quotation in the future.
57. Nostalgia derives from the Greek *nostos* (the return home) and *algos* (grief, pain, or sorrow). As Boym points out, nostalgia is not anti-modern but coeval with the modernist project. Svetlana Boym, 'The Ruins of the Avant-garde', in Andreas Schonle and Julia Hell (eds.), *The Ruins of Modernity*, Durham, NC: Duke University Press, 2008, and 'Tatlin, or Ruinophilia', *Cabinet* 28 (2007–8).
58. Paul Gilroy, *Postcolonial Melancholia*, New York: Columbia University Press, 2005.
59. See for example Michael Kimmelman, 'Kerry James Marshall at Jack Shainman Gallery', *New York Times*, 29 September 1995, section 3, p. 18.
60. When Marshall paints the interiors of these postwar homes, he depicts them with furnishings that are gaudy and busy rather than tastefully mid-century modern; they are foils for human life and relationships, rather than stage sets for privileged inaction.
61. Previous monuments include the *Deleuze Monument* (2000) in Avignon and the *Bataille Monument* (2002) in Kassel. Hirschhorn rejects the term 'participatory installation' and prefers to describe these works as 'Presence and Production': generating a situation on site for the (two- to three-month) duration of the project's existence.
62. The *Gramsci Monument* included a library of Gramsci's writings, an exhibition of objects belonging to him while in prison in the 1930s, a radio station, a bar, an internet corner, a lounge, a workshop space, and a 'platform' (open-air auditorium).
63. Fred Moten, 'The Gramsci Monument', *Social Text* 32:1 (2014), pp. 117–18.

Illustration Credits

Rugilė Barzdziukaitė, Vaiva Grainytė, and Lina Lapelytė, *Sun and Sea (Marina)*, 2018. Performance view, Teatre Lliure, Barcelona, 2022. Photography: Teatre Lliure/Sílvia Poch. © and courtesy of the artists.

Kevin Beasley, *The Sound of Morning*, 2021. Performance view, New York, 14 October 2021. Dancers: Raymond Pinto, Amadi Washington, Ley Gambucci. Photo: Paula Court. Courtesy of the artist and Performa.

Thomas Rowlandson, Auguste Charles Pugin, and John Hill, *Exhibition Room, Somerset House*, 1808. Etching and aquatint. Collection: Metropolitan Museum of Art, New York.

View of 'Cubism and Abstract Art', Museum of Modern Art, New York, 1936. Digital Image © The Museum of Modern Art/Licensed by SCALA / Art Resource, NY © 2023 Estate of Pablo Picasso / Artists Rights Society (ARS), New York. Courtesy of MoMA.

Antoine Meunier, *La Comédie-Française*, ca. 1790–1800. Pen, ink, and watercolour. Collection: Bibliothèque Nationale de France, Paris.

La vue intérieure du théâtre de Bayreuth (interior view of the theatre at Bayreuth). Illustration published alongside Édouard Dujardin's history of the Bayreuth Festspielhaus in *Revue Wagnérienne*, Paris, Vol. 5, 8 June 1885.

Charles Graham and Thure de Thulstrup, *Interior of Wallack's New Theatre (the screen scene in 'The School for Scandal')*, 1882. Wood engraving published in *Harper's Weekly*, Vol. 26, no. 1307, 7 January 1882.

David Goldblatt, *Ex-offenders at the Scene of Crime or Arrest*, 2008–16. Series of forty-eight photographs. Installation view, Pace/MacGill, New York, 2016. Photo: Pace Gallery. © The David Goldblatt Legacy Trust. Courtesy of Goodman Gallery, Johannesburg, and Pace Gallery, New York.

Hans Haacke, *Shapolsky et al. Manhattan Real Estate Holdings, a Real-Time Social System, as of May 1, 1971*, 1971. One hundred and forty-six photographic views of New York apartment buildings, six pictures of transactions, an explanatory wall panel, and maps of Harlem and the Lower East Side. Installation view, Venice Biennale, 1978. © Hans Haacke / Artists Rights Society (ARS), New York / VG Bild-Kunst, Bonn. Courtesy of the artist and Paula Cooper Gallery, New York.

Renée Green, *Import/Export Funk Office*, 1992. Mixed-media installation with metal shelf structure, books, magazines, newspapers, ephemera, BETA video cases, twenty-five hours of digitized video, two monitors, one video projection, cassette cases, sound, acrylic signs, four wooden structures, acrylic signs on four shelves, four cassette players, and thirty wooden plaques with rubber-stamped text. Installation view, Galerie Christian Nagel, Cologne, 1992. Photos (two views): Andrea Stappert. Courtesy of the artist.

Mario García Torres, *A Film Treatment (Share-e-Nau Wanderings)* (2006) and *After many casual and unscripted talks with Sher Agha, current care taker of Alighiero Boetti's One Hotel site, I asked Aman Mojadidi to formally interview him in Dari and tape his answers. A great talker, Agha went on deep about his childhood in the Share Naw neighborhood of Kabul, the people who inhabited it, their traditions and about his sporadic working relationship with the house occupants since his teens. He chatted about taking care of the house through the last few tenants and about the raise of prices of real estate in the area during the last decade. He finished by saying he had no personal recollection of a hotel being run by Italian twins* (1391, Iranian calendar). Installation view, Documenta 13, Kassel, Germany, 2012. Photo: Haupt and Binder. Courtesy of Documenta, the artist, and Jan Mot, Brussels.

Henrik Olesen, *Some Gay-Lesbian Artists and/or Artists relevant to Homo-Social Culture I–VII*, 2007. Collage, computer printouts on wooden boards. Installation view, Galerie Buchholz, Cologne, 2007. Courtesy of the artist and Galerie Buchholz.

Wolfgang Tillmans, *Truth Study Center*, 2005–. Installation with wooden tables, digital prints on paper, C-print photographs, graphite on paper, and other materials. Installation view, *The Last Newspaper*, New Museum, New York, 2010. Photo: Latitudes, Barcelona. Courtesy of the artist.

Studying Truth with Wolfgang Tillmans, 2017. Online visualizer by Nate van der Ende and Johanna Lundberg, created for the exhibition *Wolfgang Tillmans: 2017*, Tate Modern, London. Courtesy of the designers.

Forensic Architecture, *The Long Duration of a Split Second*, 2018. Mixed-media installation. Installation view, *Turner Prize 2018*, Tate Britain, London. Photo: Tate Photography/Joe Humphreys. Courtesy of the artists and Tate.

Walid Raad, *Scratching on Things I Could Disavow: Walkthrough*, 2007–. Performance view, Museum of Modern Art, New York, 5 October 2015. Photo: Julieta Cervantes.

Anna Boghiguian, *The Salt Traders*, 2015. Mixed-media installation. Installation view, Stedelijk Van Abbemuseum, Eindhoven. Photo: Peter Cox. Courtesy of the artist and Archives Van Abbemuseum. Second view photo: Nikki Columbus. Courtesy of the artist.

Merce Cunningham, *Event #45*, 1972. Performance view, Museum of Modern Art, Belgrade, 17 September 1972. Photo: James Klosty. Courtesy of Merce Cunningham Trust, New York.

Yvonne Rainer, *Continuous Project Altered Daily*, 1970. Performance view, Whitney Museum of American Art, New York. Photo: Peter Moore. © Northwestern University, Evanston, Illinois.

Maria Hassabi, *PLASTIC*, 2015. Performance view, Museum of Modern Art, New York, 2016. Performer: Maria Hassabi. Photo: Thomas Poravas. Courtesy of the artist and The Breeder, Athens.

Xavier Le Roy, *'Retrospective'*, 2012. Performance view, MoMA PS1, Queens, New York, 2014. Performers: Oisín Monaghan, K J Holmes, Eleanor Bauer, Michael Helland. Photo: Matthew Septimus. Courtesy of the artist and MoMA PS1.

Anne Imhof, *FAUST*, 2017. Performance view, German Pavilion, Fifty-Seventh Venice Biennale, 2017. Performer: Eliza Douglas. Photo: Nadine Fraczkowski. Courtesy of the artist, Galerie Buchholz, and German Pavilion 2017.

Anne Teresa De Keersmaeker/Rosas, *Work/Travail/Arbeid*, 2015. Performance view, Wiels, Brussels, 2015. Dancer: Igor Shyshko. Musician: Jean-Luc Plouvier. Photo: Anne Van Aerschot. Courtesy of Rosas, Brussels.

'Stop' (Louis Morel-Retz), *Aux Italiens* (At the Italian Theatre), 1857. Engraving published in *Le Petit Journal pour Rire*, 1857. Courtesy of the Courtauld, London (Samuel Courtauld Trust).

Audience members watch Jérôme Bel, *MoMA Dance Company*, Museum of Modern Art, New York, 2016. Photo: Claire Bishop.

3NÓS3, *Ensacamento*, 1979. São Paulo, 27 April 1979. Courtesy of Mario Ramiro.

View of 3NÓS3 exhibition, Espaço Nervo Óptico, Porto Alegre, 1980. Installation includes photographs and press cuttings about the group's interventions. Courtesy of Mario Ramiro.

Portrait of David Burliuk, 1928. Photographer unknown. Courtesy of Heritage Image Partnership Ltd/Alamy Stock Photo.

Pope.L, *Times Square Crawl a.k.a. Meditation Square Pieces*, 1978. Digital colour photograph on gold-fiber silk paper. © Pope.L. Courtesy of Mitchell-Innes & Nash, New York.

E.T.I., *TEXT*, 1991. Red Square, Moscow, 18 April 1991. Courtesy of Anatoly Osmolovsky.

Harry Gamboa Jr., *Decoy Gang War Victim*, 1974. Colour photograph of Asco intervention. © 1974 Harry Gamboa Jr.

Guillaume de La Perrière, 'Depiction of Occasio', *Le théâtre des bons engins, auquel sont contenuz cent emblèmes*, Paris: Denis Janot, 1539.

Voina, *Dick Captured by the FSB*, 2010. St Petersburg. Photo: Alexey Plutser-Sarno. Courtesy of Alexey Plutser-Sarno.

Pussy Riot, *Mother of God, Drive Putin Away*, 2012. Cathedral of Christ the Saviour, Moscow, 21 February 2012. Screengrab from livejournal.com where the video was originally posted. Courtesy of the artists.

Tania Bruguera, *#YoTambienExijo*, 2014. Reporters wait on Plaza de la Revolución, Havana, 30 December 2014. Photo: Klaus Biesenbach. Courtesy of Estudio Bruguera.

Parker Bright protests in front of Dana Schutz's *Open Casket* at the Whitney Biennial, 2017. Screengrab from gofundme.com/parkerbrightprotest.

Mel D. Cole, *Richmond, VA, 6.20.2020*, 2020. Digital photograph. Courtesy of the artist.

Kcho (Alexis Leyva Machado), *To the Eyes of History*, 1992–95. Twigs, plant fibres, and fabric coffee filter. © Kcho.

Ai Weiwei, *Fountain of Light*, 2007. Steel and glass crystals on a wooden base. Courtesy of Ai Weiwei Studio.

Chto Delat, *Untitled (Tatlin Tower)*, 2013. Installation view, *Art Turning Left: How Values Changed Making 1789–2013*, Tate Liverpool, 2013. Courtesy of the artists and Tate.

Sam Durant, *Modern Moon*, 1994. Collage on photocopy. Courtesy of the Museum of Contemporary Art, Los Angeles. Gift of the artist.

Paulina Ołowska, *Siatkarka (Volleyball Player)*, 2006. Renovated neon sign, Warsaw. Photo: Mateusz Romaszkan and Waldemar

Czapor. Courtesy of the artist and Foksal Gallery Foundation, Warsaw.

Juan Araujo, *Rivista 2G no.23 and* 24, 2006. Oil on paper and wood. Courtesy of the artist and Tate.

Günther Förg, *IG-Farben-Haus VII,* 1996. Colour photograph. Sammlung der DZ BANK im Städel Museum, Frankfurt am Main. © Estate Günther Förg, Suisse / VG Bild-Kunst, Bonn.

Amie Siegel, *Provenance*, 2013. Exhibition view © MAK/Nathan Murrell.

Judi Werthein, *This Functional Family*, 2007. Single channel video. Courtesy of the artist.

Kerry James Marshall, *Better Homes, Better Gardens*, 1994. Acrylic and collage on canvas. Collection: Denver Art Museum. Funds from Polly and Mark Addison, the Alliance for Contemporary Art, Caroline Morgan, and Colorado Contemporary Collectors: Suzanne Farver, Linda and Ken Heller, Jan and Frederick Mayer, Beverly and Bernard Rosen, Annalee and Wagner Schorr, and anonymous donors, 1995.77. © Kerry James Marshall. Courtesy of Denver Art Museum.

Thomas Hirschhorn, preparatory sketch for *Gramsci Monument*, 2013. Ink on paper. Courtesy of the artist.

Thomas Hirschhorn, *Gramsci Monument*, 2013. Forest Houses, Bronx, New York. Poetry session with Fred Moten, 14 August 2013. Photo: Romain Lopez. Courtesy of the artist and Dia Art Foundation, New York.

Index

Numbers in *italics* refer to illustrations